T0330315

A Research Agenda for Critical Political Economy

Elgar Research Agendas outline the future of research in a given area. Leading scholars are given the space to explore their subject in provocative ways, and map out the potential directions of travel. They are relevant but also visionary.

Forward-looking and innovative, Elgar Research Agendas are an essential resource for PhD students, scholars and anybody who wants to be at the forefront of research.

A Research Agenda for Critical Political Economy

Edited by

BILL DUNN

Associate Professor, Department of Political Economy, University of Sydney, Australia

Elgar Research Agendas

 **Edward Elgar**
PUBLISHING

Cheltenham, UK • Northampton, MA, USA

Published by
Edward Elgar Publishing Limited
The Lypiatts
15 Lansdown Road
Cheltenham
Glos GL50 2JA
UK

Edward Elgar Publishing, Inc.
William Pratt House
9 Dewey Court
Northampton
Massachusetts 01060
USA

A catalogue record for this book
is available from the British Library

Library of Congress Control Number: 2020942922

This book is available electronically in the **Elgar**online
Social and Political Science subject collection
http://dx.doi.org/10.4337/9781789903072

ISBN 978 1 78990 306 5 (cased)
ISBN 978 1 78990 307 2 (eBook)

Printed by CPI Group (UK) Ltd, Croydon CR0 4YY

Contents

Contributors

Bhagat, Ali, Lecturer in International Relations, University of Manchester, UK

Bittes Terra, Fábio Henrique, Associate Professor at Federal University of ABC, and Researcher at National Council for Scientific and Technological Development, Brazil

Dados, Nour Nicole, Research Fellow, Macquarie Business School, Centre for Workforce Futures, Macquarie University, Australia

Dow, Sheila, Emeritus Professor, Division of Economics, Stirling Management School, University of Stirling, UK, and Adjunct Professor, Department of Economics, University of Victoria, Canada

Dunn, Bill, Associate Professor, Department of Political Economy, University of Sydney, Australia

Ferrari Filho, Fernando, Retired Professor of Economics at Federal University of Rio Grande do Sul, and Researcher at National Council for Scientific and Technological Development, Brazil

Hargreaves Heap, Shaun P., Professor of Political Economy, King's College, London, UK

Herod, Andrew, Distinguished Research Professor, Department of Geography, University of Georgia, USA

Matthaei, Julie, Professor Emerita of Economics, Wellesley College, USA

Mezzadri, Alessandra, Senior Lecturer in Development Studies, Development Studies, SOAS, UK

Obeng-Odoom, Franklin, Associate Professor, Development Studies and Helsinki Institute of Sustainability Science, University of Helsinki, Finland

O'Hara, Sabine U., Distinguished Professor, College of Agriculture, Urban Sustainability and Environmental Sciences, University of the District of Columbia, USA

Selwyn, Benjamin, Professor of International Relations and International Development, International Relations, School of Global Studies, University of Sussex, UK

Sheppard, Eric, Distinguished Professor and Alexander von Humboldt Chair, Department of Geography, University of California, Los Angeles, USA

Soederberg, Susanne, Professor, Department of Political Studies and Department of Global Development Studies, Queen's University, Canada

Stilwell, Frank, Professor Emeritus, Department of Political Economy, University of Sydney, Australia

1 What makes critical research in political economy?

Bill Dunn

Nobody thinks of themselves as uncritical. So there is no neat definition of what constitutes critical political economy. The field is unbounded and fecund.

There are diverse schools of critical political economy – classical, Marxist, institutional, Keynesian, feminist, ecological, to name just a few – with each having many strands. Some research draws on several traditions or refuses categorisation. And while it will be suggested below that a useful understanding of what constitutes critical political economy can be approached through the negative, through opposition to the economic mainstream, some critics raid behind enemy lines to acknowledge and engage with insights from orthodoxy. Many researchers draw on different academic disciplines: on history, sociology, anthropology and political science. Research areas range across issues and across time. Some studies explicitly focus on the global economy, others on specific local contexts, with important work done at all sorts of scales in between. Therefore, critical political economists differ from their mainstream counterparts not only in terms of method, but at least as much in terms of the questions they ask, the nature and breadth of the research agenda. Neither the themes discussed in this introduction nor the chapters in this book can possibly be comprehensive.

But to begin with the negative, critical political economists believe that economics in the form that dominates university departments, at least across the Anglophone world, is profoundly flawed and profoundly conservative. At best it provides an insufficient basis for understanding complex economic realities. At worst it amounts to a crude and fanciful apology for the existing economic system. It is therefore useful to begin by offering some broad outlines of a critical research agenda in contrast to the approaches of this orthodoxy. There are now many useful books which provide much more thorough overviews and critiques of conventional economic thinking (e.g. Green and Nore 1977; Heilbroner and Milberg 1995; Lawson 1997; Milonakis and Fine 2009), and

I am delighted that contributors to this volume have resisted the considerable temptation to spend large amounts of their space venting frustration with the assumptions and practices of orthodoxy. The purpose here is to move towards a positive articulation of research agenda. But a few themes seem particularly relevant to understanding and developing such an alternative, critical, approach.

Perhaps most fundamentally, economics or political economy should be a social science. People do not behave like inanimate objects. A few things follow. First, a radical individualism makes no sense and important and interesting questions develop precisely out of thinking about the relations between individuals, institutions and social structures. Second, the methods of a natural science like physics at best provide one weapon in a critical political economist's arsenal. The economy cannot simply be studied in the same way as physical processes. Third, time and space are experienced unevenly. There is often a path dependence to economic action, not an oscillation around equilibrium. The spaces and places, the interaction over distances, the heterogeneous material world in which we live, all shape economic activity profoundly. Not only are we learning how economic activity is transforming the environment, but we are also learning how the environment shapes the economy. Fourth, and finally, political economy is not a 'neutral' academic endeavour, divorced from the object it studies. How we see the world, and what we say about the world, is inseparable from our position within it. Potentially, what we say about the world also has consequences, and can possibly be used to change that world. As Robert Cox writes, 'Theory is always for someone and for some purpose' (1981: 128). We need to ask 'who gains' from particular theories and policies.

To repeat, there is no clear dividing line between the critical and uncritical. There is however a risk of caricature. Binary depictions of us and them, of good and bad or even of fundamentally opposed 'modes' of economics (Tabb 1999) at best oversimplify. Particularly since the global financial crisis of 2008, some prominent figures have acknowledged the shortcomings of their discipline. Some famous economists can be claimed by both the mainstream and the critics. Keynes is probably the clearest example. I will quote him approvingly below, but it would be possible to find formulations where he appears to sit on the other side of the fence, or at least where he sits on the fence, as was his wont. Some of Keynes's followers, including contributors to this volume (usually seen as 'post-Keynesians'), can be radical critics of both mainstream economics and the existing economic order. Other followers have been safely absorbed back into the mainstream. Some still hover in the centre ground, claiming both a political centre and insisting that their economics is simultaneously radical and capable of satisfying the standards of orthodoxy (Davidson

1978, 2007). But I think most people would recognise the broad distinctions between orthodoxy and critical political economy, and I hope the themes that follow can help to inform the development of a critical research agenda, which is exemplified in the chapters in this book that are briefly introduced below.

Economics as a social science

It is useful to begin by saying that critical political economists see what they do as a social science. This has several dimensions. But political economy as it was originally conceived and taught in the 18th and 19th centuries was understood to be what was then called a 'moral science'. The radical separation of economics from broader historical and social concerns and the insistence that economics had distinct and proper methods were 20th-century innovations, which had some seriously deleterious consequences.

Standard definitions of economics as 'the study of scarcity, the study of how people use resources and respond to incentives, or the study of decision-making' (American Economic Association 2020) rule out most of what actually makes the economic world go round and which critical political economists want to put (back) in. Political economy should ask the questions which preoccupied the classical tradition of Adam Smith and David Ricardo about work and about how resources are produced in the first place; should ask the Marxist questions of exploitation and class; the questions of the Institutionalist and German historical schools about formal and informal institutions, not least about the nature and role of the state. It should ask about time and how the past informs the present; should ask the Keynesian questions about decisions made in conditions of uncertainty, the relation between money and the 'real' economy, and about the relations between production and demand; should ask the feminist questions about how the political economy is gendered both in fact and in the way it is conceived to prioritise some issues and undervalue others like domestic labour; should ask questions about space and land, nature and place, and the relationship between economy and ecology. Critical political economy asks much else besides. Even if no one researcher can do all this at once, a recurring theme for critical political economists is interconnectedness; of different aspects of the economy with each other and of the economy with the rest of society.

There is therefore usually a recognition of the need to engage with, and to learn from, other social scientists. At the same time this creates difficult questions about where to stop. It is impossible to know everything and the objection that 'it is more complicated than that', while never wrong, is seldom helpful. It also creates difficult questions about analytical priorities, which the postmodern moment has made people shy of declaring. But it is impossible not to prioritise in practice and far better that these priorities are made explicit and subject to criticism than driven underground. Along with a commitment to a broader approach, come responsibilities to make clear exactly what is being studied and how.

Because there are many different traditions of critical political economy, there are also often sharp disagreements. Indeed, the diversity of interpretations is one of the characteristics of the critical, a consequence of rejecting the existence of established authority on what constitutes 'proper' economics. But while this means that it is possible to find critical political economists saying mutually incompatible things, it also means that, as in other social sciences, there is broad agreement that disagreement should be allowed, even encouraged. This would be too obvious to need saying among sociologists or political scientists. It contrasts sharply with mainstream economics, where the bounds of appropriate disagreement are very narrow. The established right way of doing things, in Stephen Rousseas's phrase, allows its adherents, to 'engage themselves in the endless task of paradigm polishing' (1986: 16). For the critics, there are fewer established principles but more exciting, neglected avenues of legitimate enquiry and different ways of getting critical purchase on important issues.

Some implications of insisting that economics should a social science, not an 'objective', natural, science, seem worth developing a bit further.

Structure and agency

If interdependence is a recurring theme for critical political economists, a particularly crucial interdependence is that between human agency and social structures. We make our own world as it makes us (Onuf 1997; Marx 2010).

This contrasts sharply with most mainstream economists, who – with honourable exceptions (e.g. Arrow 1994), and if they bother to think about such philosophical questions at all – generally subscribe to methodological individualism. Crudely, to paraphrase Margaret Thatcher's famous formulation, 'there is no such thing as society, there are only individuals'. Attempting to reduce people to something akin to (19th-century) physics' atomic level, we must all be reckoned simple, selfish, rational, utility maximisers. To quote

William Stanley Jevons, one of the founders of modern marginalism, 'each person is to other persons a portion of the outward world ... Hence the weighing of motives must always be confined to the bosom of the individual' (1957: 14). Any apparent 'society' is then simply the sum of those individual parts. In principle, for the mainstream, the (unfortunate) reality of institutions can be explained away by aggregating individual utilities to give us firms (Coase 1937; Williamson 1975) or states (Tullock 1987). The insistence on methodological individualism can then also become the basis for 'economics imperialism' (Fine and Milonakis 2009), which exports the methods of a de-socialised economics to other social sciences. There are more sophisticated defences of individualism and important questions whether this is really a methodological or ontological issue (Hayek 1948). But even more subtle versions either end up with a rather banal circularity or smuggling presuppositions of the social back into their understanding of individuals (Lukes 1973).

Accordingly, most critical political economists acknowledge an inseparable relation between structure and agency, albeit they see this in different ways and put more or less stress on structure or agency. Often, they are concerned precisely with the relation between the two (Lawson 1997). Each individual is born into an already existing society and, as Keynes insists, 'the whole is not equal to the sum of the parts, comparisons of quality fail us, small changes produce large effects' (2013: 262). Keynes continues that economics should be a 'moral science':

> I mentioned before that it deals with introspection and with values. I might have added that it deals with motives, expectations, psychological uncertainties. One has to be constantly on guard against treating the material as constant and homogeneous. It is as though the fall of the apple to the ground depended on the apple's motives, on whether it is worth while falling to the ground, and whether the ground wanted the apple to fall, and on mistaken calculations on the part of the apple as to how far it was from the centre of the earth. (2012: 300)

Modern behavioural economists, more likely than most to secure a foothold in mainstream departments, have highlighted how even put in 'laboratory conditions' people seldom behave as the rational utility maximisers mainstream economics supposes. Among other things, people behave differently towards others depending on those others' social location and they value gain and loss very differently (Hargreaves Heap, Chapter 8 in this volume; Kahneman 2012).

Several advocates of methodological individualism build their arguments on a false claim that the only possible alternative is a structuralist-functionalism. Some political economies have slipped into something close to this, but, of course, opposition to radical individualism need not say that individuals do not matter. It is merely necessary to say and to investigate how our thoughts and actions are themselves social, always developed in relation to other people. This leaves open important questions of how best to research relations between structure, and the many different social structures, and agency, to which critical political economists respond in different ways.

Marxists, in particular, usually begin with the structures, particularly emphasising 'big picture' issues of class, even as these are understood to be dynamic and changing and mutable, with key research questions around how social struggles transform economic relations. Challenges, from both within and without the Marxist tradition, research how class relates to other structures, notably those of race and gender (Hartmann 1981; Walby 1986; Collins 2000; Matthaei 1996). Feminist economists have identified both the implicit assumptions in conceiving economics in terms of rational economic 'man' (Hewitson 1994) and the empirical limits of conventional categories, including conceptions of 'the household' as a suitable standard unit of analysis. At the very least, for critical political economists, questions of inequality (Stilwell, Chapter 2 in this volume) loom large, and if as political *economists* the economic is a core concern, this is multidimensional and inherently inseparable from other processes. The importance of institutions, of formal institutions but also of ideological 'regimes', has become central to many recent research agenda. Other critical political economists are more likely to begin with agency and social movements and investigate how social pressures are experienced and resisted.

Beyond physics envy and an obsession with mathematical formalism

A second way of thinking about the differences of method between critical and mainstream economics can then be couched in terms of the accusation that the mainstream suffers from 'physics envy' (Mirowski 1992). Economists themselves would be more likely to couch this in terms of 'rigour', and critical political economists, of course, are perfectly capable of writing woolly nonsense the mainstream seeks to avoid. But there are important differences in what constitutes acceptable method and profound problems with claims that economics should look more like natural science than social science.

Any such 'physics envy' is probably most conspicuous in the mainstream's penchant for complex mathematics. To quote Jevons again, '[m]y theory of Economics is entirely mathematical in character ... I do not hesitate to say, too, that Economics might be gradually erected into an exact science, if only commercial statistics were far more complete and accurate than they are at present' (1957: 14, 21). Jevons notwithstanding, for many years it remained acceptable to write in straightforward prose. Alfred Marshall, effective leader of the next generation of mainstream economists in Britain around the beginning of the 20th century and largely responsible for separating economics teaching from the 'moral sciences' at Cambridge, nevertheless famously recommended translating any mathematics into plain English, and if that proved impossible, recommended deleting the mathematics. In the US, at least until the middle of the 20th century, economics graduate students were required to read German in order to access the work of the non-mathematical German historical school (Fusfeld 2002). Most academic economics articles up to the mid-century would still have been comprehensible by non-specialists, a deficiency now radically corrected. In its turn to mathematics and in the furnishing of statistics, 150 years since he wrote these words, economics has fulfilled Jevons's ambitions more fully than he could have imagined.

Critical political economists tend to be less fond of mathematical formalism. In a sense this is just intellectual honesty. A leading mainstream economist can acknowledge that what they do is not really science but a mixture of 'fiction and journalism' (Leamer 2012). Of course, many mainstream mathematical economists who occupy prestigious positions do invaluable work. There is something particularly satisfying when statistics coming out of the International Monetary Fund (IMF) show that inequality is also bad for growth or research coming out of the World Bank acknowledges that microfinance initiatives they have promoted are counter-productive. But a wariness of abstract mathematical arguments flows from critical political economists' views of the world and their relation to it, the inherent difficulty reducing to algebra what are complex relations between individuals and social structures, concerns with history and time and space, and questions of politics and power.

This does not require an out-of-hand rejection of mathematics, let alone of precise reasoning, and critical political economists take different attitudes. Almost all would agree that the mainstream overdoes it; that it habitually assumes a specious precision unreflective of the complexities of the social world it purports to describe. At best, mathematical equations are tautologies. As such they can be useful, helping to identify which factors are reckoned to be related and how, and to suggest ways of testing those relations empirically. But they can also lend themselves to a misleading view that economic variables should be understood as effectively independent of one another (like the ground and the apple). At least some of the routine mainstream practices are manifestly flawed.

A phrase in an old introduction to calculus, a mathematics not an economics book, recently caught my attention. Having used some monetary illustrations, the author quickly adds 'but money is not a good example for the calculus, because it generally comes and goes by jumps, not by a continuous flow' (Thompson 2012: 54). A great deal of modern economics, not least Friedman's (1987) version of the quantity theory of money, seems blithely unaware that the methods so useful to physicists may be completely inappropriate.

Most critical political economists would share Keynes's wariness of formal mathematical presentation in preference for 'ordinary discourse' where 'we can keep "at the back of our heads" the necessary reserves and qualifications' (1973: 297). Some critical political economists would go further in their hostility to the mainstream use of maths, insisting on more qualitative and agent-centred approaches. But without needing to be anti-mathematical there is a predisposition to methodological pluralism. As social scientists in many other disciplines would recognise (as indeed would many natural scientists), there is no single right way of doing things. There are different paths to analytical rigour and to deep understanding.

The complexity of time and space

Among other things, questions of time and space can make social life recalcitrant to mathematical formalism. Largely overlooked by the mainstream, the irreversible nature of time is crucial to much of critical political economy (Robinson 1964). History matters and impinges on current practices. In Marx's phrase, 'the tradition of all the dead generations weighs like a nightmare on the brain of the living' (2010: 103). Research in critical political economy is often concerned with history, with how capitalism came into being, with its changing forms but also how established institutions shape current practice.

One particularly influential contribution to understanding both history and the present is the idea of 'circular and cumulative causation'. Rather than any deviation from the norm being quickly and automatically corrected by market pressures towards equilibrium, there is often a path dependency as small changes beget bigger ones. Myrdal's (1944) original example described a vicious circle of poverty among, and racism towards, black Americans. But the idea has been extended to other areas, from technological innovation to spatial agglomeration and uneven development. Rather than a static equilibrium, questions of rupture and crisis and changes of direction become particularly fascinating.

Many critical political economists go further to endorse notions of uncertainty in Keynes's sense that at least some future events are radically unknowable. Despite which, we are required to act, not only knowing that the future is unknowable but also knowing that other people, on whose actions we depend, similarly lack any secure basis for knowing the consequences of their actions. Some post-Keynesians accept that such an understanding of uncertainty can spin out into what Alan Coddington labelled 'analytical nihilism' (Coddington 1983; Shackle 1972). At the other end of the spectrum, Marxists are more likely to see capitalism both as the driver of uncertainty and volatility and as providing imperatives which are difficult to escape. For Anwar Shaikh there are 'ordered patterns' but these 'are neither steely rails nor mere constellations of circumstance. They are, rather, moving limits whose gradients define what is easy and what is difficult at any moment of time' (2016: 5). At the very least, as Davidson (1978) insists, the future is not the statistical shadow of the past. The mainstream fondness for extrapolation and economic forecasting is often fundamentally misguided, taking away the possibility of 'choice' on which it claims to be predicated.

Perhaps particularly in recent years, critical political economists have also become profoundly interested in questions of space and territory. In fairness, economists within or very close to the mainstream have also recognised the importance of spatial relations and the previously inadequate treatment of this (Krugman 1979, 1993). But critical political economists have been particularly responsive to ecological concerns and the relationship between people and the (rest of) nature and the interaction of economic processes at different scales.

Problems of 'scale' are addressed explicitly in what follows by our geographers Eric Sheppard and Andy Herod. They are also raised among others by Frank Stilwell's discussion of inequality, Sheila Dow's discussion of finance and Alessandra Mezzardi's discussion of field economics. Among other things, we have inequalities between countries but also within them, including spatial differences, which are often less well measured by conventional national accounting techniques. Stimulated in part by claims of 'globalisation' and the inadequacy of both the liberalising-globalising literature and nation-state-based alternatives, critical thinking has challenged the individual–state binary, vulnerable not least to transposing the individualist methods of the mainstream onto state structures as if they too had subjective utilities. The national bases of data collection still present formidable challenges, and potential areas of constructive research, but there is a growing awareness of the interaction of processes and actions over different scales, within countries and regions as well as simply at individual, national and global levels.

A socially concerned social science

Finally, but to return to the idea of what we do as a moral science, most critical political economists ask questions about 'for whom?'. Who gains from particular economic practices? Who gains from particular economic ideas? There are seldom universal interests in one path rather than another and economic theories which purport to identify straightforwardly better or worse ways of acting are usually misleading.

This can also be true of natural science. Rather than an objective pursuit of truth, the scientific research which is actually carried out may be that which is sponsored by the arms industry. Medical research is sponsored by pharmaceutical companies, aware that diseases of poverty are less likely to be lucrative than those of the rich. But it is probably particularly straightforward in economics. Financial models get built into the computer programs, which predict stability and are used to value assets in ways that then provoke instability. Mainstream economic theorising gets built into policies, like those of 'Inflation Targeting', which prioritise 'sound' money and the interests of wealthy asset holders over employment or welfare spending.

Most critical political economists would therefore agree that research is never neutral. But questions of what is to be done, perhaps the most vital dimension raised by Cox's aphorism that theory is always for somebody and for some purpose, bring out some vivid differences. There is little consensus on questions of for whom or to what end do we research or of strategies for change.

Economists of the Austrian School (followers of the likes of Ludwig von Mises and Friedrich Hayek) would share many of the criticisms of mainstream, marginalist, equilibrium approaches raised above. But they can draw right-wing libertarian or even fascist conclusions. While the Austrians are not represented in what follows, and most critical political economists, like most social scientists, would today position themselves somewhere from the political centre leftwards, that leaves a very wide space and scope for very different priorities. Most critical political economists favour more egalitarian outcomes. Some write explicitly in class terms. Others prioritise gender inequalities and redressing them. An emphasis on the Global South and its disadvantage or exploitation and in overcoming this is the focus for many writers. These goals may be complementary, but there can also be tensions between them, which tensions themselves provide the basis for important research projects.

In terms of strategy, too, critical political economists, including contributors to this volume, answer in different ways. Some envisage better policies for national economies. Many writers share Keynes's vision of national interests and of an essentially benign state, or at least of a state capable of reform and potentially receptive to better advice. Jonathon Goldstein and Michael Hilliard go so far as to see heterodox economists as required to 'provide sound policy recommendations' (2009: 4). Other critical political economists, without necessarily rejecting the potential for policy reform, are more likely to point to the failures of the state and to emphasise non-state, social movement activism (Gibson-Graham 1996; Matthaei, Chapter 15 in this volume). The Marxist tradition, of course, while not necessarily opposed to either reform strategy, sees them as inherently limited without more radical, revolutionary change. But most critical political economists at least try to keep in the back of their minds that what they write is not a neutral scientific endeavour and to think about the implications for economic and political practice.

For the most part, economic thinking today is dominated by an individualised and abstractly mathematical mainstream which purports to maintain a disinterested scientific objectivity. Against this, other critical political economists would construct different lists of alternative principles from those above. The critics are a relatively small but diverse minority. A few manage to sustain departments where critical economic thinking is encouraged. Some survive and work within otherwise mainstream economics departments, others find shelter in other disciplines. These institutional settings shape what research is possible, but in different ways there is an attempt to create a more socially aware and more socially responsible economic research agenda.

Some avenues for enquiry, some done and undone research

The following chapters provide a flavour of critical research in political economy, sketching a research agenda in different ways. Some set out the 'state of the art', some identify problems and domains of done and undone research and questions worth pursuing, some draw on specific examples of their own research to illustrate how further work might be done. Several address the normative dimensions and suggest what might be done better not only in research but in practice. The chapters are short and broadly speak for themselves, so here the content of each can be introduced briefly.

Frank Stilwell's chapter on inequality (Chapter 2) is concerned with both causes and consequences. In both cases the chapter argues for the need for clarity in developing concepts and theories. There are linked but distinct inequalities of wealth and of income. Stilwell invokes Myrdal's (1944) 'circular and cumulative causation' to argue how rather than being pulled back to an equilibrium, inequalities of wealth tend to build inequalities of income, reinforcing inequalities of wealth. He sees a need for broad political economy research concerned with social structures and processes to be linked with 'more micro-scale research undertaken by sociologists and anthropologists'. Stilwell is also concerned with strategies and policies for a more equal society. His emphasis is on how public policy and the state can make a difference, but he also sees a role for the labour movement and non-governmental organisations (NGOs). Stilwell also raises questions of scale, of inequality within and between countries, an important theme developed in several of the following chapters.

Benjamin Selwyn's chapter (Chapter 3) argues that something as apparently simple as 'growth', so commonly assumed to be a universal good, needs to be critically interrogated. In particular, the acceptance of growth as a goal obscures the social class relations on which it is predicated. Growth is achieved by exploiting labour, and (as is now being more widely acknowledged) the way it has hitherto been achieved ultimately undermines ecological sustainability. Selwyn uses Marx to examine questions of development and poverty and how two distinct but related processes, of dispossession and of labour exploitation, produce new forms of poverty. He points to a vicious cycle where growth is seen as the means to overcome poverty and inequality but the means by which growth is achieved themselves generate poverty and inequality. Selwyn emphasises the problems of conceiving alternatives to mainstream individualism in national and nation-state-based terms and considers alternatives to growth-based development. At least, we should deprioritise and contextualise growth in our research agenda.

Sheila Dow (Chapter 4) develops a critical research agenda on money, finance and the state. She discusses the importance of financial institutions and institutional change, pointing out that 'the subject matter does not stand still'. The emergence of cryptocurrencies is a telling case in point. Reflecting on the implications of the 2008 global financial crisis, Dow considers the role of policy and central banks in promoting financial but also social stability. '[M]oney's nature is social', so there is an interconnectedness of state and private institutions, of monetary and financial policy, and of these with the broader economy. Dow's approach contrasts not only with the mainstream but with some other heterodox writers who insist on a rigid exogenous/endogenous or state/market distinction. As Dow (1996) herself argued previously, for the critical political economist nothing bar 'acts of god' is truly exogenous and part of the research task is to understand, not exclude, the state. Here she considers the role of state monopolies of money, including proposals for central bank digital currencies, and the role of regulation. She argues that, given systemic financial instability, as identified by Minsky, 'it is up to the state to intervene to moderate it'. Policy, Dow argues, also needs to address environmental concerns, and while most of the research (including heterodox research) on money and finance has taken the Western system as its model, the situation may be very different in developing countries.

Nour Dados says much more on this in her chapter on Southern theory (Chapter 5). She looks at how the Global South has been central to capitalism's history while indigenous economies and knowledges have been disrupted and destroyed. The chapter describes an uneven creation and circulation of knowledge, embedded in a global division of intellectual labour, itself built upon the violence of colonialism, imperialism and economic domination. But Dados also describes attempts to recuperate subaltern epistemologies and how these can inform contemporary research agenda, arguing that the contributions of post-colonial intellectuals and Global South perspectives are vital to understanding global capitalism and knowledge creation in the neo-colonial, neoliberal world.

Bill Dunn (Chapter 6), sketching a potential critical research agenda on international trade, is probably more sympathetic than most to a constructive, critical engagement with mainstream trade theory, but argues that it needs to be put in its place; that it is also necessary to examine how international trade relations are constructed, both historically and in relation to other social and economic processes. Like Selwyn, he identifies the problems with national-based alternatives to liberalism, which share many of the same presumptions about national interest and 'growth' as if it were something straightforwardly desirable. He argues that a pervasive 'methodological nationalism' has been an obstacle to developing a genuinely critical research agenda on international trade, leaving un-investigated many important dimensions of trade's causes and consequences.

Alessandra Mezzadri's work on sweatshop economics (Chapter 7) epitomises the conceptual pay-off for 'fieldwork economics', looking beneath apparently equitable trade relations to investigate how those relations are constructed and what they mean for the workers involved. Where mainstream trade theory assumes that countries have 'factor endowments', Mezzadri asks how those factors, particularly labour, are produced and reproduced very differently within countries, based on complex social differentiation and power relations, among other things according to gender and caste. She contests the individualism of conventional microeconomics and the broad sweeps and generalisations of macroeconomics. Her field-based research agenda draws on sociology, human geography and development studies and shows how the study of production, exchange and inequality must transcend rigid divisions between the global, the national and the local.

Shaun Hargreaves Heap's chapter (Chapter 8) addresses some similar themes of structure and agency while adopting an apparently radically different research strategy. Experimental economics puts volunteers in 'laboratory' situations to consider how they behave in different circumstances. Hargreaves Heap is able to show, in a controlled way, how the 'social, institutional or historical framing', how questions of social identity and context, affect what appear to be 'individual' decisions. His discussion of 'chat opportunities' shows that deliberative procedures are conducive to the public good, with implications for formal democracy but also, surely, for how resistance can be built. '[P]eople behave differently in the same situation depending on whether they are interacting with a fellow member of their group or with someone who belongs to another.' One implication that Hargreaves Heap draws from this is that in-group identity with the rich may make people less likely to support egalitarian reform, which would be in their interest. Hargreaves Heap's experimental results also show that people appear less likely to favour redistribution if they feel that inequality derives from individual decisions rather than luck, potentially shedding light on why health care is widely supported but also differences between European attitudes and those in the US, where income is more likely to be attributed to individual effort or skill. But as Hargreaves Heap concludes, 'there is a key question that needs addressing about how people come to hold views on the relative contribution of each in determining outcomes'. He ends with an elegant liberal argument for equality. If individual autonomy is the objective, it matters equally for all individuals and can only be achieved in an egalitarian society.

The following three chapters raise 'big picture' issues concerned with space and time. Andrew Herod (Chapter 9) explores how different conceptualisations of time, space and the geographical scale at which social life is organised have implications for understanding the geography of capitalism and hence for political economy. He examines how different conceptions of time and space, among philosophers, scientists and social scientists, have important implications for how we conduct research. He describes how 'the different ways in which scales are described can shape how we understand the world to be organised geographically and so what we consider politically possible'.

Questions of time have been particularly crucial to critical thinking about money in the post-Keynesian tradition, and Fernando Ferrari Filho and Fábio Henrique Bittes Terra (Chapter 10) turn to Keynes's views on uncertainty and its implications for modern financial markets. They show how an understanding of uncertainty as more than a probabilistic risk contrasts with that of the mainstream and undermines claims of the efficient market theory. The chapter shows that, once 'speculation is essentially an "activity of forecasting the psychology of the market"', in an entrepreneur economy, the organisation of the financial market, given uncertainty, faces a severe trade-off between liquidity and speculation. It then shows how for this approach there are necessary links between the financial market and the real economy. Ideas of money's 'neutrality' are unsustainable, and the implication is that a research agenda needs to incorporate analyses of money and the 'real'.

Eric Sheppard (Chapter 11) explores the implications for Marxist political economy of thinking geographically about capitalism. He argues that 'in the wild' capitalism is inherently geographical. Uneven geographical development is less the result of place-based geographical characteristics than it is of the asymmetric and uneven connectivities between places and across scales. Socio-spatial poverty and marginalisation continue to be reproduced in different ways and are exacerbated by cultural and biophysical processes that exceed attempts to commodify them.

Similar themes are developed more concretely in the next three chapters. Sabine O'Hara's chapter (Chapter 12) advocates developing more context-conscious measures of economic performance. The chapter develops themes raised by feminist and ecological economics and advocates strategies of localisation and 're-embedding' the economy, at the same time as stressing the need for national and global levels of action. O'Hara gives the important example that '[c]heap food produced in industrial-scale farms may not be cheap at all, but may come at the expense of ecosystems and human health that carries enormous social costs'. The growing virtual economy is seen as providing the basis for localising solutions and an important arena for further research.

Franklin Obeng-Odoom (Chapter 13) proposes a Georgist political economy for understanding and redressing problems of urban land in Africa. Henry George was a US political economist of the late 19th century who emphasised the importance of land and advocated land taxes. Obeng-Odoom suggests a Georgist approach provides the basis for a critique of a mainstream agenda based on privatisation and individual property rights, and a mainstream practice based on financialisation and increasing debt. Obeng-Odoom's Georgist political economy emphasises that research questions should not simply be about private versus public but about whose interests are being pursued. It is also necessary to ask about the nature of political intervention in the economy and about who pays, in class terms and inter-generational terms. Public guarantees of financial interests exacerbate problems of urban indebtedness. The chapter's evidence focuses on Accra, Ghana, but also touches on similar research done in South Africa and Uganda, suggesting a research agenda applicable to the urban economy more generally, particularly in the growing cities of the Global South.

Ali Bhagat and Susanne Soederberg (Chapter 14) focus on refugees in the European Union to examine the political economy of displacement governance. Using empirical examples of Berlin and Paris as host cities, they explore questions of race and class and of space and scale. The chapter asks who benefits and why to describe the so-called refugee crisis and the depiction of refugees as a 'trope' which masks underlying issues of shelter insecurity and which is underpinned by systematic racial exclusion.

Julie Matthaei's provocative final chapter (Chapter 15) argues for a reconstructed Marxist–feminist–anti-racist–ecological economics and for 'thinking beyond capitalism'. Matthaei maintains that we live in times of epic crises and transformation and that political economists need to be active participants in change, through both their teaching and their research. Such a political economy can inform a solidarity economy, involving liberatory practices and institutions already emerging within capitalism even in its US heartlands. Theory and practice, as so often for critical political economists, are inseparable.

Other critical political economists including contributors to this volume would reach different strategic conclusions, but Matthaei's reference to crises prompts an important final coda. I am completing this introduction in London, in March 2020, as the UK follows other countries into lockdown in response to the Covid-19 virus. My sympathies with those who are ill and solidarity with those who are battling the disease in different ways. It is too soon to be confident about the course of the pandemic or about its broader impact. Beyond the horrors of the rising death toll, already we have seen employers seize an opportunity to lay off workers and to impose worse working conditions. We have seen governments find resources they said were unavailable while still the most vulnerable seem to get least. We know that when resources were suddenly found in 2008 to rescue the banks, it was not the financiers who were expected to pay later. But the response to the virus has also shown glimpses of better alternatives, community responses to look after their vulnerable, collective refusals to work where profit was trumping health. We are in an extraordinary crisis, which can make worrying about the best ways of doing political economy look frivolous, but which also makes critical reflection on how the world works, and how we can make it a better world, more pressing than ever.

References

American Economic Association (2020) What is economics, available at https://www.aeaweb.org/resources/students/what-is-economics, accessed 18 March 2020.

Arrow, K.J. (1994) Methodological individualism and social knowledge, *American Economic Review*, 84(2): 1–9.

Coase, R.H. (1937) The theory of the firm, *Economica*, 4(16): 386–405.

Coddington, A. (1983) *Keynesian Economics: The Search for First Principles*, London: George Allen & Unwin.

Collins, P.H. (2000) Gender, black feminism, and black political economy, *Annals of the American Academy of Political and Social Science*, 568: 41–53.

Cox, R.W. (1981) Social forces, states and world orders, *Millennium: Journal of International Studies*, 10(2): 126–155.

Davidson, P. (1978) *Money and the Real World*, 2nd ed., London: Macmillan.

Davidson, P. (2007) *Interpreting Keynes for the 21st Century, Volume 4: The Collected Writings of Paul Davidson*, Basingstoke: Palgrave Macmillan.

Dow, S.C. (1996) *The Methodology of Macroeconomic Thought: A Conceptual Analysis of Schools of Thought in Economics*, Cheltenham, UK and Brookfield, VT, USA: Edward Elgar Publishing.

Fine, B. and Milonakis, D. (2009) *From Economics Imperialism to Freakonomics: The Shifting Boundaries between Economics and Other Social Sciences*, Abingdon: Routledge.

Friedman, M. (1987) Quantity theory of money, in Eatwell, J., Milgate, M. and Newman, P. (eds) *The New Palgrave Dictionary of Economics*, Vol. 4, London: Macmillan, pp. 3–20.

Fusfeld, D.R. (2002) *The Age of the Economist*, Boston, MA: Addison-Wesley.

Gibson-Graham, J.K. (1996) *The End of Capitalism (As We Knew It)*, Cambridge, MA: Blackwell.

Goldstein, J.P. and Hilliard, M.G. (2009) Introduction: a second-generation synthesis of heterodox macroeconomic principles, in Goldstein, J.P. and Hilliard, M.G. (eds) *Heterodox Macroeconomics: Keynes, Marx and Globalization*, London: Routledge, pp. 3–23.

Green, F. and Nore, P. (eds) (1977) *Economics: An Anti-Text*, London: Macmillan.

Hartmann, H. (1981) The unhappy marriage of Marxism and feminism: towards a more progressive union, in Sargent, L. (ed.) *The Unhappy Marriage of Marxism and Feminism*, London: Pluto Press, pp. 19–33.

Hayek, F.A. (1948) *Individualism and Economic Order*, Chicago: University of Chicago Press.

Heilbroner, R. and Milberg, W. (1995) *The Crisis of Vision in Modern Economic Thought*, Cambridge: Cambridge University Press.

Hewitson, G. (1994) Deconstructing Robinson Crusoe: a feminist interrogation of 'rational economic man', *Australian Feminist Studies*, 9(20): 131–149.

Jevons, W.S. (1957) *The Theory of Political Economy*, 5th ed., New York: Sentry Press.

Kahneman, D. (2012) *Thinking, Fast and Slow*, Harmondsworth: Penguin.

Keynes, J.M. (1973) *The General Theory of Employment, Interest and Money*, London: Macmillan.

Keynes, J.M. (2012) *The Collected Writings of John Maynard Keynes, Volume XIV: The General Theory and After: Part II. Defence and Development*, Johnson, E. and Moggridge, D. (eds) Cambridge: Cambridge University Press.

Keynes, J.M. (2013) *The Collected Writings of John Maynard Keynes, Volume XX: Activities 1929–1931: Rethinking Employment and Unemployment Policies*, Moggridge, D. (ed.) Cambridge: Cambridge University Press.

Krugman, P.R. (1979) Increasing returns, monopolistic competition, and international trade, *Journal of International Economics*, 9: 469–479.

Krugman, P.R. (1993) *Geography and Trade*, Leuven: Leuven University Press.

Lawson, T. (1997) *Economics and Reality*, London: Routledge.

Leamer, E.E. (2012) *The Craft of Economics: Lessons from the Heckscher–Ohlin Framework*, Cambridge, MA: MIT Press.

Lukes, S. (1973) *Individualism*, Oxford: Basil Blackwell.

Marx, K. (2010) *Marx and Engels Collected Works*, Vol. 11, Lawrence & Wishart, ebook.

Matthaei, J. (1996) Why feminist, Marxist and anti-racist economists should be feminist-Marxist-anti-racist economists, *Journal of Feminist Economics*, 2(1): 22–42.

Milonakis, D. and Fine, B. (2009) *From Political Economy to Economics: Method, the Social and the Historical in the Evolution of Economic Theory*, Abingdon: Routledge.

Mirowski, P. (1992) Do economists suffer from physics envy? *Finnish Economics Papers*, 5(1): 61–68.

Myrdal, G. (1944) *An American Dilemma: The Negro Problem and Modern Democracy*, 7th ed., New York: Harper & Brothers.

Onuf, N. (1997) A constructivist manifesto, in Burch, K. and Denemark, R.A. (eds) *Constituting International Political Economy*, Boulder, CO: Lynne Rienner, pp. 7–17.

Robinson, J. (1964) *Economic Philosophy*, Harmondsworth: Pelican

Rousseas, S. (1986) *Post Keynesian Monetary Economics*, Basingstoke: Macmillan.

Shackle, G.L.S. (1972) *Epistemics and Economics: A Critique of Economic Doctrines*, Cambridge: Cambridge University Press.

Shaikh, A. (2016) *Capitalism: Competition, Conflict, Crises*, Oxford: Oxford University Press.

Tabb, W.K. (1999) *Reconstructing Political Economy*, London: Routledge.

Thompson, S. (2012) *Calculus Made Easy*, London: Palgrave Macmillan.

Tullock, G. (1987) Public choice, in Eatwell, J., Milgate, M. and Newman, P. (eds) *The New Palgrave: A Dictionary of Economics*, London: Macmillan, pp. 1040–1044.

Walby, S. (1986) *Patriarchy at Work*, Cambridge: Polity Press.

Williamson, O. E. (1975) *Markets and Hierarchies*, New York: Free Press.

2 The political economy of inequality: research to deepen understanding

Frank Stilwell

Introduction

Now is a key moment for researching inequality from a critical political economic perspective. Widening rich–poor gaps in many countries, alongside profound problems of climate change, economic insecurity and financial instability, have generated growing public concern. Political economy, as an analytical approach that probes connections between economic issues, social wellbeing and political processes, is uniquely placed to reveal what is happening and what could make a difference.

The modern study of inequality builds on the contributions of pioneering political economic thinkers who sought to understand 'who got what'. Two centuries ago, David Ricardo described the study of income distribution between the classes as the 'central question in political economy'. Karl Marx analysed it as a structural feature of an economic system under the rule of capital. J.S. Mill thought that, whereas production had to operate according to economic laws, political choices could determine the distribution of the incomes thereby generated. Thorstein Veblen wryly observed how the extreme inequalities associated with the rise of a 'leisure class' led to wasteful forms of consumption. J.M. Keynes considered that the economy would function better with less inequality once society adjusted to the change. J.K. Galbraith pointed to the adverse consequences of not pursuing greater distributional equity, including the persistence of poverty in affluent societies.

Whereas sociologists have typically stressed the multi-dimensional characteristics of inequalities, the political economists' primary focus has usually been more directly on income and wealth, seeking to illuminate the material foundations of the social inequalities and tensions that bedevil deeply divided societies. Extending and deepening our knowledge of these matters is as crucial as ever, perhaps even more so now because of the dominant contemporary trend towards increased intra-national inequalities.

It is therefore important to take stock of what we know and what we still need to know about economic inequalities. Some research questions relate to theoretical issues, such as how we conceptualise the relationship between income and wealth. Others are more directly empirical, concerned with evidence about inequality and its measurement. Yet others concern causal relationships, seeking to understand the drivers of inequality and how it connects with social problems and political processes. Finally, there are questions about policy effectiveness and alternative strategies for creating a more egalitarian society. This chapter explores these concerns sequentially, beginning with a stocktaking of what we already know before moving on to consider the theoretical, empirical and policy issues that researchers need to address.

Taking stock

Analysis of economic inequalities has surged since the global financial crisis. The publication of Thomas Piketty's book *Capital in the Twenty-first Century* (2014) gave major stimulus to both public interest and professional debate on this topic. Other important contributions during the last decade have come from political economists and interdisciplinary scholars, including Galbraith (2012), Bowles (2012), Stiglitz (2013, 2015), Atkinson (2015), Zucman (2015), Di Muzio (2015), Milanovic (2016), Schneider et al. (2016), Dorling (2017), McCain (2017) and Wilkinson and Pickett (2018). These contributions have helped us to understand the nature, causes and consequences of inequality.

We know that, while greater wage disparities have driven increased income inequalities, there is also growing inequality of incomes from property ownership, creating a compounding effect. Exploring the stock–flow relationships between incomes and wealth is crucial for understanding the relative income shares of capital, land and labour and the inequalities of incomes and wealth between households.

We also have increasingly good data showing the multiple geographical scales at which inequalities of incomes and wealth exist – global, international, intra-national and sub-national. Of these scales, the first two are best known because most data about the distribution of incomes and wealth is collected by national governments, before being assembled and reconciled by international agencies and collaborative research teams. The data reveals substantial changes in international inequalities during the last few decades. In many countries, especially in sub-Saharan Africa, the stresses of underdevelopment and widespread poverty remain pervasive and acute (Obeng-Odoom 2017); but some previously poor nations, such as India and China, have experienced rapid overall economic growth. More often than not, however, the intra-national inequalities of income and wealth have increased, as the wealth has become more concentrated in rich elites. That tendency has been particularly pronounced in India and China, the world's two most populous nations. Meanwhile, in most of the advanced capitalist countries, intra-national inequalities have also tended to increase, most glaringly so in the US.

Trying to assess whether global inequality – looking at the whole of the world's population irrespective of location, race or gender – is increasing or decreasing is difficult in these circumstances, since it requires measurement of the net effects of the international and intra-national shifts. A prerequisite has been to get the nation-based economic data into a reasonably consistent global form, a task that has motivated major studies by Bourguignon (2015), Milanovic (2016), Solt (2016) and the team of researchers producing the *World Inequality Report* (Alvaredo et al. 2018; World Inequality Lab 2019). The result has been significant progress in monitoring the global, international and intra-national trends, revealing a kaleidoscope of shifting disparities within a strikingly unequal world.

Improved data is one thing: understanding the human and social implications of the revealed inequalities is another. Here too, significant progress has been made in social science research, showing significant connections between economic inequality and social problems such as physical and mental ill-health, crime and incarceration, environmental degradation and poor educational outcomes (Wilkinson and Pickett 2009, 2018; Dorling 2017; Stilwell 2019). This work extends our knowledge of how inequality impacts on the wellbeing of individuals and societies. Thus, it shows why inequality matters. Yet, determining the best ways of conceptualising, measuring and monitoring inequality's connections with wellbeing remains a significant research concern.

Turning to what could be done to reduce inequality raises different questions about the effectiveness of policy instruments. Consider fiscal redistribution through taxation and transfer payments, for example. Most countries do it, but its impact on inequality varies considerably, ranging from high in Ireland, where fiscal redistribution reduces inequality of 'market' incomes by about

40 per cent, to very low in Chile, where its estimated reduction of inequality is a mere 5 per cent (Causa and Hermansen 2017). We also have increasingly good information on the effectiveness of other policy instruments that can re-shape particular types of inequality. For gender inequalities, for example, there is research comparing the trends in the gender pay gap between societies with different regulatory and affirmative action policies (Blau and Kahn 2017). For racial inequalities, we have useful data on average incomes and wealth of racial groups within individual nations, showing how deep divisions may persist despite anti-discrimination laws (e.g. Leiman 2010; Chetty et al. 2018; Corlett 2017).

This empirically based knowledge is substantial, helping to reveal the patterns, processes, problems and policies associated with economic inequalities. These are the dimensions of knowledge that I sought to synthesise when writing *The Political Economy of Inequality* (Stilwell 2019). While doing that stocktaking, however, I became aware of various aspects of the topic requiring further research. This chapter is therefore a sequel to the book, identifying knowledge gaps and suggesting directions for future research. Its central theme is the importance of extending knowledge into deeper understanding that leads to action.

Considering conceptual issues

A necessary starting point is to consider how understanding inequality can be most effectively framed. Clear conceptualisation of the wealth–income relationship is crucial. In popular discourse, income and wealth are terms that are often used interchangeably, but wealth as a stock of assets has to be carefully distinguished from income as a flow. More generally, we need an analysis that distinguishes five key dimensions of wealth and income inequalities, focusing on:

1. the relationship between public wealth and private wealth;
2. inequality in the distribution of private wealth;
3. the shares of labour, land and capital in total income;
4. inequality of incomes among waged workers, among landowners and among the owners of capital; and
5. the resulting distribution of household incomes.

Looked at in this stepwise manner, the income inequalities between rich and poor households (i.e. the last of the items above) can be understood in terms of the preceding four dimensions. First, the relative sizes of public and private wealth indicate the extent to which people's needs are catered for collectively (e.g. through state provision of goods and services) rather than by people depending on their individual economic resources. Second, how unequal is the distribution of private wealth – is it widely spread or concentrated among relatively few individuals or corporations? Third, how is the total income split between classes – as payments to workers and to the owners and managers of capital and land? Fourth, what about inequalities of income *within* each of the classes – inequalities among the workers and among the capitalists and landowners? Together, all these factors shape the extent of inequality in the distribution of household incomes.

Much follows from this way of seeing. It takes us beneath the 'surface appearances' of personal income inequalities to the underlying structural determinants. It directs attention to how the differential ownership of labour, land and capital impacts on incomes and wealth. It shows how people with high incomes can accumulate wealth and how that wealth then expands possibilities for gaining even higher incomes. Thus it leads into an interpretation of poverty and wealth as mutually reinforcing. It also creates a foundation for understanding the processes of circular and cumulative causation that make inequality and poverty such pervasive and deeply rooted phenomena.

Conceptual and empirical issues arise at each of the five analytical steps. Take step three, for example: identifying and measuring the shares of income going to labour, capital and land – the so-called 'functional distribution of income'. In practice, distinguishing between labour and non-labour incomes is easier said than done. Are the incomes of senior executive officers in large corporations properly regarded as wage incomes (as official statistical agencies usually classify them) or are they payments to the managers of capital? How are 'mixed incomes' to be allocated, such as those going to owners of small businesses as a result of their personal labour as well as capital ownership? And can we unpack the total non-wage share of national income – the 'gross operating surplus' – into its component parts, such as the payments to landed capital, industrial capital and finance capital? Although attempts at that sort of disaggregation have been made (e.g. Karabarbounis and Neiman 2017; Peetz 2018), the research is still at an exploratory stage.

Extending empirical research

Data on inequalities information needs to be consistent over long periods of time (to facilitate time-series analyses) and between different places (to facilitate comparative cross-country and cross-regional studies). Building on the considerable progress that has already been made in these respects (as reviewed by World Inequality Lab 2019), the following five points may be helpful in guiding future research.

First, choosing the most appropriate measures of inequality requires careful consideration. Among the many measurement options are (1) percentage shares (e.g. the share of the top 1 per cent or top 10 per cent of households in the total income or wealth); (2) comparative shares (e.g. the share of the top 10 per cent as a ratio of the bottom 10 per cent); (3) comparative percentile measures (e.g. the P10:P90 ratio, which is the income of the household 10 per cent from the top of the distribution expressed as a multiple of the income of the household 10 per cent from the bottom); and (4) statistical artefacts, such as the Gini coefficient, that represent distributions in terms of their deviation from an hypothetical norm, such as complete equality. Each of them has its own rationale, depending on which aspect of inequality is under considera-tion. However, the different indicators do not necessarily generate consistent empirical rankings when applied to cross-country comparisons.

Should the Gini be the preferred choice? It still has the 'inside-track running' because of its widespread use. However, it is under increasing challenge. Clemanti et al. (2019) argue that it is conceptually flawed because 'apart from concentration, it cannot grasp other relevant features of inequality like hetero-geneity and asymmetry'. The Gini is also more sensitive to changes occurring at the centre of the distribution than at the tails, which makes it ill-suited to studying recent distributional shifts where the main action is at the top end (Alvaredo 2011). Measures such as the income and wealth shares going to the top 1 per cent have become increasingly widely used in preference to the Gini (or alongside it), especially by those motivated to show who are the principal beneficiaries of the distributional shifts. Greater standardisation on this basis would help with consistency in the treatment and presentation of data.

Second, there is the question of how the empirical data itself could be improved. Reliance on whatever information is available from official national and international agencies seems inescapable. However, the official data tends to be deficient in showing the extent of concentration at the top end. The statistical problem of under-sampling is compounded by the tendency for rich people to conceal their incomes and wealth in tax havens and other tax-avoidance processes. One estimate is that some 8 per cent of global wealth is hidden through such means (Zucman 2015). Progress towards better data is therefore inseparable from progress in economic reform – meaning, in this case, the implementation of globally enforceable policies to limit the means by which wealthy people protect their wealth from public scrutiny and redistributive policies.

Third, the development of distributional accounts deserves strong support as a means of creating more internationally consistent empirical data. Pursuing this ambition would be a mission comparable to the standardisation of national income accounts that occurred in the mid-20th century when, building on the conceptual initiatives of economists like Keynes, Kuznets and Clark, consistent national income accounting practices were adopted worldwide. A comparable push for distributional accounts, based on the pioneering work already undertaken for the US by Piketty et al. (2018), would be timely. Linked to national income accounts, distributional accounts can show the interconnection between macroeconomic and distributional variables, providing a basis for analysis of the impacts of different types of public policy.

Fourth, there could be more focus in empirical research on the 'intersectionality' of class, race and gender. Getting the best possible national data on distributional inequality of incomes and wealth is necessary but not sufficient. As nearly all analysts in this field of inquiry acknowledge, income and wealth inequalities interact with socio-economic and personal attributes. Two types of connection are involved. First, relationships of class, gender and race structure the overall extent of inequality and the forms that it takes in different regions and nations. Second, where any individual is positioned in the overall distribution depends on their class, gender and race. Studies of intersectionality emphasise that these dimensions of inequality are commonly multiplicative, not merely additive, in their effects (e.g. Lokuge and Hillhorst 2017). Social science research needs to link political economic analysis of the systemic features of inequality with more micro-scale research undertaken by sociologists and anthropologists.

Finally, it is important to consider the spatial dimension of inequality. All empirical studies of inequality focusing on international differences have a spatial element in that countries are geographically bounded entities. With each nation, however, cities, towns, villages and rural areas often differ dramatically in their residents' economic conditions and opportunities. Paying more attention to these sub-national inequalities would show the importance of locality as the spatial scale at which macroeconomic forces most directly interact with the social features of class, race and gender. It would also bring inequalities in cost of living more explicitly into focus. Wellbeing, even in a narrow economic interpretation, depends substantially on how much has to be outlaid for key items of consumption, such as housing. Because the price of housing – whether owned or rented – often differs strikingly between rural and urban locations, the relative incidence of urban poverty almost invariably looks higher if housing costs are considered. Concurrently, wealthy urban landowners commonly reap enormous capital gains as urbanisation inflates the market values of land and housing, further concentrating the accumulation of wealth (Christophers 2018). Spatial analysis, linked to the study of people's ownership (or non-ownership) of land and housing in different localities, can help to draw out these influences on the forms that inequality takes.

Analysing drivers of inequality

Explaining the changing patterns of inequality often proceeds on a case-by-case basis, focusing on the experiences of individual nations (e.g. Joyce and Xu 2019; Collins 2018; Stilwell 2019: chs 3,4) or clusters of countries (e.g. Alvaredo et al. 2018: 83–168 and 236–276; Babones and Elsenhans 2017). Nation-specific political economic narratives abound. Where attempts are made to identify more universal drivers of inequality the influence of theoretical perspectives is yet more evident. Mainstream economists tend to put technology and markets at the centre of their analyses, identifying winners and losers according to the relationship between people's 'human capital' and the shifting patterns of rewards in the marketplace caused by technological changes. As Semuels (2016) writes, 'their view is generally that globalisation and technology created a world in which high-skilled people did well and others did not'. Other economists like Stiglitz (2013, 2015), favouring a liberal reformist variant of neoclassical economic reasoning, emphasise monopoly, asymmetric information and 'rent-seeking' behaviours that cause 'market distortions'. Radical political economic perspectives dig deeper, putting greater emphasis on the economic outcomes arising from the shifting power relations between capital and labour, including the effects of globalisation, financialisation and neoliberalism (Stilwell 2019: chs 6,7).

Piketty has presented the most influential framing of these issues. While his analysis has engendered mixed responses from political economists (e.g. Pressman 2015; Morgan 2015; Sheil 2015; King 2017), he is to be applauded for digging deeper than those who simply attribute economic inequality to successes or failures in the marketplace. His macroeconomic perspective centres on the general tendency for the rate of economic growth to exceed the rate of return on capital, producing his famous r > g formulation of the principal driver of increased inequality. Yet, from a political economic perspective, his explorations of the factors shaping wealth concentration are probably the more fundamental contribution. Indeed, even within the more restricted r > g story, the extent of inequality depends crucially on how concentrated is the ownership of wealth. Inequality does not significantly increase as a result of r being greater than g if the ownership of capital is broadly spread across the population. The smaller the group getting the capital income, the greater the inequality resulting from each set of values for r and g. This is why political economic research needs to focus on the drivers of that increasing concentration. This would also reveal the intergenerational wealth transmission processes that operate through inheritance and/or transfers made to children in wealthy families who use the 'bank of mum and dad' to facilitate the purchase of expensive properties that children in poorer households could never afford.

Ideally, we would assess the strength of each of these political economic factors – including globalisation, financialisation, neoliberalism, technological change, urbanisation and inheritance – in terms of their impacts on inequality. Some economists might advocate econometric work to provide quantitative estimates for the explanatory variables. However, while it is easy to posit possible causal connections, it is much harder to specify these relationships in a manner that is amenable to empirical testing. None of the explanatory variables mentioned above is reducible to a single numerical value, and most, if not all, of them are interdependent. Indeed, it is unrealistic to imagine that social science could ever be conclusive about quantitative apportionment of shifts in the extent of inequality to causal factors that are so broadly defined and where there are so many interconnecting channels of influence. There is probably more to be learned from an historical-institutional approach, focusing on the qualitative changes and shifting power relations in successive waves of political economic change. This would include consideration of the effects of colonialism and its continuing legacy in post-colonial societies, helping to redress the neglect of 'Southern perspectives' in political economic inquiry.

Identifying the consequences of inequality

Somewhat similar concerns arise when turning from inequality's causes to its consequences. Improving our understanding of the nature and range of inequality's impacts on wellbeing and sustainability is necessary. However, the causal connections, though crucially important, are numerous, complex and not easily isolated. Yet research is essential because herein lies the 'should we care?' question (Bushey et al. 2017: 13). As concerned social scientists, we need to consider and explain why the extent of inequality, not just the existence of poverty at one end of the inequality spectrum, should be of social and political concern.

More carefully constructed cross-country comparisons are the obvious priority, investigating whether and why more equal nations have fewer socio-economic problems. Much has already been done, including studies that refute the claims commonly made by neoclassical economists and conservative politicians about the necessity for substantial economic inequalities as incentives for work, higher productivity and faster economic growth. Research emanating from the International Monetary Fund (IMF) shows that countries with less inequality tend to have generally superior macroeconomic outcomes (Berg and Ostry 2011; Berg et al. 2012; Ostry et al. 2014, 2018). These research findings have been widely cited, not least because they emanate from an international agency that has long been regarded as a contributor to the global inequality problem.

We also have increasingly good cross-sectional international studies of the association between economic inequality and other social variables (Wilkinson and Pickett 2009, 2018; Dorling 2017) and extensive consideration of the ways in which extreme inequality impairs the functioning of democracy (e.g. Stiglitz 2013). The nature of the causal connections is open to continuing debate, of course. There are well-known problems of isolating the effects of particular variables because everything else cannot be held equal, particularly where major differences of geography and culture exist. However, the evidence continues to expand, now also including how inequality relates to societal problems in individual countries, such as the recent study of different forms of addiction in the US (Sachs 2019). Concurrently, further study of people's capabilities and wellbeing, building on the pioneering work of Sen (1999), can help to show how inequality impairs the health and happiness of the societies in which those people live.

Taking that step into the analysis of inequality's connections with (un)happiness is a controversial suggestion, because some would say it goes beyond the field in which political economists can claim expertise. Yet it has wry appeal to critics of neoclassical economics because it 'brings it all back home' to that theory's origins in theorising about 'utility' (Cook 2018). If subjective measures of people's welfare (utility) show a negative correlation with inequality, we may infer that mainstream economists have been backing the wrong horse, even by their own standards, when they prioritise economic growth rather than distributional equity as the principal goal of economic policy. Recognising the diverse views on how inequality relates to happiness (e.g. Piekalkiewicz 2017; Powdthavee et al. 2017; Stevenson and Wolfers 2008), an empirically based way forward needs to be found, one that identifies what actually increases people's wellbeing. One possibility is to develop nation-based wellbeing accounts to supplement national income accounts and the distributional accounts advocated above. If, on similar reasoning, a further set of accounts on environmental quality were also added, that would comprise a formidable database – four interlinked accounts on national income, inequality, social wellbeing and environment for each country. This sounds like a very tall order, but if achieved it would be an unprecedented set of data for monitoring and analysing how distributional variables relate to macroeconomic conditions, wellbeing and sustainability.

Prescribing policies and assessing political possibilities

Turning from the questions of 'why should we care?' and 'what do we need to know?' to 'what should we do next?' raises yet more deep-seated dilemmas. While it is not difficult to identify particular types of public policy that *could* make a difference, it is much harder to identify the political economic conditions under which such policies could actually operate.

What are the policy options? Broadly, they can be grouped in two categories: redistribution and pre-distribution. The former seeks to ameliorate inequality through policies such as progressive taxation and public expenditures that benefit poorer people, either by direct transfers or by providing improved public services and infrastructure, thereby reducing the adverse effects of existing 'market' inequalities on wellbeing. The latter involves strategies that dig deeper into the determinants of the 'market' inequalities themselves, such as setting minimum wage rates, putting caps on executive remuneration, limiting corporate power, enhancing the wage-bargaining capacities of trade unions or fostering the development of worker and community co-operatives. Some potential public policies straddle both redistribution and pre-distribution. Public provision of basic income is a case in point, reducing poverty by 'raising the floor' in the distribution of income but simultaneously expanding the range of citizens' rights (Standing 2017; van Parijs and Vanderborght 2017; Haagh 2019).

Assessing the effectiveness of different policies for reducing inequality is never simple. The difficulty of running large-scale controlled experiments pervades the social sciences. Even practical trials, such as have occurred in relation to basic income policies, have their limitations as a means of assessing the viability of policies on a broader society-wide basis. However, internationally comparative studies can usefully focus on seeing how countries with markedly different structures of taxation and industrial relations compare in terms of their macroeconomic performance and other social indicators. Historical studies can also be useful adjuncts, for example looking back to periods such as the 1950s and 1960s when income tax rates in the advanced capitalist countries were very much higher than they are today, or at countries with different rates of inheritance taxation and their effectiveness in reducing intergenerational inequalities. Thus, both the spatial and temporal dimensions of research into policy effectiveness can add to the stock of policy-relevant knowledge.

Knowledge is even better if it leads to effective action. The difficulties associated with the politics of making progressive change are all too evident, however. Looking at the situation from a political economic perspective, the question of agency is paramount. Who is the 'we' in the question 'what ought we to do next?' (Bushey et al. 2017: 19). Formally, the state represents the collective interest and has the capacity to develop and implement policies that would reduce inequality. However, in a class-structured society, the relevant 'we' may need to be seen quite differently – as comprising people active in the labour movement and in non-governmental organisations (NGOs) pressing for more progressive distributional arrangements. What research agendas are implied? One option is study of how inequality impacts on support for different types of political parties and public policies, taking us into the study of public opinion formation, social attitudes and political commitments (e.g. Piketty 2018, 2020; Petach 2017; Solt 2012; Ritter and Solt 2019). This line of inquiry raises questions about the future prospects for social democratic and labour parties that are losing their traditional bases of reliable support in the working class. The recent growth of right-wing populism in many nations and the corresponding difficulty in getting support for social democratic reformist policies brings such concerns into increasingly sharp focus. Another research agenda is more explicitly strategic, exploring potentially effective strategies for driving egalitarian political economic change. Such focus on 'the politics of the possible' (Stilwell 2015) takes a more prescriptive approach to seeing what can be done even in the most difficult political economic contexts.

Conclusion

Progress in understanding economic inequality and its diverse dimensions is possible. As indicated in this chapter, various forms of research can add usefully to our knowledge of the relevant patterns, processes, problems, policies and politics. However, as is commonly the case in social sciences, progress also depends upon the changing material conditions in the real world. Issues relating to inequality are inevitably intertwined with interests, ideologies and institutions. We cannot blithely assume that improved knowledge will translate into social improvement. Advances in knowledge need to interact with human agency that is capable of driving progressive social change.

It has been wisely said that 'with most problems nowadays the economic answers are only political questions' (Robinson 1980: 275). In this case, the key questions are 'what type of society do we want?' and 'how are we going to get it?' Researching inequality from a critical political economy perspective can make a useful, albeit not decisive, contribution in this context. A purely academic exercise cannot suffice. We also need to research – and work to change – public perceptions and power relationships if we want to move beyond knowledge to the deeper forms of understanding that lead to purposeful action. In other words, alongside an analytical agenda, assessing the causes and consequences of inequality in contemporary capitalist societies is an important area for visionary post-capitalist thinking and actions. Not all researchers can be expected to engage in these activist elements, but making the connection is ultimately essential if knowledge is to have social purpose and impact.

References

Alvaredo, F. (2011) A note on the relationship between top income shares and the Gini coefficient, *Economic Letters*, 110: 274–277.

Alvaredo, F., Chancel, L., Piketty, T., Saez, A. and Zucman, G. (2018) *World Inequality Report 2018*, Cambridge, MA: Belknap Press of Harvard University Press.

Atkinson, A. (2015) *Inequality: What Can Be Done?* Cambridge, MA: Harvard University Press.

Babones, S. and Elsenhans, H. (2017) *BRICS or Bust? Escaping the Middle-Income Trap*, Stanford, CA: Stanford University Press.

Berg, G. and Ostry, J. (2011) *Inequality and Sustainable Growth: Two Sides of the Same Coin?* IMF Staff Discussion Note SDN/11/08.

Berg, G., Ostry, J. and Zettlemeyer, J. (2012) What makes growth sustained? *Journal of Development Economics*, 98(2): 149–166.

Blau, F.D. and Kahn, L.M. (2017) The gender wage gap: extent, trends and explanations, *Journal of Economic Literature*, 53(3): 789–865.

Bourgignon, F. (2015) *The Globalisation of Inequality*, Princeton, NJ: Princeton University Press.

Bowles, S. (2012) *The New Economics of Inequality and Redistribution*, Cambridge: Cambridge University Press.

Bushey, H., Delong, J.B. and Steinbaum, M. (eds) (2017) *After Piketty: The Agenda for Economics and Inequality*, Cambridge, MA: Harvard University Press.

Causa, O. and Hermansen, M. (2017) *Income Redistribution through Taxes and Transfers across OECD Countries*, OECD Economics Department Working Papers, 1453, OECD Publishing, Paris.

Chetty, R., Hendren, N., Jones, M.R. and Porter, S.R. (2018) *Race and Economic Opportunity in the United States: An Intergenerational Perspective*, US Census Bureau, April.

Christophers, B. (2018) Intergenerational inequality: labour, capital and housing through the ages, *Antipode*, 50(1): 101–121.

Clemanti, F., Gallegati, M., Gianmoena, L., Landini, S. and Stiglitz, J.E. (2019) Mis-measurement of inequality: a critical reflection and new insights, *Journal of Economic Interaction and Coordination*, 14: 891–921.

Collins, C. (2018) *Is Inequality in America Irreversible?* Cambridge: Polity Press.

Cook, E. (2018) The great marginalisation: why twentieth century economists neglected inequality, *Real-World Economics Review*, 83: 20–34.

Corlett, A. (2017) *Diverse Outcomes: Living Standards by Ethnicity*, Resolution Foundation, available at https//:www.resolutionfoundation.org/app/uploads/2017/08/Diverse-oucomes.pdf, accessed 22 September 2018.

Di Muzio (2015) *The 1% and the Rest of Us: A Political Economy of Dominant Ownership*, London: Zed Books.

Dorling, D. (2017) *The Equality Effect: Improving Life for Everyone*, Oxford: New Internationalist Publications.

Galbraith, J.K. (2012) *Inequality and Instability*, New York: Oxford University Press.

Haagh, L. (2019) *The Case for Universal Basic Income*, Cambridge: Polity Press.

Joyce, R. and Xu, X. (2019) *Inequalities in the 21st Century: Introducing the Deaton Review*, Institute for Fiscal Studies, Nuffield Foundation, UK.

Karabarbounis, L. and Neiman, B. (2017) The global decline of the labour share, *Quarterly Journal of Economics*, 129(1): 61–103.

King, J. (2017) The literature on Piketty, *Review of Political Economy*, 29(1): 1–17.

Leiman, M. (2010) *The Political Economy of Racism*, Chicago: Haymarket Books.

Lokuge, G. and Hillhorst, D. (2017) Outside the net: intersectionality and inequality in the fisheries of Trincomalee, Sri Lanka, *Asian Journal of Women's Studies*, 23(4): 473–497.

McCain, R.A. (2017) *Approaching Inequality: What Can Be Done about Wealth Inequality?* Cheltenham, UK and Northampton, MA, USA: Edward Elgar Publishing.

Milanovic, B. (2016) *Global Inequality: A New Approach in the Age of Globalisation*, Cambridge, MA: Belknap Press of Harvard University Press.

Morgan, J. (2015) Piketty's calibration economics: inequality and the dissolution of solutions, *Globalisations*, 12(5): 803–823.

Obeng-Odoom, F. (2017) The myth of economic growth in Africa, *Review of African Political Economy*, 44: 466–475.

Ostry, J.D., Berg, A. and Kothari, S. (2018) *Growth–Equity Trade-Offs in Structural Reforms*, IMF Working Paper WP 18/5.

Ostry, J.D., Berg, A. and Tsangarides, N. (2014) *Redistribution, Inequality and Growth*, IMF Staff Discussion Note SDN/14/02.

Peetz, D. (2018) The labour share, power and financialisation, *Journal of Australian Political Economy*, 81, Winter: 34–51.

Petach, L. (2017) Politics, preferences and prices: the political consequences of inequality, *Real-World Economics Review*, 80: 2–15.

Piekalkiewicz, M. (2017) Why do economists study happiness? *Economic and Labour Relations Review*, 60(1): 3–22.

Piketty, T. (2014) *Capital in the Twenty-first Century*, Cambridge, MA: Harvard University Press.

Piketty, T. (2018) *Brahmin Left vs Merchant Right: Rising Inequality and the Structure of Political Conflict*, World Inequality Working Paper, available at http://piketty.pse .ens.fr/files/Piketty2018.pdf, accessed 22 September 2018.

Piketty, T. (2020) *Capital and Ideology*, Cambridge, MA: Harvard University Press.

Piketty, T., Saez, E. and Zucman, G. (2018) Distributional national accounts: methods and estimates for the United States, *Quarterly Journal of Economic*, 133(2): 553–609.

Powdthavee, N., Burkhauser, R.V. and De Neve, J.E. (2017) Top incomes and human well-being: evidence from the Gallup World Poll, *Journal of Economic Psychology*, 62, October: 246–257.

Pressman, S. (2015) *Understanding Piketty's Capital in the Twenty-first Century*, London: Routledge.

Ritter, M. and Solt, F. (2019) Economic inequality and campaign participation, *Social Science Quarterly*, 100(3): 678–688.

Robinson, J. (1980) *Collected Economic Papers*, Vol. 2, Oxford: Basil Blackwell.

Sachs, J. (2019) Addiction and unhappiness in America, in Helliwell, J.F., Layard, R. and Sachs, J.D. (eds) *World Happiness Report*, New York: Sustainable Development Solutions Network, pp. 123–135.

Schneider, M., Pottinger, J. and King, J. (2016) *The Distribution of Wealth: Growing Inequality?* Cheltenham, UK and Northampton, MA, USA: Edward Elgar Publishing.

Semuels, A. (2016) Why so few American economists are studying inequality, *The Atlantic*, available at https://www.the atlantic.com/business/archive/2016/09/why-so -few-american-economists-are-studying-inequality/499253/, accessed 22 September 2018.

Sen, A. (1999) *Commodities and Capabilities*, 2nd ed., Delhi and New York: Oxford University Press.

Sheil, C. (2015) Piketty's political economy, *Journal of Australian Political Economy*, 74: 19–37.

Solt, F. (2012) The social origins of authoritarianism, *Political Research Quarterly*, 65(4): 703–713.

Solt, F. (2016) The Standardised World Inequality Database, *Social Science Quarterly*, 97(5): 1267–1281.

Standing, G. (2017) *Basic Income: And How We Can Make It Happen*, London: Penguin.

Stevenson, B. and Wolfers, J. (2008) Economic growth and happiness: reassessing the Easterlin paradox, *Brookings Papers on Economic Activity*, Spring: 1–87.

Stiglitz, J.E. (2013) *The Price of Inequality: How Today's Divided Society Endangers Our Future*, New York: W. W. Norton & Company.

Stiglitz, J.E. (2015) *The Great Divide: Unequal Societies and What We Can Do about Them*, New York: W. W. Norton & Company.

Stilwell, F. (2015) Towards a political economy of the possible, in Sprague, J. (ed.) *Globalisation and Transnational Capitalism in Asia and Oceania*, London: Routledge, pp. 302–317.

Stilwell, F. (2019) *The Political Economy of Inequality*, Cambridge: Polity Press.

van Parijs, P. and Vanderborght, Y. (2017) *Basic Income: A Radical Proposal for a Free Society and a Sane Economy*, Cambridge, MA: Harvard University Press.

Wilkinson, R. and Pickett, K. (2009) *The Spirit Level: Why More Equal Societies Almost Always Do Better*, London: Allen Lane.

Wilkinson, R. and Pickett, K. (2018) *The Inner Level: How More Equal Societies Reduce Stress, Restore Sanity and Improve Everyone's Well-Being*, London: Allen Lane.

World Inequality Lab (2019) Measuring inequality in income and wealth, in *Human Development Report 2019*, New York: UNDP, pp. 103–143.

Zucman, G. (2015) *The Hidden Wealth of Nations: The Scourge of Tax Havens*, Chicago: Chicago University Press.

3 Economic growth and the ideology of development

Benjamin Selwyn

1. Introduction

Anyone engaged in the study of development will be familiar with how economic growth represents a common-sense foundation of human progress. For example, *The Economist* (1 June 2013) claims that '[m]ost of the credit [for global poverty reduction] … must go to capitalism and free trade, for they enable economies to grow – and it was growth, principally, that has eased destitution.' The Sustainable Development Goals (SDGs) posit limited growth as a principal cause of poverty:

> A continued lack of decent work opportunities, insufficient investments and under-consumption lead to an erosion of the basic social contract underlying democratic societies: that all must share in progress. Even though the average annual growth rate of real GDP per capita worldwide is increasing year on year, there are still many countries in the developing world that are decelerating in their growth rates and moving farther from the 7% growth rate target set for 2030. (United Nations 2020)

Global capitalism is an immense wealth-generating system. Despite the chronic global economic crisis that emerged in 2007, total global wealth (the sum total of money and other assets) continues to multiply. In 2013 it reached an all-time high of US$241 trillion, an increase of 68 per cent since 2003. The Swiss-based financial organisation Credit Suisse (2015) estimates that total global wealth will reach US$345 trillion by the mid-2020s. While some of this wealth is a product of new financial technologies and instruments, and might thus be labelled fictitious, growth, driven by systemic wealth accumulation, represents a general trend within capitalism. Capitalism's growth dynamic is so powerful that the world economy is set to triple in size by 2050 – entailing three times more production, consumption and trade based upon current trends (Hawksworth and Chan 2015).

However, while economic growth is inscribed into the capitalist system, it also reproduces poverty (Pogge and Reddy 2010; Pritchett 2006; Sumner 2016; Selwyn 2017) and wreaks havoc on the natural environment (Klein 2015).

What is the role of economic growth in capitalist development? How does the ideology of growth influence development policies? Are there alternatives to this growth-based mindset? This chapter addresses these questions as follows. Section two outlines how economic growth is central to the ideology of development. Section three shows how capitalist expansion generates new forms of labouring class poverty. Section four sketches out how, across the political spectrum, growth-based development ideologies justify labour repression and exploitation. Section five concludes by considering alternatives to capitalist growth-based development.

2.   Economic growth and capitalist development

Despite ever-expanding growth, the capitalist system and the ideologies promoting it are characterised by a seeming double paradox. On the one hand, capitalism's inner social relations of competitive capital accumulation ensure that it achieves higher, permanent and cumulative rates of economic growth than any previously existing social system, generating an ever-greater global accumulation of social wealth. On the other hand, proponents of capitalism and growth-based development strive continuously to achieve yet more growth.

The second paradox inherent in capitalist ideologies is between their emphasis upon individual freedom and their emphasis upon systemic imperative. From Adam Smith onwards, albeit with various nuances, pro-capitalist theorists have emphasised the individual freedoms that capitalism generates via the market mechanism, and how such choice in turn sustains further capitalist expansion (Smith 1976; Friedman and Freidman 1980). According to these theories of human betterment, individual choice functions best through the market. Withdrawal from the market, resistance to market integration or collective actions to limit the effects of market competition, are portrayed by most development theories as rigidities, or barriers, which will disrupt the ability of other individuals to exercise their freedoms of choice.

Such pro-market ideologies legitimate non-market actions in (at least) two, asymmetric ways. On the one hand, actions such as strike-breaking, harsh labour-discipline and the political imposition of low (often below subsistence) wages are supported in the name of imposing market discipline upon populations who attempt collectively to reject it. On the other hand, large-scale subsidies to corporations – such as the US $5.3 trillion (or 6.5 per cent of global GDP) in 2015 to the fossil fuel industry (Coady et al. 2017: 21) – are justified as enabling the latter sectors to perform their market-enhancing activities.

The apparent dual paradoxes of pro-capitalist theory – where freedom and benefits from economic growth can only be achieved through the subordination of the majority of society to the accumulation objectives of a small minority – represent a potential stumbling block to capitalist hegemony. This stumbling block is partially flattened through the paradigm of economic growth. As Gareth Dale explains:

> [G]rowth serves as an *idealised refiguration* of capitalist social relations; it serves to naturalise and justify the prevailing social order ... Discussion of the economic by way of biological analogy implies continuity (gradual change), and unity (it is the 'social whole' that grows). When represented through the discourse of growth, the interests of capital come to be identified with the common good, because the profitability of capital ... appears as a necessary condition for the satisfaction of all other interests. Without profitable enterprises there will be no investment, no employment, no taxation, and no money for workers to pursue their goals. (2012: 106, emphasis in original)

While capitalism's productive dynamism represents a potential source of real human development, its exploitative and competitive social relations preclude such possibilities. Because of this unpalatable fact, most capitalist theory rests upon the continued obfuscation of human social relations under capitalism. As Kidron and Gluckstein (1974: 35) put it, 'as a system of competition capitalism depends on the growth of capital; as a class system it depends on obscuring the source of that growth'.

3.   Capitalist expansion and labouring class poverty

What are the social relations that determine how economic surpluses under capitalism are distributed, and how they benefit a tiny minority at the expense of the majority?

While rapid economic growth is inscribed into the DNA of capitalism, the benefits of growth are distributed very unevenly. As David Woodward (2015: 50) observes, 'the poorest 30% of the world population received just 1.2% of the additional income generated by global GDP growth between 1999 and 2008, the poorest 60% received 5.0%, while 95% accrued to the richest 40%'. Given such an extreme rationing to the poor of the benefits of growth, Woodward calculates that it will take centuries to come anywhere near global poverty eradication. Moreover, the damage to the natural environment caused by several more hundreds of years of capitalist growth would wipe out any gains in poverty reduction, and would represent an existential threat to the continued existence of humanity (Spratt and Dunlop 2019).

Why does capitalist expansion and economic growth reproduce labouring class poverty in new ways?

Endless competitive accumulation imposes productivity drives upon individual units of capital (firms). Those that fail to increase their productivity risk bankruptcy as other more competitive firms appropriate their market share with more cheaply produced goods. Under capitalism, productivity drives are not intended to improve the living standards of workers, but to cut costs, in particular wage costs. Increases in their productivity reduce workers' *relative wage* – the difference between the value (wages) that they retain and the value that they produce. The polarisation of wealth, upon which the capital–labour relation is established initially, is thus continuously reinforced.

Firms attempt to maintain their profitability at, or raise it above, the sector-wide profit rate in two inter-related ways. The first strategy requires the spatial expansion of capital – through ever more extensive markets and access to resources, and through drawing into those markets activities that were previously external to them (Harvey 1981). Such expansion entails (full or partial) dispossession of assets and property, such as common lands, that are not (yet) subordinate to capital accumulation.

But such strategies are only one side of the coin of capitalist competition. The other is (strict) labour management. The 'inner secret', as Marx (1990) put it, of capitalist profit is capital's ability to reap a greater portion of value from workers' labour power (surplus value) than the cost of its initial purchase. Firms can increase the surplus value appropriated from workers in four broad, often combined ways, through increasing rates of (1) relative surplus value extraction (intensification of the working day); (2) absolute surplus value extraction (lengthening the working day); (3) immiseration (by pushing down wages); or (4) super-exploitation (presiding over a labour regime where wages do not satisfy workers' subsistence requirements). This second strategy requires raising the rate of labour exploitation and expanding the size of the labour force (actually or potentially) exploitable by capital, to ensure continuous surplus value extraction from labour.

Capitalist expansion, therefore, is generative of at least two historically novel forms of labouring class poverty: poverty caused by dispossession from the means of production (often through privatisation of the commons), and the payment of poverty wages (super-exploitation). Contemporary globalisation combines these dynamics in novel forms. From the imposition of structural adjustment programmes in the 1980s onwards, hundreds of millions of rural dwellers have been forced off the land in the most recent wave of capitalist enclosures (Delgado-Wise and Veltmeyer 2016), often forced to find new ways of living in the 'planet of slums' (Davis 2006). Conjointly, the expansion of the global labouring class under conditions of indecent work represents the sub-structure of the contemporary world economy – demonstrated most clearly in China's eastern seaboard, the new workshop of the world (Cantin and Taylor 2008; Chan et al. 2013).

Foster and McChesney (2012) capture the specificity of this combination of partial dispossession and super-exploitation in contemporary China:

> In Beijing around 40 percent of the population in 2011 were migrant workers, with temporary residence. In the city of Shenzhen nearly 12 million out of a total population of 14 million people are rural migrants. In addition to receiving much lower pay, rural migrants lack the benefits provided to urban-based workers in the cities, and frequently live and work at the factory in dormitory conditions. The vast majority of rural migrant laborers are under thirty-five years of age – in 2004 the average age was twenty-eight. They work in industrial centers under superexploitative conditions (i.e., receiving wages below the normal reproduction costs of workers) for a few years and then typically return to the land and their peasant origins.

4.   Pro-growth development theory: freeing the economy, regulating labour

This section outlines how most development theories posit capitalist economic growth as the basis of development and attempt to stimulate even further growth. In doing so they often justify the reproduction of social relations where labour is subordinate to capital. They represent an elite subject–subordinate object (ES–SO) conception of social transformation, where elite subjects are conceptually allocated decision-making power, while subordinate objects are conceived of as achieving social betterment by following rules established by elite subjects.

The ES–SO conception of development represents what Cowen and Shenton describe as an 'intent to develop through the exercise of trusteeship *over society*. Trusteeship is the intent which is expressed, by one source of agency, to develop the capacities of another' (Cowen and Shenton 1996: ix–x, emphasis added). This process entails the 'exercise of power in which the capacity to state the purpose of development *is not accompanied by accountability*' (Cowen and Shenton 1996: 454, emphasis added).

However, as noted above, capitalist growth-based development is beset by a dual paradox: it is the most dynamic, expanding, system in human history, and yet such rapid growth is never sufficient to satisfy pro-capitalist policy-makers, let alone labouring class needs, the world over. And while such market-based growth is portrayed as enhancing individual freedom, such freedoms must complement the imperatives of market expansion, that is, they are highly circumscribed freedoms that permit only a narrow range of human actions.

This dual paradox is embodied in the concept of stages of development: while each stage represents a new summit of economic growth and human potential, deviating from such a pre-ordained schema of social transformation is ideologically and politically off the cards. For example, at the birth of industrial capitalism in Britain in 1762, Adam Smith explained to his students how human societies developed through stages: 'first, the Age of Hunters; secondly, the Age of Shepherds; thirdly, the Age of Agriculture; and fourthly, the Age of Commerce' (quoted in Davidson 2006). For Smith the progress from one stage to another occurred through the cumulative increase in population, the rising extent and complexity of the division of labour, and increasingly efficient production techniques. Smith's stagist conception of historical change represented and generated further restricted conceptions of human agency, propounded by various development theories in the 20th century.

One of the most influential conceptions of ES–SO stagist development theories was W.W. Rostow's (1960) post-Second World War modernisation theory, produced at the high point of what Philip McMichael (2000) calls the 'development project'. It is one of the clearest ES–SO theorisations of the intent to impose capitalist social relations upon subordinate populations while eliminating other possible routes to human development.

Rostow's *The Stages of Economic Growth: A Non-Communist Manifesto* posited five stages of economic growth (traditional society; preconditions for take-off; take-off; drive to maturity; age of high mass consumption) through which all countries could pass, provided they followed the correct (non-socialist) policies. The key concern for the US state identified by Rostow was to ensure that 'modernisation' would occur in the countries of the South in ways that would incorporate them into global capitalism while precluding other forms of development based upon workers' and peasants' revolution. As Rostow (1960: 163) warned:

> It is in ... a setting of political and social confusion, before the take-off is achieved and consolidated politically and socially as well as economically, that the seizure of power by Communist conspiracy is easiest; and it is in such a setting that a [pro-capitalist] *centralised dictatorship* may supply an essential technical precondition for take-off and a sustained drive to maturity. (Rostow 1960: 163, emphasis added)

The power of Rostow's perspective was neither its historical accuracy nor its ability to predict the future course of poor countries' development experiences. Rather, it represented a guide to action for the US state, and its allies in rich and poor countries alike. The theory justified postponing social welfare measures for the poor until an undefined future, while implementing development strategies designed to subordinate populations to imperatives of world-market-orientated economic growth.

This axiom – the delay of the benefits of growth to labouring classes while the latter are subordinated to continued growth-orientated employment – lies at the heart of many capitalist development theories. Greater freedom for capital at the expense of labour is portrayed as the precondition for widespread social betterment, even when workers already enjoy some collective benefits. As Robert Solow noted for neoliberal theory:

> A labour market is inflexible if the level of unemployment-insurance benefits is too high or their duration is too long, or if there are too many restrictions on the freedom of employers to fire and to hire, or if the permissible hours of work are too tightly regulated, or if excessively generous compensation for overtime work is mandated, or if trade unions have too much power to protect incumbent workers against competition and to control the flow of work at the site of production, or perhaps if statutory health and safety regulations are too stringent. (1988: 190)

From the above perspective, ensuring labour market flexibility represents a baseline for successful economic development. Moreover, it is held to contribute to increasing freedoms of individuals that comprise a national society. Friedrich Hayek expressed this logic with brutal clarity following General Pinochet's murderous 1973 coup against Chile's democratically elected president Salvador Allende: 'I have not been able to find a single person even in much-maligned Chile who did not agree that personal freedom was much greater under Pinochet than it had been under Allende' (cited in Selwyn 2015).

Historically, the main alternative to liberal theory has been an advocacy of the primacy of the state in fomenting economic growth and catch-up development. Statist political economy (SPE) is rooted in the work of Alexander Hamilton, Friedrich List and the post-Second World War emergence of development economics, encompassing thinkers such as Alexander Gerschenkron, Nicholas Kaldor, Albert Hirschman and others. Contemporary advocates of SPE, drawing on Chalmers Johnson's concept of the developmental state, include Robert Wade, Ha-Joon Chang, Alice Amsden, Atul Kohli and Peter Evans, among others (see Selwyn 2014 for an overview).

SPE undermines liberals' faith in the division of labour and free markets generating meaningful development. Instead it shows that, historically, all successful cases of catch-up development have been achieved by strong states. While such policies generated high rates of economic growth and structural transformation, they were often based on brutal ES–SO conceptions of social change. For example, while South Korea is often held up as one of the most successful cases of catch-up development, Atul Kholi compares it to inter-war European fascist states, highlighting their common features: 'Generally right-wing authoritarian ... [these states] ... prioritize rapid industrialization as a national goal, are staffed competently, work closely with industrialists, systematically discipline and repress labour, penetrate and control the rural society, and use economic nationalism as a tool of political mobilisation' (2004: 381).

Alice Amsden located such authoritarian tendencies in a broader, world historical, framework, noting how 'Labour repression is the basis of late industrialization everywhere' and that '[c]heap labour is the anchor of late industrialization. Labour has been available in "unlimited" supply, generally politically powerless, and educated to a level unknown in former industrial revolutions. The discipline of labour by the state lies at the heart of all late industrialization' (1990: 18).

While liberalism and statist perspectives have dominated theories of development, various forms of Marxism have sometimes represented a contender ideology. However, Marxism has been divided into rival camps – of socialism from above versus socialism from below (Draper 1966). Socialism from above, despite its Marxist phraseology, represents another case of ES–SO theory, replicating stagist, growth-first and labour-repressive tropes.

The socialism from above perspective became an almost religious doctrine in Russia following Stalin's assumption of total leadership of the USSR in 1928 and the deployment of state-implemented five-year industrialisation plans to enable it to compete militarily with the West. Stalin justified the ruthless nature of these plans in terms of survival: 'The pace must not be slackened!' he said in February 1931. 'On the contrary we must quicken it as much as is within our powers and possibilities ... We are fifty or a hundred years behind the advanced countries. We must make good this lag in ten years. Either we do it or they crush us' (Stalin, quoted in Deutscher 1961: 328, and see Selwyn 2017 for a longer discussion). This explanation, and the five-year plan strategy for catch-up development, struck a chord with newly independent countries following the Second World War as they struggled to find their geopolitical and economic footing.

The developmental 'successes' – in particular rapid industrialisation and militarisation – of 'really-existing' socialist states certainly influenced academic conceptions of Marxism. Whether or not they subscribed to Stalinist development strategies, these variants of Marxism portrayed capitalism and capital accumulation as a dynamic and progressive force in human developmental terms. For example, in John Sender and Sheila Smith's (1986) prognosis for sustained economic growth in Africa, the authors argue that 'rapid accumulation is unlikely to be achieved without significant reductions in the real incomes of a substantial proportion of the population'. To achieve such accumulation African states must become viable political entities, entailing the containing of 'sub-nationalist pressures' through '[a] combination of hegemonic official nationalism and the military means to reinforce this ideology ... [A] method must be devised for the appropriation for sufficient surplus to ensure the smooth functioning of the military and repressive apparatus' (Sender and Smith 1986: 77, and see Selwyn 2017 for further discussion).

As the above examples suggest, growth-based ES–SO theories of capitalist development – whether Liberal, Statist or Marxist – 'distort the worker into a fragment' of a person (Marx 1990: 799). Perhaps the ultimate paradox of these theories is that while they propound a desire of social betterment, they seek to do so through instituting and reproducing unequal, repressive and exploitative relations between capital and labour.

5.   Real human development: beyond economic growth, beyond capitalism

Capitalism is the most dynamic socio-economic system in human history, one that generates continual and cumulative economic growth. If economic growth and accumulated wealth alone are the benchmarks of developmental success, then capitalism has won the day. This, indeed, is the core argument of all pro-capitalist development theories.

However, capitalism is simultaneously a system of endless competitive capital accumulation, exploitation, oppression and environmental destruction. These social relations will more certainly wreck the planet, create new forms of mass poverty and reproduce mega-inequalities than deliver the dream of well-being for all.

Mainstream theories of development may differ on the weight they allocate to markets and states in the development process. They concur, however, that labour exploitation (and repression) are necessary ingredients of capitalist development.

Is there an alternative to capitalist growth-based development? Marx argued for the need to create an alternative political economic system organised to achieve maximum collective and individual fulfilment, based on 'the absolute working out of [her] creative potentialities', where 'the development of all human powers [is] ... the end itself' (Marx 1993: 488). This system would establish a society where 'the free development of each is the condition for the free development of all' (Marx and Engels 1967: 105). Social relations enabling such forms of development could not be exploitative or competitive as they are under capitalism but would have to be based on new forms of social co-operation.

The bridge between the present and a genuinely democratic future based upon real human development can only be constructed by mass, democratic, collective action. Without such a driving force, it risks establishing another ES–SO form of development. During such a transition period there will be myriad trade-offs – for example, between the need for immediate increases in labouring class consumption and the need to radically reduce and redistribute working hours emerging from the necessity to overcome the enforced austerity derived from prior subordination to capital. While it is almost impossible to predict how such trade-offs will be resolved, it is central to the quest for demo-cratic human development that their resolution is a collective process.

How could resources be mobilised and allocated to achieve real human devel-opment in a new society? New forms of human development could be pursued by eliminating socially unnecessary expenditure, re-orientating industrial production towards socially useful rather than profitable objectives, reducing the working week, redistributing wealth, generating and rolling out green technologies and, above all, finding ways to live in harmony with the earth's ecosystem (and see Selwyn 2018). Such outcomes could be sought based upon new, co-operative as opposed to competitive and exploitative, social relations. For such an historical epoch to commence, the power of capital must be overturned.

References

Amsden, A. (1990) Third World industrialization: 'Global Fordism' or a new model? *New Left Review*, 182: 5–31.

Cantin, E. and Taylor, M. (2008) Making the 'workshop of the world': China and the transformation of the international division of labour, in Taylor, M. (ed.) *Global Economy Contested: Power and Conflict across the International Division of Labour*, London: Routledge, pp. 51–76.

Chan, J., Pun, N. and Selden, M. (2013) The politics of global production: Apple, Foxconn and China's new working class, *New Technology, Work and Employment*, 28(2): 100–115.

Coady, D., Parry, I., Sears, L. and Shang, B. (2017) How large are global fossil fuel subsidies? *World Development*, 91: 11–27.

Cowen, M. and Shenton, R. (1996) *Doctrines of Development*, London: Taylor & Francis.

Credit Suisse (2015) *Global Wealth Report 2015*, available at https://www.allianz.com/v_1444215837000/media/economic_research/publications/specials/en/AGWR2015_ENG.pdf, accessed 13 June 2018.

Dale, G. (2012) The growth paradigm: a critique, *International Socialism*, 134, available at http://www.isj.org.uk/index.php4?id=798&issue=134, accessed 21 May 2020.

Davidson, N. (2006) Enlightenment and anti-capitalism, *International Socialism*, 110, available at http://isj.org.uk/enlightenment-and-anti-capitalism/, accessed 21 May 2020.

Davis, M. (2006) *Planet of Slums*, London: Verso.

Delgado-Wise, R. and Veltmeyer, H. (2016) *Agrarian Change: Migration and Development*, Fernwood: Nova Scotia.

Deutscher, I. (1961) *Stalin: A Political Biography*, Colección: A Pelican Book.

Draper, H. (1966) *The Two Souls of Socialism*, Highland Park, MI: International Socialists.

Foster, J.B. and McChesney, R.W. (2012) The global stagnation and China, *Monthly Review*, 63(9).

Friedman, M. and Friedman, R. (1980) *Free to Choose*, Harmondsworth: Penguin.

Harvey, D. (1981) The spatial fix – Hegel, von Thunen, and Marx, *Antipode*, 13(3): 1–12.

Hawksworth, J. and Chan, D. (2015) *The World in 2050: Will the Shift in Global Economic Power Continue?* PricewaterhouseCoopers, available at https://www.pwc.com/gx/en/issues/the-economy/assets/world-in-2050-february-2015.pdf, accessed June 2019.

Kidron, M. and Gluckstein, E. (1974) Waste: US 1970, in Kidron, M. (ed.) *Capitalism and Theory*, London: Pluto Press, pp. 35–60.

Klein, N. (2015) *This Changes Everything: Capitalism vs. the Climate*, New York: Simon & Schuster.

Kohli, A. (2004) *State-Directed Development: Political Power and Industrialization in the Global Periphery*, Cambridge: Cambridge University Press.

Marx, K. (1990) *Capital: A Critique of Political Economy*, Vol. 1, London: Penguin.

Marx, K. (1993) *Grundrisse*, London: Penguin.

Marx, K. and Engels, F. (1967) *The Manifesto of the Communist Party*, London: Penguin.

McMichael, P. (2000) *Development and Social Change: A Global Perspective*, 2nd ed., Thousand Oaks, CA: Pine Forge Press.

Pogge, T. and Reddy, S. (2010) How not to count the poor, in Anand, S., Segal, P. and Stiglitz, J. (eds) *Debates on the Measurement of Global Poverty*, Oxford: Oxford University Press, pp. 42–85.

Pritchett, L. (2006) Who is not poor? Dreaming of a world truly free of poverty, *World Bank Research Observer*, 21(1): 1–23.

Rostow, W.W. (1960) *The Stages of Economic Growth: A Non-Communist Manifesto*, Cambridge: Cambridge University Press.

Selwyn, B. (2014) *The Global Development Crisis*, Cambridge: Polity Press.

Selwyn, B. (2015) Freidrich Hayek: in defense of dictatorship, Open Democracy, available at https://www.opendemocracy.net/benjamin-selwyn/friedrich-hayek-dictatorship, accessed January 2017.

Selwyn, B. (2017) *The Struggle for Development*, Cambridge: Polity Press.

Selwyn, B. (2018) A manifesto for socialist development in the 21st century, *Economic and Political Weekly*, 53(36): 47–55.

Sender, J. and Smith, S. (1986) *The Development of Capitalism in Africa*, London: Methuen.

Smith, A. (1976) *The Wealth of Nations*, 2 Vols, Chicago: University of Chicago Press.

Solow, R. (1988) What is labour-market flexibility? What is it good for? Keynes Lecture, *Proceedings of the British Academy*, 97: 189–211.

Spratt, D. and Dunlop, I. (2019) *Existential Climate-Related Security Risk: A Scenario Approach*, Breakthrough – National Centre for Climate Restoration, available at https://docs.wixstatic.com/ugd/148cb0_a1406e0143ac4c469196d3003bc1e687.pdf, accessed June 2019.

Sumner, A. (2016) *Global Poverty: Deprivation, Distribution and Development*, Oxford and New York: Oxford University Press.

United Nations (2020) Sustainable Development Goals. Decent work and economic growth, available at https://www.un.org/sustainabledevelopment/economic-growth/, accessed 17 March 2020.

Woodward, D. (2015) Incrementum ad absurdum: global growth, inequality and poverty eradication in a carbon-constrained world, *World Economic Review*, 4: 43–62.

4 Money, finance and the state: potential routes for further development of research

Sheila Dow

Introduction

The financial crisis and its fallout have had a dramatic impact on thinking about money, banks and monetary policy, that is, about the relationship between money, finance and the state. Before then, during the 'great moderation' period, there had been remarkable complacency over mainstream macroeconomic theory which disregarded money and finance and supported the 'new consensus' approach to monetary policy. But the crisis changed all that. There is now debate about the nature and role of money and proposals for new forms of money. Some mainstream macroeconomic theory now incorporates the behaviour of banks, something which had previously been absent. Further, there has been a major rethinking of the role of central banks, with attention shifting from inflation targeting to financial stability and further to economic stability and social stability.

Non-mainstream theory was better equipped to address the crisis, having a theory – Minsky's (1986) financial instability hypothesis – which explained it, with a central role for banks. In addition, there is a substantial non-mainstream, or political economy, literature on the social nature of money and on its real economic role, which contrasts with the traditional mainstream view of money as a veil (Ingham 2004). Long before the crisis, non-mainstream theory was advocating a much broader role for monetary policy than inflation targeting, not only emphasising the central bank's duty to promote financial stability, but also the scope for central banks to provide the kind of fiscal finance generally ruled out by central bank independence (Dow 2017).

But the subject matter does not stand still. Not only have new ideas been emerging, but the financial sector itself has been evolving in ways which raise new challenges. The purpose here is to focus on issues which pose particular challenges for future research on money, finance and the state. While reference will be made, as appropriate, to mainstream thinking, the emphasis will be on the political economy literature and where it might go from here.

We start with the big issue raised by the banking crisis of whether the state should provide less support for banks, enforcing market discipline, or more to promote trust in bank deposits as the main form of money. We pursue further, in the following section, the nature and role of money and the role of the state with respect to money and banking. The emergence of private cryptocurrencies has encouraged central banks to consider issuing their own digital currencies. We explore the issues this raises, both for the future of banking and for financial inclusion. At the same time, the rise of shadow banking has made it harder for the state to promote financial stability; we consider the issues raised in the fourth section.

Then, given the return by central banks, *de facto* if not *de jure*, to concern with economic stability as well as monetary stability, we consider issues posed by the potential for complementarity between fiscal and monetary policy. Particular attention is paid to the contribution from ideas associated with what has been called Modern Monetary Theory (MMT), and to the implications for central bank independence. Finally, along with the recognition of the real economic impact of central banking, a growing awareness of its social and environmental role has emerged. In this final set of topics we consider how money and finance and the state might co-operate to promote social and environmental goals.

Lender-of-last-resort facility and 'too big to fail'

Within an economy, money is whichever asset is generally accepted in final settlement of contracts (Davidson 1972). In modern economies, money has taken the form primarily of bank deposits denominated in the national currency; contracts are normally settled by the payee's claim on the bank, which is settled through the payment-clearing mechanism. The system thus relies on confidence that banks can honour their liabilities. But the crisis seriously punctured that confidence. There were runs on banks (like Northern Rock in the UK) by customers concerned about loss of deposits, while nervousness among banks themselves about lending to each other caused the interbank market to freeze for a time. Yet the reliability of money is crucial to the functioning of a commercial society built on contracts. Central banks thus intervened to inject liquidity into financial markets. But the asset price falls caused by the banking crisis meant that an illiquidity problem was turning into an insolvency problem. Governments therefore intervened by injecting capital into failing banks, at huge fiscal cost.

The predominant reaction, supported by mainstream theory, was that banks had taken on undue risk because of their confidence that the state would not allow them to fail: moral hazard. The solution therefore had to include a clear signal that in future banks should not expect such support. The emphasis was then on setting up procedures for dealing with bank failure in the expectation that market discipline would limit excessive risk-taking. The central bank's lender-of-last-resort facility, if preserved at all, was to be limited to ring-fenced retail banking.[1]

But the political economy reaction was very different. There is common ground in arguing that the lender-of-last-resort facility should apply only to retail banking as the locus of money. But the facility itself is regarded in a much more positive light, as part of a system of central bank support for retail banking which should prevent failures. This system includes regulation to restrict exposure of retail banking to systemic risk, enforced through monitoring and supervision. It represents a social contract between central banks and retail banks, built up in many cases over centuries, whereby banks accept portfolio restrictions in exchange for access to the lender-of-last-resort facility and the benefits of the high redeposit ratio which accompanies deposits being used as money.

This alternative approach to the role of the state is built on a different theory of money and finance based on the prevalence of fundamental uncertainty. If uncertainty prevents any identification of 'true' risk then market pricing is inevitably conventional. Therefore market 'discipline' cannot prevent undue risk-taking and, ultimately, crises. While there may well have been an element of moral hazard, this would have meant that banks had actually recognised the unsustainability of their portfolios. In fact banks had undue confidence in their own pricing of risk, to the extent that some bank CEOs themselves were over extended with their personal investments when the crisis struck. Given the systemic nature of the crisis, with the extent of interdependent portfolios greatly enhanced by the prevalence of new opaque structured products, any preventative (or mitigative) action required a macro view being taken. We explore this crucial role for the state further below when we consider financial stability more generally. But first we consider the issues raised by the emergence of cryptocurrencies.

Financial innovation and central bank digital currencies

The development of cryptographic techniques, combined with blockchain technology, has underpinned the emergence of new assets and asset-transfer mechanisms. The aim has been to rival state-issued money and conventional payments mechanisms. Indeed, the first mover, Bitcoin, was explicitly pitched in Hayekian libertarian terms (Nakamoto 2008). Since then, however, the sector has consolidated, dominated by large operations; it is the tech giants such as Facebook which are now leading the way in seeking to provide an alternative, private sector money. The earlier cryptocurrencies did not in fact meet the requirements for money: stable value relative to other assets and ease of exchange. Speculation meant that values were particularly unstable, and exchange was generally cumbersome. But proposals now are for cryptocurrencies in the form of stablecoins which are fully backed by state currency (as in a currency board system) and which operate on a global scale which would make payments relatively easy.

There had already been consideration within central banks about issuing their own digital currencies because of the loss of seigniorage due to reduced cash usage. Doubts about the usefulness to central banks of blockchain technology had held the process back, although digital currencies need not use blockchains. However, the proposals for private sector stablecoins have pushed the issue up the agenda, with or without blockchain. Central banks are concerned that there is scope for a large-scale private money to compete with national currencies, subvert national monetary policies and risk facilitating fraud and causing financial instability.

Replacing cash with digital currency is not just a technical matter. It would profoundly affect retail banking in a way which finds support particularly in some mainstream analyses of the banking crisis. Currently, banks have the ability to create credit as much as they do because their liabilities form the major part of society's money. If the crisis was due to excessive bank credit creation, then the solution would appear to be to curtail banks' ability to create credit. This could be achieved by providing digital accounts at the central bank for transactions balances and payments.[2] Then banks would become pure financial intermediaries rather than credit creators. Rather than trust in money relying on banks' prudence, it would be assured by a state monopoly (see e.g. Clarke 2018).

But it can be argued that the capacity of banks to create credit has been a beneficial institutional development which has helped to spur economic development. The key distinction is between bank credit creation which finances investment ahead of the generation of the savings to fund it, on the one hand, and financial intermediation which requires prior savings, on the other. Operated effectively, the traditional provision by central banks of liquidity support, regulation, monitoring and supervision should ensure trust in bank deposits as money, and thus the capacity to create credit. Even though financial transactions are increasingly being conducted in digital form, settlement still occurs predominantly through bank deposits, interbank settlements and ultimately digital bank reserves with the central bank.

If final settlement occurred instead directly between accounts with the central bank, then banks would lose the capacity to create credit. According to some proposals, new credit would instead be directed by the central bank through the banking system, while others see it intermediated on the basis of new money creation. Indeed, many proposals see it as an advantage of a central bank digital currency that its supply can be controlled. Yet again, this presumes a mainstream view of money as being held for transactions purposes only. Once we allow for changes in liquidity preference, which tend to be discrete and unpredictable in response to a jump in uncertainty, demand for money cannot confidently be forecast, removing the rationale for control of its supply. In any case, the argument presumes that the state can actually monopolise money.

This discussion has presumed a sharp divide between banking and non-banking, but this too is an area of significant change which poses challenges for future research. Money is the most liquid asset, but when risk perception is low in rising markets, other assets can become more liquid; there is confidence that their value will be upheld (i.e. that they will continue to be liquid). This has been the case for the liabilities of financial institutions outside the regulated banking sector such that non-bank financial intermediaries have been acting as if they were banks: major suppliers of credit and transformers of maturity. If nothing else these institutions are adept at supplying liquidity as required, as long as markets are favourable, subverting any attempts by central banks to control the supply of credit and thus money. Such a response can be expected to be fuelled if retail bank deposits are replaced by central bank digital currencies, subverting any thought of the state enforcing a monopoly over money (see further Dow 2019).

In developing countries informal finance has been particularly important for meeting financial needs unmet by the formal banking system, most notably in the form of microcredit, but also microdeposits and microinsurance. Digital payments systems, often using mobile phone networks, have also been helping those without bank accounts to function more effectively in commercial society. There is considerable attention to promoting financial inclusion as a development strategy, with central bank digital currencies potentially playing a significant part. But Gabor and Brooks (2017) argue that financial inclusion, and thus financialisation, at the same time serves to extend the profit potential of the formal banking system. Further, Settle (2020) argues that financial inclusion can pose risks, particularly in developing countries, for those who become reliant on formal banks and thus national interest rates and volatile national currencies. She documents how the unbanked (in Pakistan) have developed their own, more effective, means of mitigating risk.

Promoting financial stability

The proliferation of money assets and finance outside the formal banking system poses huge problems for the state in its efforts to promote financial stability. These developments were spurred on by financial liberalisation and attendant financialisation, which in turn had been validated by the pro-market stance of mainstream finance theory. There had been confidence that competitive markets would produce socially optimal outcomes; sophisticated, high-tech arbitrage activity would ensure that deviations from equilibrium would be corrected. New Keynesian theory suggested that the crisis was due to impediments to these market forces, whose removal would restore financial stability. But Minsky's (1986) financial instability hypothesis rather showed financial instability to be systemic, with stability actually creating the conditions for instability. Stability creates overconfidence in risk assessment (in spite of uncertainty), encouraging increasingly leveraged borrowing fuelling rising asset prices. The fragility so created means that any small reversal in expectations which prompts asset sales sets off a reversal of the whole process.

Given that this instability is systemic, it is up to the state to intervene to moderate it. The first step is to ensure the safety of the core of the system: retail banks and their liabilities. Moves have been made in this direction, with macroprudential policies governing portfolio composition, ring-fencing retail banking from investment banking, and so on. Regulated banks continue to be core in that payments are still predominantly routed through them and non-banks hold reserves with them. But two particular factors cause concern. First, the source of instability is increasingly outside this core, with more credit being created by lightly regulated financial institutions – shadow banks. While non-bank financial intermediaries used not to engage in maturity transformation, the thirst for both credit and liquidity has allowed a greater degree of maturity transformation, which exposes these institutions to particular risk. Second, the financial sector, regulated and unregulated, is now so interconnected, often in very opaque ways which conceal risks, that the scope for instability is greatly enhanced. In particular, both types of bank operate in the unregulated market for repos (short-term borrowing, usually against sovereign debt), where the same collateral effectively backs borrowing many times over (Gabor and Vestergaard 2016).

The appropriate policy response seems to be two-fold. First, bring as many institutions as possible inside the regulatory net in order to limit scope for excesses. Since such efforts encourage further financial innovation to avoid regulatory restrictions, regulation needs to be updated continually to address new threats to stability. Second, central banks need to trade directly in key markets as dealer-of-last-resort in order to prevent these markets from collapsing (Mehrling 2011).

Economic stability and monetary stability

While monetary stability has been the primary goal of central banks in recent decades, often expressed in the form of an inflation target pursued by an independent central bank, this has been an aberration in the history of central banking (see e.g. Goodhart 2011). Traditionally, central banks have also been concerned with financial stability and economic stability. The crisis meant that these two goals took priority. Monetary stability (stable and low inflation) requires that the dominant money assets (bank deposits) are safe, that is, meet the requirement of money. It also requires that the economy does not tip into recession due to collapsing asset values. So central banks injected liquidity into the financial system and, initially, governments injected more expenditure into the economy. While lip-service had to be paid to monetary stability (because of formal mandates), it was not the primary concern. Indeed, while some were concerned that quantitative easing programmes addressed to liquidity shortage would be inflationary, this has not transpired. It is evident that, even over several years, a massive injection of liquidity into the banking system has not caused inflation with respect to consumer prices. Rather, it has caused inflation in asset prices as the extra liquidity found its way more into financial asset purchases than into business and household credit. This in turn has contributed to the increased skewing of income and wealth distribution towards the owners of financial assets.

Indeed, it is debatable whether targeting inflation was ever actually within the power of the central bank, particularly operating independently of government as is now the normal formal requirement. The monetarist argument that central banks can orchestrate aggregate expenditure relative to the economy's productive capacity by (directly or indirectly) controlling the money supply has been challenged theoretically – as well as empirically in light of the experience of quantitative easing. It is now widely accepted that the central bank cannot control the money supply, that is, it is endogenous to some degree (even if only in a limited sense, as the outcome of interest-rate policy, or through the money multiplier). It is a key feature of a political economy approach that the money supply is more fundamentally endogenous, as the outcome of bank credit creation.[3] Indeed the emergence of money itself is endogenous to the evolution of society.[4]

In any case the connection between the money supply, or even interest rates, and expenditure is loosened by changes in the expectations which govern expenditure and borrowing decisions and by fluctuations in liquidity preference as confidence in those expectations fluctuates. Both factors are profoundly affected by financial instability and by economic instability. In terms of causal priority therefore, the logical priority for pursuing monetary stability is to ensure financial stability and economic stability.

Whatever the formal arrangements, it has been evident in the wake of the crisis that central banks need to co-operate and co-ordinate with governments in order for each to be more effective. Monetarist theory had promoted the primacy of monetary policy over fiscal policy to the extent that the latter was severely limited in terms of ceilings on fiscal deficit/GDP ratios and debt/GDP ratios (as in the Eurozone for example). Now that active fiscal policy is back on the agenda, issues arise as to how the relationship between fiscal and monetary policy should be handled. Particular thought is being put into establishing fiscal rules which give much more latitude to fiscal policy than the type of strictures imposed on the Eurozone by the Maastricht Treaty. Just as monetary policy could be more effectively attuned to the business cycle, for example by pro-cyclical capital requirements, so any rules for fiscal policy could promote more expenditure during economic contractions than expansions.

Before the ascendancy of monetarist theory and policy, it was uncontroversial for government deficits to be financed by borrowing directly from the central bank (money creation), as well as by borrowing on the bond market. Support for a return to this practice is growing, challenging central bank independence in the form of prohibition on government finance. It is agreed that net fiscal expansion should only be pursued according to the availability of unemployed resources or else it would be inflationary. The potential for borrowing is not limitless either, but is constrained by the capacity to finance the debt-service burden itself and its implications in turn for the cost of new debt.

The case for money-financed expenditure has been made most prominently by supporters of MMT, for whom tying expenditure to a job guarantee to ensure full employment is central.[5] Fiscal expansion in times of economic recession, to ensure full employment, is a classic Keynesian policy. But the MMT case for money-financed expenditure is not uncontroversial, because of the monetary theory which underpins it. MMT builds on a state theory of money whereby money is defined as whatever is acceptable for paying taxes. While (other) Post Keynesians share a focus on the role of the state in the development of monetary systems, it is the acceptability in the final settlement of *all* contracts which is taken to identify any asset or assets as money (Davidson 1972). Further, there is a spectrum of assets whose liquidity changes with market conditions and financial innovation, and according to expectations of asset prices. As we have seen particularly with the growth of shadow banking, and the dramatic change during the crisis in what assets were regarded as liquid, the stock of what society regards as money is beyond state control. Changes in liquidity preference as confidence in expectations changes mean that demand for money itself is not tied to private sector expenditure plans. This does not invalidate the argument for money-financed fiscal expansion in time of recession, but rather means that the state cannot enforce a monopoly of what in practice is regarded as money, or use that to steer aggregate demand. Private sector cryptocurrencies are a direct threat to state money, but, as we argued above, central bank digital currencies are not the answer either.

Social and environmental stability

New challenges are posed for central banks by what is now seen by many to be a need for them to attend also to social and environmental stability.[6] Quite apart from the (significant) implications of instability in either sphere for the three more conventional goals of economic, financial and monetary stability, there is a growing sense that public institutions need to address issues of social justice and the survival of the planet. At the same time, non-mainstream theorists make the case that, whether it is admitted or not, no economic theory is value-free.[7] Far from providing positive, technical advice for politicians to add their normative judgements, economists inevitably incorporate their own, conventional, judgements, even if these are to exclude consideration of questions relating to income distribution and climate change. The recognition of the real social effects of monetary policy justifies an abandonment of the principle of central bank independence from government (see further Dow 2013 and 2017).

It has always been the case that money's nature is social and that monetary policy has social consequences, even while mainstream theory treated money as a veil. As far as social stability is concerned, the issues are multi-faceted and are connected with money, finance and the state in different ways. The most direct connection was made between monetary policy and worsening trends in income and wealth distribution, something directly discussed by Bank of England Governor Mark Carney (2014). The top of the income and wealth distribution consists primarily of major asset-holders who have gained from the central bank policy of quantitative easing. Rather than filtering through to easier credit conditions for businesses and households, the liquidity has served primarily to fuel further expansion of the financial sector and increases on asset prices. So the policy has failed also with respect to economic stability and, given the resumption of growth in the financial sector fuelled by quantitative easing, financial stability.

In the meantime, not only had mainstream finance theory indicated that free competitive operation of financial markets would ensure optimal social-welfare outcomes, but that this would include financial flows equalising returns across space, in different types of economy. Yet, just as the crisis was a refutation of the first, so are persistent structural disparities across space a refutation of the second. Dymski and Kaltenbrunner (forthcoming) argue that analysis of the role of banking and finance in aggravating these disparities needs to highlight the role of disparities in socio-economic power between spatial areas, and their irreversible consequences. Again, we conclude that market liberalisation cannot be expected to promote social stability.

In the interests of social stability (as well as improved national economic performance), central banks are well placed to take the macro view of the financial structure within the relevant nation. The social nature of money and the granting of credit is particularly evident in the case of mutual, co-operative financial institutions, which in general proved to be particularly robust during the crisis. The state can promote and support such institutions to serve peripheral areas and populations which are not well served by conventional commercial banking. It can set up development banks in order to intervene directly in particular areas and sectors. And it can direct retail banks to target credit at particular areas and sectors as part of the social contract between them. Turner (2012) argues that such measures should be integrated into macroprudential controls, attending to the composition as well as the volume of credit.

Further, nation states can co-operate in the international institutions such as the International Monetary Fund (IMF) and World Bank in order to reduce disparities in credit and liquidity conditions in peripheral countries (see e.g. Davidson 1992–93). In the meantime, policy has been designed to address the extent to which a population is unbanked, something which is particularly an issue for developing countries: the financial inclusion agenda. But we recall Settle's (2020) argument outlined above that the unbanked may well have protected their interests more effectively by pursuing alternative strategies to seeking banking services. There may be a role for the state here too, in supporting some forms of informal finance.

Finally, social justice issues arise also from climate change, given that much of the cost of the climate crisis will fall on low-income communities which are ill-equipped to protect themselves, requiring an international response, not least in the provision of adequate credit to finance mitigation efforts. But central banks have a particular responsibility in considering the way in which financial markets deal with climate change. Mainstream finance theory had posited full rationality, taking account of full available information, in financial markets. But, in the face of ample evidence, climate change has been absent until recently from valuations of projects', companies' and governments' vulnerability to climate change costs. It has mainly been up to central banks to take the lead in pointing out the urgent need to price climate risk (see e.g. Carney 2019). This applies to current risks, but also to the long-term costs of a strategy to mitigate climate risks in the future, all in the face of short-termism on the part of markets and the state.

Both sets of issues have taken on general political significance, and direct pressures are being put on companies, not only by activists, but also by shareholders and customers. There has thus been a response in the form of some shifting in corporate culture. In particular, there is a growing focus on Environmental, Social and Governance (ESG) criteria by which investors can judge corporate activity, and on efforts to promote ESG-compliant activity and products. Much of this is now mapped out regularly by the *Financial Times* Moral Money initiative.[8]

Conclusion

We have touched here on some of the many issues regarding money, finance and the state which have been thrown up by the financial crisis and which require a theoretical response. At the same time, the way in which financial institutions and markets have been evolving and growing in scale poses particular challenges for policy – as well as for developing theory attuned to the modern context. Given the complexity of the financial sector and its interaction with economic activity, there is particular force in the political economy argument for a plurality of theoretical approaches. There is also force in the argument for policy plurality whereby no one strategy (such as a central bank monopoly on money, or regulation alone) can be effective; the open-system context rather requires a 'belt-and-braces' approach which, in a closed system, would be over-determined. Such an approach to theory and policy intrinsically invites controversy.

We have explored a series of controversial issues calling out for further research: the proper relationship between a central bank and the banks; the emergence of cryptocurrencies and the implications of central banks' interest in creating their own digital currencies; the responsibility of central banks with respect to financial stability and how that can be promoted in a modern financial system; the responsibility of central banks to use their influence on the real economy in co-operation with governments' fiscal policy, and the implications for central bank independence; the responsibility of central banks to engage with efforts to promote social and environmental stability.

The change in context for theorising has been particularly dramatic in recent years, requiring careful consideration of how best to develop theory. But this is a reminder that economic systems always evolve and that theory needs to adapt accordingly.

Notes

1. The deregulation of banks since the 1970s had encouraged the consolidation of retail banking with much riskier investment banking.
2. Some suggest that these accounts could be administered by private sector banks.
3. While McLeay et al. (2014) support a focus on credit creation as the mechanism for money supply changes, they nevertheless conclude that the money supply can be controlled indirectly through interest-rate control.
4. See Dow (forthcoming) for a fuller discussion of endogenous money from a variety of perspectives.
5. See issue 89 of the *Real-World Economics Review*, 'Modern monetary theory and its critics', 3 October 2019, for a sample of different positions on MMT.
6. Chick (2018) identified these as two of the challenges now facing economic theory more generally.
7. See Peil and van Staveren (2009) for a range of views.
8. https://www.ft.com/moral-money.

References

Carney, M. (2014) Inclusive capitalism: creating a sense of the systemic, paper presented at the *Conference on Inclusive Capitalism*, London, 27 May.

Carney, M. (2019) Remarks given during the UN Secretary General's Climate Action Summit, available at https://www.bankofengland.co.uk/speech/2019/mark-carney-remarks-at-united-nations-climate-action-summit-2019, accessed 20 November 2019.

Chick, V. (2018) The relevance of *The General Theory* at 80: economic change and economic theory, in Dow, S., Jespersen, J. and Tily, G. (eds) *The General Theory and Keynes for the 21st Century*, Cheltenham, UK and Northampton, MA, USA: Edward Elgar Publishing, pp. 1–15.

Clarke, D. (2018) *The Future of Cash*, London: Positive Money.

Davidson, P. (1972) *Money and the Real World*, London: Macmillan.

Davidson, P. (1992–93) Reforming the world's money, *Journal of Post Keynesian Economics*, 15(2): 153–179.

Dow, S.C. (2013) The real (social?) experience of monetary policy, in Pixley, J. and Harcourt, G.C. (eds) *Financial Crises and the Nature of Capitalist Money: Mutual Developments from the Work of Geoffrey Ingham*, London: Palgrave Macmillan, pp. 178–195.

Dow, S.C. (2017) Central banking in the 21st century, *Cambridge Journal of Economics*, 41(6): 1539–1557.

Dow, S.C. (2019) Monetary reform, central banks and digital currencies, *International Journal of Political Economy*, 48(2): 153–173.

Dow, S.C. (forthcoming) Endogenous money and ideas for monetary reform, *European Journal of Economics and Economic Policies: Intervention*. https://doi.org/10.4337/ejeep.2020.0059.

Dymski, G. and Kaltenbrunner, A. (forthcoming) Space in Post-Keynesian monetary economics: an exploration of the literature, in Bonizzi, B., Kaltenbrunner, A. and Ramos, R. (eds) *Emerging Economies and the Global Financial System: Post-Keynesian Analysis*, London: Routledge.

Gabor, D. and Brooks, S. (2017) The digital revolution in financial inclusion: international development in the fintech era, *New Political Economy*, 22(4): 423–436.

Gabor, D. and Vestergaard, J. (2016) Towards a theory of shadow money, UWE and DIIS mimeo, available at https://ineteconomics.org/uploads/papers/Towards_Theory_Shadow_Money_GV_INET.pdf, accessed 27 May 2020.

Goodhart, C.A.E. (2011) The changing role of central banks, *Financial History Review*, 18(2): 135–154.

Ingham, G. (2004) *The Nature of Money*, Cambridge: Polity Press.

McLeay, M., Radia, A. and Thomas, R. (2014) Money creation in the modern economy, *Bank of England Quarterly Bulletin*, Q1: 1–14.

Mehrling, P. (2011) *The New Lombard Street: How the Fed became the Dealer of Last Resort*, Princeton, NJ: Princeton University Press.

Minsky, H.P. (1986) *Stabilizing an Unstable Economy*, New Haven, CT: Yale University Press.

Nakamoto, S. (2008) Bitcoin: a peer-to-peer electronic cash system, mimeo.

Peil, J. and van Staveren, I. (eds) (2009) *Handbook of Economics and Ethics*, Cheltenham, UK and Northampton, MA, USA: Edward Elgar Publishing.

Settle, A. (2020) *Risk and the Rupee in Pakistan's New Economy: Financial Inclusion and Monetary Change in a Frontier Market*, Cambridge: Cambridge University Press.
Turner, A. (2012) Credit creation and social optimality, *International Review of Financial Analysis*, 25: 142–153.

Knowledge, power and the Global South: epistemes and economies after colonialism

Nour Nicole Dados

Introduction

'We live in a postcolonial neo-colonized world' declared social theorist Gayatri Spivak in 1990. Spivak's statement speaks to a plurality of geopolitical histories that are at once global, ubiquitous and connected. In our post-colonial world, the creation and circulation of knowledge is uneven. It is embedded in a political economy of knowledge production and a global division of intellectual labour built upon the violence of colonialism, imperialism and economic domination. The creation and circulation of knowledge is as much about power as it is about the content or cultural origins of the ideas being exchanged. This chapter examines the contributions of post-colonial intellectuals and Global South perspectives to understanding global capitalism and knowledge creation in the neo-colonial, neoliberal world. It is organised in five sections. The first looks in general terms at the problem of knowledge, the disruption and destruction of indigenous economies and knowledge systems, and at attempts to recuperate subaltern epistemologies. The second considers economic models which centre the Global South and the interdependence of core–periphery relations, the third at the centrality of imperialism to capitalism and the essential but hidden Southern role, the fourth at alternative economic strategies developed after World War II and the fifth at more recent Southern responses to neoliberalism.

The problem of knowledge: epistemes and economies

Post-colonial and Southern theory approaches to the social sciences centre the experiences and knowledge of colonised people – 'the subaltern' (Spivak and Harasym 1990) or 'the wretched of the earth' (Fanon 1967) – within the uneven geographies of knowledge production (Connell 2007; Sousa Santos 2007; Bhambra 2014; Collyer et al. 2019; Mignolo 2007). These approaches disrupt disciplinary orthodoxies and conceptual singularities by revealing the imperial foundations of contemporary domains of knowledge, economic models and political power, as well as challenges and alternatives to them.

Post-colonial theories, which emerged in the 1970s with the publication of Edward Said's (1995 [1978]) *Orientalism*, identify the colonial encounter as the point at which indigenous knowledge systems were disrupted and destroyed, or reinscribed as an inferior 'other' to colonial knowledge. The complete destruction of indigenous economies and knowledge systems, described as 'epistemicide' by Boaventura de Sousa Santos, continues today through 'abyssal thinking', the tendency of modern Western thinking to create invisible distinctions that determine what exists as knowledge, and what vanishes 'on the other side of the line' (Sousa Santos 2007; Bhambra 2014; Said 1993; Mignolo 2007; Connell 2007).

This has serious consequences for the formation of disciplines and domains of knowledge and requires an interrogation of the social, economic and political dynamics of knowledge production (Connell 2018; Collyer et al. 2019; Bhambra 2014; Connell 2007; El Shakry 2007). While there are some variations in how post-colonial, Southern theory and decolonial approaches are applied, all seek to recuperate intellectual contributions of the periphery, both before and since the colonial encounter.

Post-colonial approaches describe the ways that modern knowledge systems, owing to their cultural, economic and political entanglement with colonialism and imperialism, divide the world into the binaries of 'West' and 'East', 'metropole' and 'colony', 'centre' and 'periphery', assigning values and attributes to these categories that imbues them with authority. This system of knowledge production derives from the nexus of knowledge and power within colonial rule. To be subjugated, the colonised must be known, and to be known, the colonised must be known through the coloniser's systems of knowledge (Said 1995 [1978], 1993; Go 2013; Bhambra 2014). Knowledge about the colonial 'other' filters into general cultural consciousness as 'fact'. It also forms the foundation of economic, political and military power, enabling various forms of domination and hegemony, since, 'to have knowledge of such a thing is to dominate it, to have authority over it' (Said 1995 [1978]: 32; Go 2013; Bhambra 2014).

Southern theory, while sharing similarities with post-colonial studies, is concerned with the global division of intellectual labour between the Global North and the Global South (Connell 2014, 2007; Connell et al. 2017; Collyer et al. 2019; Dados and Connell 2018). The political economy of knowledge production is an outcome of the colonisation of the world and the expansion of neoliberalism (Connell et al. 2017). In this formation, the periphery supplies data, while the metropole creates the theory and exports it back to the periphery, establishing and reinforcing the institutional hegemony of the Global North (Connell et al. 2017; Connell 2014, 2007). Southern theory encompasses various approaches, since '[t]he argument for southern theory isn't mainly about different propositions, but about different knowledge practices' (Connell 2014: 219). These knowledge practices include tracing the intellectual lineages of established disciplines and arenas of knowledge, and identifying the North-centric patterns of knowledge production (Connell et al. 2017; Connell 2014, 2007).

Decolonial thought, for example in the work of the coloniality/modernity group (Quijano 2000; Mignolo 2007), locates the political economy of the post-colonial world within an imperial regime of racial difference. The constructed racial inferiority of the colonised world is more than a political tool in the service of empire. It serves as an economic basis for contemporary capitalism through the racialised geopolitical differentiation of the world (Quijano 2000). The decolonial school, also drawing on debates from dependency and world-system theories, calls for a delinking of the colonised world (Mignolo 2007).

Post-colonial, Southern theory and decolonial interventions highlight the 'imperialistic unconscious' of knowledge (Go 2013: 49; Connell 2007; Mignolo 2007). This is examined in detail by Raewyn Connell's *Southern Theory* (2007), which maps the formation of sociology in light of its imperial foundations. Connell traces the emergence of sociology as an academic discipline and intellectual discourse in the final decades of the nineteenth century, noting the near total erasure of the epistemological complexity of the discipline's establishment by its canonisation and the allocation of founding texts and founding fathers (Connell 2007: 11). Connell points out that while the foundational story of the discipline focuses on industrial modernisation as the driver, social theorists at the time were much less concerned with modernity. Of approximately 2400 reviews published in Emile Durkheim's *L'année sociologique* in 1913, roughly two-thirds concerned themselves with 'ancient and medieval societies, colonial or remote societies, or global surveys of human history' (Connell 2007: 7). The central idea present in these surveys is what Connell identifies as 'global difference', that is, 'the difference between the metropole and other cultures whose main feature was their primitiveness' (Connell 2007: 7).

The concept of progress at the heart of sociology reflected 'the social relations of imperialism' and global racial hierarchies (Connell 2007). As all social questions came to be refracted through it, the problems of the metropole and the periphery were conflated (Connell 2007: 17–18). The establishment of a canon and the development of modern general theory came later, erasing the experience of empire and imperialism in the historical narrative of disciplinary formation. General theory is 'Northern theory': it claims universality but does not examine its location in the metropole, it builds models of the world based on the view from the centre, it excludes voices from the periphery, and it erases the experience of the majority world (Connell 2007: 44–47).

This bias raises serious questions about how we apply concepts and adapt theoretical proposals (Collyer et al. 2019; Connell and Dados 2014). Many studies of capitalism, globalisation and neoliberalism continue to focus on the Global North while claiming a universality that has been described as thinly disguised 'provincialism' (Chakrabarty 2000). Southern intellectuals have posited a range of responses, from recognising 'autonomous' traditions of knowledge (Alatas 2006), to locating epistemes within broader 'ecologies of knowledge' (Sousa Santos 2007). While there are many differences in these approaches, they all concur that the history of colonialism and imperialism, and the continuing legacy of neo-colonialism, should be at the centre of how we create knowledge and models of the world (Bhambra 2014; Go 2013; Connell 2007; Said 1995 [1978]). The remainder of this chapter assesses how theories of capitalism, imperialism and neoliberalism have dealt with these questions.

Centring the South in economic models

Economic models that centre the Global South take a critical view of normative analyses of the world economy and propose alternatives to neo-classical theories of the development of capitalism. Not surprisingly, these models see imperialism and colonisation as central to understanding development and inequality.

World-system analysis, an approach that has been highly influential in the Global South, views nations as operating in an interlocking network of exchange, the world-system (Wallerstein 1980 [1974]; Amin 1991; Frank and Gills 1993; Chase-Dunn and Grimes 1995). Structural inequality shapes social, political, cultural and economic interactions between the developed, wealthy 'core' countries, the partially developed 'semi-periphery', and the underdeveloped 'periphery'. Economic, political and military power is concentrated in the core countries, resulting in their economic and political domination of the periphery. Powerful states, or *hegemons*, emerge among the core countries and dominate the world-system by exerting economic, military and political pressure that maintains a system of 'unequal exchange' with 'periphery' and 'semi-periphery' countries (Wallerstein 1980 [1974]; Amin 1991; Chase-Dunn and Grimes 1995).

For Wallerstein, the economic interaction between different societies is structured around the necessary exchange of goods and materials required for everyday life, a relationship that is ultimately expressed in trading patterns (Wallerstein 1980 [1974]; Chase-Dunn and Grimes 1995: 389–390). The economic development of semi-periphery and periphery countries is constrained by structural inequality within the world-system, producing and reproducing an uneven international division of labour and a flow of primary resources and surplus value from the periphery to the core countries (Wallerstein 1980 [1974]; Amin 1991; Frank and Gills 1993; Chase-Dunn and Grimes 1995). This system of exchange reproduces the subordinate status of periphery countries, regardless of the policies they adopt at a local level, resulting in dependency (Amin 1974, 1990 [1985], 1991).

Dependency theory extended the work of Raul Prebisch and Hans Singer ('the Singer–Prebisch thesis'; Prebisch 1951; Singer 1950), which contends that the incorporation of the periphery into the international economy leads to the decline of the purchasing power of underdeveloped countries over time, owing to the deterioration of terms of trade. This occurs because the value of raw materials exported from underdeveloped countries to wealthy countries decreases over time, whereas the value of manufactured goods imported by peripheral countries from developed countries increases (Prebisch 1951; Singer 1950). The Singer–Prebisch thesis demonstrated that, far from being an equaliser, international trade between 'the industrial centre and agrarian periphery' (Love 1980: 45) creates a relationship of dependency that compels underdeveloped countries to trade valuable resources for the acquisition of necessary manufactured goods that they do not have the capacity to produce. This pattern of disadvantageous trade relations transfers wealth from the periphery to the centre, creating a dynamic of unequal exchange in which

increased productivity in peripheral countries is not reabsorbed through economic development or a rise in real incomes (Prebisch 1951; Love 1980; Singer
1950: 484–485). Later theories of unequal exchange expanded on the transfer
of surplus and profit from the peripheries to the centres as a result of wage
differentials being greater than differentials in productivity (Emmanuel 1972;
Amin 1974, 1990 [1985]: 107–108).

The modern world-system is understood by Wallerstein (1980 [1974], 1974)
as emerging with the rise of capitalism in Europe between 1450 and 1550,
as the first truly global capitalist system. It is seen as substantively different
from pre-capitalist societies and sixteenth-century empires like that of the
Ottomans, which tended towards coercion rather than economic domination.
In the modern world-system, economic domination, rather than political
power and violence, is foregrounded during the centuries of European colonial
expansion. While the problem of imperialism is central to world-system and
dependency perspectives, it is primarily encountered as a response to the crisis
of capital accumulation in the form of ongoing primitive accumulation, or
accumulation by dispossession (Harvey 2003; Luxemburg 1951; Amin 1990
[1985]; Wallerstein 1980 [1974], 1974).

Others have similarly conceptualised the relationship between economic
domination and imperialism with reference to European colonisation. Walter
Rodney's (1972) *How Europe Underdeveloped Africa* examines underdevelopment in the context of African neo-colonialism, providing an account of how
the dependency relationship was etched in the history of colonial expansion.
For Samir Amin the modern capitalist system signifies a qualitative break and
a fundamental reversal in which the economic emerges as more dominant than
the political or the ideological (1991: 352). By comparing the modern system to
pre-capitalist organisation, however, Amin (1991) argues strongly against the
view that there is historical continuity with pre-capitalist society, a view which
places importance on long-term, worldwide patterns and trends, understood
as cycles of expansion, contraction, rise and decline (Denemark and Gills 2012;
Arrighi 2010 [1994]; Braudel 1972). For Amin there is a structural logic which
reproduces core/periphery relations. Capitalism is imperialistic because it
requires a ceaseless construction of peripheries that can be dominated (Amin
1989, 2010). New cultural discourses, like democracy, operate as a form of
legitimation that reinforce the hegemonic relationship between centre and
periphery (Amin 2010).

Imperialism and the history of capitalism

The centrality of Europe in the concept of the modern world-system has led to contention and critique. Unlike world-system analysis, world-system history does not see the modern capitalist system as fundamentally unique, nor 'the rise of capitalism in Europe [as] the appropriate starting point for understanding the present era' (Denemark and Gills 2012: 166–167; Arrighi 2010 [1994]; Braudel 1972). This view gives precedence to cyclical change and historical continuity, arguing that capital accumulation long predated the modern system and that capitalist practices were common to both East and West for most of world history, cautioning that to view European capitalism as unique is to continue to reproduce Eurocentric social theory (Denemark and Gills 2012; Arrighi 2010 [1994]; Braudel 1972).

The caution against Eurocentrism is upheld by Amin, who while concurring with Wallerstein that the modern world-system constitutes a decisive break with pre-capitalist societies, does not see the emergence of European capitalism as geographically contiguous or uniquely European in its evolution (Amin 1989). Amin emphasises the existence of regional and even world-systems prior to the sixteenth century, stressing that the image of a universal history based on the notion that European capitalism is the first system to unify the world is Eurocentric (Amin 1991, 1989). He contends that, '[t]he system conquers the world but does not make it homogenous' (Amin 1991: 353).

The experiences of other regions highlight the point. The Ottoman Empire, for example, 'falls between the cracks of the fault lines that determined world politics in the nineteenth century' (Deringil 2011 [1999]: 3). Despite the loss of territory and infiltration by Western economic interests, it continued to exert significant military, political and economic power (Deringil 2011 [1999]; Göçek 1996; Karpat 2002; Hanssen 2005). Its relationship with Europe was shaped by historical continuity, and local adaptation to European innovation had long been the norm (Deringil 2011 [1999]; Göçek 1996; Karpat 2002; Dados forthcoming).

As Kirsten Alff (2018) demonstrates in new research on Levantine joint-stock companies in the nineteenth century, the success of capital accumulation for Ottoman companies was shaped by strategies rooted in the Ottoman social formation. Alff argues that the features of capitalism in the eastern Mediterranean, as elsewhere, depended on specific cultural, political and social factors. While the strategies employed by the Levantine joint-stock companies resembled those of European and American competitors, and were often more successful, they continue to be characterised as backward or feudal, and capitalist practices in the Ottoman world continue to be seen as pre-capitalist, non-capitalist or anti-capitalist (Alff 2018: 175–176).

Similarly, for the Latin American modernity/coloniality group (Quijano 2000; Mignolo 2007), the tension between economic domination and imperialism is not sufficiently resolved in world-system and dependency theory perspectives. Rather than seeing colonialism as an expansion of capitalism from a European core to an integrated world economy, the modernity/coloniality group see colonialism as formative in the emergence and expansion of capitalism globally. This is captured in the theory of the 'coloniality of modern world power', or simply 'the coloniality of power' (Quijano 2000), and 'the colonial matrix of power' or 'matrix of modernity' (Mignolo 2007). Anibal Quijano (2000) and Walter Mignolo (2007), two key figures of the modernity/coloniality group, view colonial power as generative of the emergence of capitalism and national-ist modernities on a world scale. While Quijano is concerned with questions of economic power, Mignolo's focus is the coloniality of knowledge.

In contrast to Wallerstein's (1974) view of the world-system as 'a unit with a single division of labour and multiple cultural systems', Quijano (2000) iden-tifies two interlocking systems that emerge simultaneously with the expansion of European colonisation: a capitalist economy and a racialised geopolitical hierarchy. Importantly, racial hierarchies are not seen simply as the applica-tion of colonial power to ensure economic domination, but as a form of social differentiation that is integral to the control of work on a world scale (Quijano 2000: 216–219). As new forms of work are articulated towards a global capital-ist system during European colonial expansion, they are organised by a 'racial distribution of work' grounded in new 'racial geocultural identities' (Quijano 2000: 218). Quijano's (2000) emphasis is on the operation of race as a form of social reproduction arising from the coloniality of modern power. Racial hierarchies enable the incorporation of relationships of servitude and slavery, which, as for Wallerstein (1980 [1974], 1974), are seen not as anomalous rem-nants of feudalism, but as forms of work integrated within the capitalist mode of production, in a geopolitical configuration that is concentrated in the Global South (Quijano 2000).

Mignolo asserts that the project of modernity is irrecuperable for the peoples of the South, and proposes nothing short of a radical 'de-linking' to shake 'the most fundamental belief of modernity: the belief in abstract universals' (Mignolo 2007: 500; Quijano 2000). With a nod to Fanon, Mignolo places coloniality at the centre of the critique of modernity by resurrecting the subjec-tivity of the 'damnés' (from Fanon's (1967) 'wretched of the earth') (Mignolo

2007: 483). Decoloniality rejects post-colonial thought as an inadequate trans-formation of the academy, without a geopolitical transformation of society, proposing instead that decolonisation must be enacted from the perspective of the 'damnés'. Without this, the damnés 'would be deprived of their "right" to liberate and de-colonize and be compelled to await the generous gifts of the colonizer' (Mignolo 2007: 458).

While decoloniality is an epistemic and political project, it demands a complete break from economic and political principles based on Western categories of thought, including Marxism. From this perspective, the very notion of centres and peripheries simply reinforces Eurocentric coloniality and the legacy of imperialism. In practical terms, the coloniality of knowledge is reinforced in the relationships of dependency that foreclose economic, institutional and educational development. The export of European knowledge, whether through the establishment of European educational institutions in the Global South or the adherence to European theoretical frameworks, has long been seen as an obstacle to emancipation and progress (Mazrui 1975; Connell 2018; Hountondji 1997). In a case study of Local Economic Development strategies in post-apartheid South Africa, Ndlovu and Makoni (2014) employ a decolo-nial paradigm to examine the asymmetrical global power relations that value European concepts of development and democracy over other elements of human progress. They argue that development paradigms are haunted by the spectre of coloniality, reproducing inequalities because they do not account for local specificities and subaltern experience (Ndlovu and Makoni 2014).

Alternatives to Northern hegemony

In the interwar years, as the colonial world marched towards independence, the League Against Imperialism was breathing life into what would become known as the Third World Project. With the outbreak of World War II, plans to unite the colonial world under an anti-colonial umbrella were delayed until the Bandung Conference in Indonesia in 1955, before coming to form the Non-Aligned Movement (NAM) through the United Nations in 1961 (Prashad 2012).

The demands of the Third World Project, articulated through the NAM, were for peace, bread and justice (Prashad 2012). Third Worldism, as a project, envisaged a united resistance against capitalism and imperialism that sought alternative forms of post-colonial sovereignty. In the words of Frantz Fanon

(1967), the Third World did not want 'to catch up' with anyone, it wanted to start a new history.

After World War II, this new movement sought new economic models and development strategies that would overcome impoverishment and underdevelopment in the Global South. In 1947, a group of Latin American economists and social and political scientists succeeded in establishing ECLAC or CEPAL, the Economic Commission for Latin America and the Caribbean (Comisión Económica para América Latina y el Caribe), a United Nations organisation dedicated to studying the economic development of the colonised world. Among them were development economists Raul Prebisch and Celso Furtado, whose intellectual contributions to development economics have left a lasting legacy beyond Latin America.[1] Among the most important proposals made by ECLAC/CEPAL to remedy the structural constraints of dependency and uneven development, and pursued widely from Latin America to Africa, were government-led Import Replacement Industrialisation (IRI) and common regional market arrangements, designed to boost employment and guard emerging economies against cyclical downturns (Prebisch 1951; Espinos 2014; Mallorquin 2007).

As a statesman and economist in the government of Gen. Jose Uriburu in the 1930s, Prebisch witnessed the declining terms of trade first hand, noting in 1934 that the economic downturn now meant that 'Argentina had to sell 73 percent more than before the Depression to obtain the same quantity of (manufactured) imports' (Love 1980: 50). Up until the Great Depression, Argentina had pursued a policy of export-led growth based on the principle of comparative advantage. But Prebisch's direct experience of the downturn led him to conclude that export-oriented growth was not a viable path for economic development because the trade cycles of peripheral countries were dependent on those of their trading partners in the centre (Love 1980: 52; Prebisch 1951). Prebisch advocated organised state planning, emphasising that the differences in social structure and the imbalance of power between centre and periphery could not be overcome by pursuing neo-classical economic models (Prebisch 1951; Dados and Connell 2018).

Other radical visions that challenge Northern hegemony, like Samir Amin's concept of 'de-linking' (with a different emphasis from the way the term is used by the modernity/coloniality group), build on these proposals. In articulating an alternate path for development, Amin called for a rejection of 'the imperatives of worldwide expansion' by the countries of the periphery, and the pursuit of an economic system 'founded on a law of value on a national basis with popular relevance' rather than 'the world capitalist law of value' (Amin 1990 [1985]: 62–63).

For the majority of post-colonial states in the post-independence era, however, the national question dominated the path of development and articulated it in cultural discourses, in an attempt to protect 'fragile sovereignties' (Gupta 1992: 71). The focus on the nation became a powerful tool, both in the hands of reformist governments in North Africa (Zghal 1985; Amin 1978 [1976]), and ideologues of 'national security' in South America (Calvo 1979; Connell and Dados 2014). The solidarity of the Third World Project, weakened by the pursuit of conflicting nationalist interests, dissipated with the imposition of structural adjustment programmes and ascendant neoliberalism, often directed by the same post-colonial elites who had championed autonomous development.

Southern responses to neoliberalism and post-colonial capitalism

The rise of neoliberalism in the Global South has posed new challenges for post-colonial states, and for knowledge. While Chile was one of the first countries to pursue a substantively neoliberal programme after the military coup of Augusto Pinochet, theories of neoliberalism generally perceive it as a set of ideas and practices emanating from the Global North, reinforcing the hegemony of Northern models and theories of the world (Dados and Connell 2018; Connell and Dados 2014; Collyer et al. 2019; Connell 2007).

Connell and Dados (2014: 118) argue that social science needs to be re-oriented towards the social experience of the Global South and recognise the intellectual and theoretical contributions of Southern scholars. Focusing on development state strategies, world trade and the reorganisation of global agriculture, they demonstrate that 'neoliberalism is not a projection of Northern ideology or policy, but a re-weaving of worldwide economic and social relationships' (Connell and Dados 2014: 124). One way to understand the operation of neoliberalism from the perspective of the Global South is to focus specifically on what it offered post-colonial elites and development states. This was 'an alternative development strategy that broadly served the interests of local ruling classes, while having some attractions to wider constituencies' (Dados and Connell 2018: 30).

Research on authoritarian neoliberalism has highlighted the prevalence of coercion and force, rather than economic domination, in securing capital accumulation in the periphery (Tansel 2017; Ness 2013; Garreton 1989; Calvo 1979; O'Donnell 1973). The 'reformist dictatorships' of Latin America (for example, Juan Carlos Ongania's *Revolución Argentina* (1966–1973), Brazil's military regime (1964–1985) and Chile's Pinochet regime (1973–1990)) used foundational violence as a mechanism of social change (Garreton 1989; Calvo 1979; O'Donnell 1973). Guillermo O'Donnell characterises these regimes as 'authoritarian-bureacratic states', combining technocratic authority with military power, primarily, in O'Donnell's view, for the purpose of eradicating IRI-centred development models (O'Donnell 1973). In the face of powerful anti-capitalist movements, widespread worker resistance and movements for autonomy across the Global South today, neoliberal capitalism continues to maintain its economic domination through coercion, repression and force (Ness 2013; Tansel 2017).

In India, Kalyan Sanyal (2014, 2012) and Partha Chatterjee (2008) examine the political settlement of post-colonial capitalism under global neoliberalism, with reference to the radically different conditions of capitalist production in the Global South (Sanyal and Chatterjee 2016). Sanyal's contention is that accumulation by dispossession, albeit in a different form to that described by Harvey (2003), dominates the cycles of capitalist accumulation under neoliberalism, requiring that anti-capitalist politics focus primarily on dispossession rather than exploitation (Sanyal 2014, 2012). This is because those who are dispossessed by new waves of accumulation in the Global South cannot be absorbed within the domain of capital as sellers of labour power (Sanyal 2014, 2012; Chatterjee 2008). They must instead be 'allowed to subsist' through the establishment of a 'need-economy' made possible by a political settlement and that is not equivalent to the welfare state of social democracy (Sanyal 2012).

While the capitalist class maintains hegemony over civil society, principally through a bureaucratic-managerial class, the urban middle classes and political parties, the proletarianisation of peasants through dispossession is managed by 'temporary, contextual and unstable arrangements arrived at through direct political negotiations' and a 'globally circulating technology of poverty management' (Chatterjee 2008: 55–57). Ultimately, this settlement is about securing the stability of the state, without which capitalist accumulation cannot be guaranteed (Sanyal and Chatterjee 2016; Sanyal 2014).

While the Third World Project has receded, South-led responses and South–South co-operation continue to produce new initiatives and perspectives, many of them focused primarily on the creation of epistemological resources and economic models that centre the experience of the Global South. The *South Commission*, conceived in the 1980s as an extension of the NAM and charged with formulating intellectual concepts and policy initiatives, highlighted the neo-colonial burden placed on the South by the economic metropolises of the world (in collaboration with the World Bank and the IMF) through the misattribution of the development crisis to domestic policies in the periphery (The South Commission 1990). In response, it advocated a programme of industrial reform to boost manufacturing exports and promote import substitution (The South Commission 1990). Yet even where these policies have succeeded, they have been pursued by state elites within a setting of 'Neoliberalism with Southern Characteristics' (Prashad 2012) that continues to reproduce inequality and impoverishment for the majority of people.

Nonetheless, South–South co-operation continues to grow, as do new intellectual projects focused on South-led initiatives. Three such initiatives, briefly discussed here, provide ample resources to continue this discussion and inform future research. *Southern Responses to Displacement*[2] focuses on the Middle East and the creation and perception of Southern-led models and responses to migration and displacement. *Southern Perspectives* and *Southlink*[3] promote intellectual thought that offers alternatives to Western universalism and globalised development. The *Tricontinental Institute for Social Research*,[4] named for the revolutionary conference hosted in Cuba in 1966, provides a platform for South-based social and political philosophy, advocating that the struggle against imperialism 'must expand out from the South'. Aptly, the *Tricontinental*, following in the legacy of the NAM, ties the quest for peace, bread and justice by the people of the world to the emancipation of Fanon's (1967) 'wretched of the earth'.

Notes

1.   Many of the documents published by the organisation over its 70-year history can be found on this digital depository: https://repositorio.cepal.org.
2.   https://southernresponses.org, accessed 22 March 2010.
3.   https://www.southernperspectives.net/southlink, accessed 22 March 2010.
4.   https://www.thetricontinental.org, accessed 22 March 2010.

References

Alatas, S.F. (2006) *Alternative Discourses in Asian Social Science: Responses to Eurocentrism*, New Delhi: SAGE.

Alff, K. (2018) Levantine joint-stock companies, trans-Mediterranean partnerships, and nineteenth century capitalist development, *Comparative Studies in Society and History*, 60(1): 150–177.

Amin, S. (1974) *Accumulation on a World Scale: A Critique of the Theory of Underdevelopment*, translated by B. Pearce, 2nd ed., New York: Monthly Review Press.

Amin, S. (1978 [1976]) *The Arab Nation*, translated by M. Pallis, London: Zed Books.

Amin, S. (1989) *Eurocentrism*, translated by R. Moore, New York: Monthly Review Press.

Amin, S. (1990 [1985]) *Delinking: Towards A Polycentric World*, London: Zed Books.

Amin, S. (1991) The ancient world-systems versus the modern capitalist world-system, *Review (Fernand Braudel Centre)*, 14(3): 349–385.

Amin, S. (2010) The battlefields chosen by contemporary imperialism: conditions for an effective response from the South, *Kasarinlan: Philippine Journal of Third World Studies*, 25(1–2): 5–48.

Arrighi, G. (2010 [1994]) *The Long Twentieth Century: Money, Power and the Origins of Our Times*, London and New York: Verso.

Bhambra, G.K. (2014) *Connected Sociologies*, London: Bloomsbury Academic.

Braudel, F. (1972) *The Mediterranean and the Mediterranean World in the Age of Philip II*, translated by S. Reynolds, New York: Harper & Row.

Calvo, R. (1979) *La Doctrina Militar de la Seguridad Nacional: Autoritarismo politico you neoliberalismo economico en el cono sur*, Caracas: Universidad Catolica Andres Bello.

Chakrabarty, D. (2000) *Provincializing Europe: Postcolonial Thought and Historical Difference*, Princeton, NJ: Princeton University Press.

Chase-Dunn, C. and Grimes, P. (1995) World-systems analysis, *Annual Review of Sociology*, 21: 387–417.

Chatterjee, P. (2008) Democracy and economic transformation in India, *Economic and Political Weekly*, 43(16): 53–62.

Collyer, F., Connell, R., Maia, J. and Morrell, R. (2019) *Knowledge and Global Power: Making New Sciences in the South*, Clayton, Victoria: Monash University Publishing.

Connell, R. (2007) *Southern Theory: The Global Dynamics of Knowledge in Social Science*, Crows Nest, NSW: Allen & Unwin.

Connell, R. (2014) Using southern theory: decolonizing social thought in theory, research and application, *Planning Theory*, 13(2): 210–223.

Connell, R. (2018) *The Good University: What Universities Actually Do and Why It's Time for Radical Change*, Clayton, Victoria: Monash University Publishing.

Connell, R., Collyer, F., Maia, J. and Morrell, R. (2017) Towards a global sociology of knowledge: postcolonial realities and intellectual practices, *International Sociology*, 32(1): 21–37.

Connell, R. and Dados, N. (2014) Where in the world does neoliberalism come from? The market perspective in Southern perspective, *Theory and Society*, 43(2): 117–132.

Dados, N. (forthcoming) Mapping empire: knowledge production and government in the last Ottoman century, in Strohmaier, A. and Kiwani, A. (eds) *Mobile Media and*

New Cartographies in the Middle East and North Africa, Amsterdam: University of Amsterdam Press.

Dados, N. and Connell, R. (2018) Neoliberalism in world perspective: Southern origins and Southern dynamics, in Cahill, D., Cooper, M., Konings, M. and Primrose, D. (eds) *The SAGE Handbook of Neoliberalism,* Los Angeles and London: SAGE, pp. 28–39.

Denemark, R.A. and Gills, B.K. (2012) World-system history: challenging Eurocentric knowledge, in Babones, S. and Chase-Dunn, C. (eds) *Routledge Handbook of World-Systems Analysis: Theory and Research,* London and New York: Routledge, pp. 163–171.

Deringil, S. (2011 [1999]) *The Well-Protected Domains: Ideology and the Legitimation of Power in the Ottoman Empire 1876–1909,* London and New York: IB Taurus.

El Shakry, O. (2007) *The Great Social Laboratory: Subjects of Knowledge in Colonial and Postcolonial Egypt,* Stanford, CA: Stanford University Press.

Emmanuel, A. (1972) *Unequal Exchange: A Study of the Imperialism of Trade,* translated by B. Pearce, New York: Monthly Review Press.

Espinos, J.D. (2014) Development and inequality: reflections on Celso Furtado, *International Journal of Political Economy,* 43(4): 33–43.

Fanon, F. (1967) *The Wretched of the Earth,* London: Penguin.

Frank, A.G. and Gills, B.K. (eds) (1993) *The World System: Five Hundred Years or Five Thousand?,* London: Routledge.

Garreton, M.A. (1989) *The Chilean Political Process,* Winchester: Unwin Hyman.

Go, J. (2013) For a postcolonial sociology, *Theoretical Sociology,* 42(1): 25–55.

Göçek, F.M. (1996) *Rise of the Bourgeoisie, Demise of Empire: Ottoman Westernization and Social Change,* Oxford: Oxford University Press.

Gupta, A. (1992) Song of the non-aligned world: transnational identities and the reinscription of space in late capitalism, *Cultural Anthropology,* 7(1): 63–79.

Hanssen, J. (2005) *Fin de Siècle Beirut: The Making of an Ottoman Provincial Capital,* Oxford: Clarendon Press.

Harvey, D. (2003) *The New Imperialism,* Oxford: Oxford University Press.

Hountondji, P. (1997) *Endogenous Knowledge: Research Trails,* Dakar: CODESRIA.

Karpat, K.H. (2002) *Studies on Ottoman Social and Political History: Selected Articles and Essays,* Leiden, Boston, Köln: Brill.

Love, J.L. (1980) Raul Prebisch and the origins of the doctrine of unequal exchange, *Latin American Research Review,* 15(3): 45–72.

Luxemburg, R. (1951) *The Accumulation of Capital,* translated by A. Schwarzschild, New Haven, CT: Yale University Press.

Mallorquin, C. (2007) Celso Furtado and development: a brief outline, *Development in Practice,* 17(6): 807–819.

Mazrui, A.A. (1975) The African university as a multinational corporation: problems of penetration and dependency, *Harvard Educational Review,* 45(2): 191–210.

Mignolo, W. (2007) 'Delinking', *Cultural Studies,* 21(2–3): 449–514.

Ndlovu, M. and Makoni, E.N. (2014) The globality of the local? A decolonial perspective on local economic development in South Africa, *Local Economy,* 29(4–5): 503–518.

Ness, I. (2013) *Southern Insurgency: The Coming of the Global Working Class,* Chicago: University of Chicago Press.

O'Donnell, G.A. (1973) *Modernization and Bureaucratic Authoritarianism: Studies in South American Politics,* Berkeley, CA: Institute of International Studies, University of California.

Prashad, V. (2012) *The Poorer Nations: A Possible History of the Global South*, 2nd ed., London and New York: Verso.

Prebisch, R. (1951) *Economic Survey of Latin America 1949*, New York: Secretariat of the Economic Commission for Latin America, United Nations.

Quijano, A. (2000) Coloniality of power and Eurocentrism in Latin America, *International* Sociology, 15(2): 215–231.

Rodney, W. (1972) *How Europe Underdeveloped Africa*, London: Bogle-L'Ouverture Publications.

Said, E.W. (1993) *Culture and Imperialism*, New York: Vintage Books.

Said, E.W. (1995 [1978]) *Orientalism: Western Conceptions of the Orient*, London and New York: Penguin.

Sanyal, K. (2012) Accumulation, exclusion and hegemony: capital and governmentality in the era of globalization, UniNomade, 11 March, available at http://www .uninomade.org/accumulation-exclusion-and-hegemony, accessed 22 March 2020.

Sanyal, K. (2014) *Rethinking Capitalist Development: Primitive Accumulation, Governmentality and Post-Colonial capitalism*, London: Taylor & Francis.

Sanyal, K. and Chatterjee, P. (2016) Rethinking postcolonial capitalist development: a conversation between Kalyan Sanyal and Partha Chatterjee, translated by P. Chatterjee, *Comparative Studies of South Asia, Africa and the Middle East*, 36(1): 102–111.

Singer, H. (1950) The distribution of gains between investing and borrowing countries, *American Economic Review, Papers and Proceedings*, 40: 473–485.

Sousa Santos, B. (2007) Beyond abyssal thinking: from global lines to ecologies of knowledge, *Review*, 30(1): 45–89.

Spivak, G.C. and Harasym, S. (1990) *The Post-Colonial Critic: Interviews, Strategies, Dialogues*, New York: Routledge.

Tansel, C.B. (2017) *States of Discipline: Authoritarian Neoliberalism and the Contested Reproduction of the Capitalist Order*, London and New York: Rowman & Littlefield International.

The South Commission (1990) *The Challenge to the South: The Report of the South Commission* (chaired by Julius Nyerere), Oxford and New York: Oxford University Press.

Wallerstein, I. (1974) The rise and future demise of the world capitalist system: concepts for comparative analysis, *Comparative Studies in Society and History*, 16(4): 387–415.

Wallerstein, I. (1980 [1974]) *The Modern World-System*, Vols 1–3, New York: Academic Press.

Zghal, A. (1985) Why Maghrebi peasants don't like land reform, in Ibrahim, S.E. and Hopkins, N.S. (eds) *Arab Society: Social Science Perspectives*, Cairo: American University in Cairo Press, pp. 322–335.

6   For a critical political economy of international trade

Bill Dunn

Introduction

In this chapter I do four things. First, I argue that international trade offers an important but neglected area of research for critical political economy. The importance is easy to show. The neglect is less conspicuous, but despite some important critical scholarship, including by contributors to this volume, the subject remains dominated by mainstream economists and political scientists. Second, I identify a particular problem in a pervasive methodological nationalism, the challenging of which potentially pays substantial epistemological dividends. Third, I sketch a framework for a research agenda based on Marx's ideas about abstraction and concretization, arguing how thinking about trade can be informed by, and help to inform, thinking about other social relations. Fourth, at greater length, I exemplify this.

The importance of trade and its neglect by critical political economists

Trade's importance needs little emphasis. The rise of recent decades is spectacular. This also provokes debates that have moved to the forefront of political agenda, notably in US–China relations. But, amongst many other things, trade has been central to debates around the rise of capitalism, slavery and industry; the establishment of European empires; the collapse of 19th-century liberalism into the Great Depression and the drive to war; and persistent poverty in developing countries. It has been central to recent discussions of 'global imbalances' and economic crises, and of environmental destruction.

Given these issues and the expansive literature surrounding them, my claim of neglect might seem peculiar. But the stress is on neglect by critical political economists. Some of the contributors to important historical work on trade, most conspicuously the principals in the Dobb–Sweezy debate about the origins of capitalism, were eminent Marxist political economists. But they are exceptions. For the most part, trade has remained the preserve of mainstream economists and to a lesser extent political scientists. There is less social theory of trade. A quick reference to major generalist texts of either sociology or political economy (e.g. Beckert and Zafirovski 2006; Cohen and Kennedy 2000; Dowd 2004; Stilwell 2006) confirms that interest in trade remains peripheral. Trade usually remains the preserve of neo-classical economists and political scientists, who say much that is important but whose field of vision is restricted.

A pervasive methodological nationalism

International trade raises important conceptual issues. In particular, the way it is understood as border-crossing exchanges posits nation states as the relevant unit of analysis. 'Society' can be a slippery concept, but here, as often, there is regress to an association with 'the nation'. Rosenberg suggests this occurs '[t]ime and again – under the several rubrics of "methodological nationalism" in sociology ..., "the territorial trap" in geography ..., the "myth of the primitive isolate" in anthropology ... and the "prejudice of the nation-state" in political theory' (2010: 169). All this is 'empirically untenable and conceptually dysfunctional' (Rosenberg 2010: 169). Recent work on corporate 'globalization' makes clear that social agents are only conditionally national, but the point is fundamentally conceptual rather than historical (Bartelson 2009; Maclean 2000). Ultimately, society only makes sense as a global whole, albeit a multiply differentiated whole.

This implies particular problems for trade theory, which is almost always, and almost by definition, conceived in specifically national terms. International trade becomes inter-societal, something that happens between societies (plural) rather than itself being an intrinsically social activity. But long-distance trade predates the modern nation state by at least a couple of millennia (Curtin 1984; Findlay and O'Rourke 2007) and capitalism's subsequent development, in cities and states and in the interactions between them, is incomprehensible simply in national terms. Today, businesses rather than states actually do most of the trading. Methodological nationalism is bound to beget an inadequately social theory of trade.

One problem seems particularly acute. Almost all academic economists subscribe to methodological individualism (but see Arrow 1994). This is needed to sustain modern marginalism's subjectivist theory of value. Leaving aside the broader issues, methodological individualism creates a profound problem in relation to international trade. In principle, there might be a careful working-up from the individuals to the institutions, the corporations and the states, but this is seldom if ever attempted. Instead, trade is conceived by radical extrapolation, transposing individualist methods onto that particular collectivity that is the nation state (e.g. Krugman and Obstfeld 2003). At least by implication, states are taken to have 'wants' and 'utilities' in the same sense as people. This leaves conventional trade theory suspended over a precipice between methodological individualism and methodological nationalism, hanging only by the thinnest of assumptions that costs and 'opportunity costs', measured in price terms, are a sufficient proxy for utility. Money, originally a means to an end (e.g. Smith 1999; Jevons 1957), becomes a sufficient end in itself. The economic reasoning becomes circular and self-contradictory. For example, where at an individual level, neo-classical economists posit a trade-off, with money reckoned to overcome preferences for leisure over work up to a point of happy equilibrium, at a national level, no comparable process is conceivable. The mainstream must reckon a country more leisured but making fewer dollars as unambiguously poorer than its harder-working counterpart.

Without attempting a review, at least certain strands of the political science literature replicate economists' assumptions, with states reckoned sufficiently rational in the face of competition that the methods of mainstream economics and competitive individualism can be transposed onto their interaction. A similar intellectual fragility ensues (Guzzini 1998).

Unfortunately, much of the ostensibly radical trade theory suffers from similar problems. What Skocpol (1977) calls a 'mirror image trap' leaves the critics engaging with orthodoxy on the latter's terms. Trade ceases to be an unqualified good but becomes an equally unqualified bad, at least for poorer countries. A systemic logic of world trade imposes social structures on those poorer countries (Wallerstein 1974; Frank 1978), but the primary criteria for success and failure usually remain the standard measures of economic growth, similarly conceived in national terms with similarly little sense of trade itself as a contested social achievement.

Apart from anything else, the state-centred vision is reinforced by the overwhelmingly national bases of data collection. Abundant data provide researchers with attractive resources. In most cases there is nothing remotely comparable for levels of intra-national exchange, for trade between states or cities within the same country, even where these may be orders of magnitude greater than those between distant countries which are detailed (albeit often inaccurately) to the last dollar. Uncovering these levels of intra-national trade presents a formidable and worthwhile project of its own, but one of considerable labour and uncertain reward.

Fortunately, despite the difficulties, the state-centred views are being challenged and a fertile field of research is now being ploughed. Amongst other things, there is a substantial literature on global value chains, on food and food regimes (e.g. McMichael 2005) and on the global trade regime, including the role of corporate power in shaping this. Trade receives considerable attention from ecologists of various stripes. There are useful commentaries on the social movements against globalization, for fair trade and on the World Trade Organization and other institutions. Conceptually, many scholars of Economic Sociology and International Political Economy (IPE) emphasize the social construction of 'the international', including international trade relations. Gereffi's (2005) discussion of the global economy incorporates trade, and his strategy of considering different levels, macro (international), meso (countries and firms) and micro, has similarities with the approach advocated below. So what follows makes no claim to particular originality, but suggests there is both much useful work to be done in developing a more adequately social understanding of trade and a conceptual pay-off in potentially providing critical purchase on wider issues of political economy, not least in terms of situating 'the national'.

A framework for a research agenda

In social and economic life, everything influences everything else. The problem then becomes how to say something useful about anything specific. On the one hand, there can be a vacuous holism, in which nothing can be known until everything is known, in contemporary guise, a postmodern determinism-hunting, always able to sneer that 'it is more complicated than that'. On the other hand, specialization, as the economists would have it, allows gains through developing disciplinary comparative advantage and a depth of knowledge. But we imagine we know the thing 'in itself' without knowing its relations, while entrenching techniques and notions of suitable subject matter.

Marx's ideas of movement between the abstract and general and the concrete and specific seem particularly useful in this context, providing the basis for an ordered but multi-dimensional and social understanding of trade. Amongst some slightly different formulations, the *Grundrisse* posits five 'levels' of analysis:

> (1) the general, abstract determinants which obtain in more or less all forms of society ... (2) The categories which make up the inner structure of bourgeois society and on which the fundamental classes rise. Capital, wage labour, landed property. Their interrelation ... (3) Concentration of bourgeois society in the form of the state ... (4) The international relation of production. International division of labour. International exchange. Export and import. Rates of exchange. (5) The world market and crises. (Marx 1973: 108)

I am not claiming a royal road to science, paved by Marx. Both the ordering and the detail of such passages are eminently questionable. But this sort of schema has some obvious attractions in developing a more adequate under-standing of international trade, particularly in its explicit bridging between the generally social and the level of international relations, including international trade relations.

Marx advocates a movement from the abstract and general to the concrete and specific, not an often-imputed economic determinism. It is also immediately apparent from the preceding pages of the *Grundrisse* that the abstract ideas do not themselves descend from heaven or Marx's intuition. The method encourages us to think about different analytical levels and about their interaction. There is a two-way process with an interaction and scrutiny of concepts and evidence in moving between levels. This, in principle, requires an iterative process of mutual interrogation with conclusions reached at one level understood as provisional and requiring re-interrogation considering more concrete investigations at the next (Murray 1997: 42). Rather than defending the method in detail, here it is simply posited as a framework for a research agenda. It seems broadly compatible with Gereffi's (2005) Weberian approach or Cox's (1981) neo-Gramscian insistence on the mutual interdependence of states, social forces and world order, but the specifically Marxist ordering helps illuminate a range of important questions.

One of the points about positing this as a framework for a research project is that rather than trying to do everything simultaneously, research can operate at a particular level, making assumptions about other relations, even as these are recognized as provisional and open to a more or less radical subsequent revision. What we know at one level might be used to generate hypotheses that can be tested at the next and the results used to reflect on what we knew, or thought we knew, at the previous conceptual levels. What follows is simply illustrative, sweeping from the most general to the more specific according to Marx's schema, to outline some potentially useful research themes.

Illustrating a research agenda

The generally social

There are problems invoking a 'generally social': 'backwards' problems of imputation that what exists at other times and places are just different versions of what has become familiar within modern capitalism (Gibson-Graham 1996), and 'forwards' problems of imagining a realm of untrammelled social life, as if there were some non-capitalist margin in which it was now possible to gambol. But even in a society colonized and dominated by capital, much remains irreducible to economic imperatives and thinking about trade can both be informed by and contribute to the broader discussion about how capitalism grows out of, and in dynamic relations with, a non-capitalist 'outside'.

Pressing environmental issues have foregrounded this. Humans' relationships with (the rest of) nature continue to condition production and trade in fundamental ways. Importantly, there are ineliminable associations between land and the production and trade of certain products. Since pre-historic times, people have imported materials they could not produce themselves. Other goods can only be produced with great difficulty. Smith's (1999) famous discussion of the inadvisability of producing grapes and thence wine in his native Scotland (using glass houses and heaters) still resonates. The semi-natural elements retain a considerable intuitive plausibility, with most textbook examples of the theory of comparative advantage conveniently depicting primary products as at least one of the two commodities to be traded. Many vital resources, rare metals and fuels, are only found in specific locations. Of course, agricultural land is itself made or destroyed by human action and social and economic interests fight over where oil wells are sunk, but many activities are more easily conducted in particular environments. The spatial materiality of exchange and transport, within countries as well as across any borders, also matters in ways often overlooked. Trade often involves important semi-natural elements, facilitated for example by means of transport along rivers or across oceans. But non-human nature has been shaped by human intervention in path-dependent ways that can often be traced back over centuries, and which would be worth tracing back in more detail, and breaking from established patterns may only be possible through more or less radical ruptures.

Many activities continue to escape monetary measures, which measures therefore provide a necessarily inadequate basis for assessment. Trade epitomizes how market exchanges still operate alongside other redistributive mechanisms (Dale 2010; Polanyi 2001; Simon 1991), with large proportions conducted as within-firm transfers. Amongst other things, this induces scepticism about many quantitative evaluations, with customs declarations potentially deeply misleading (Buckman 2005; Sikka and Willmott 2010). More broadly, conceptions of social 'goods' vary. There are important normative questions around what constitute legitimate objects of trade (slaves? opium? uranium?), the answers to which change over time. There are also non-trivial positive questions about what constitutes trade. The rise of 'services' has changed what was previously conceived in more narrowly material terms. Corporations, global institutions and recent agreements attempt to include investment and intellectual property, even migration. This raises challenges for conventional theory, with comparative advantage hanging on assumptions of factor immobility but also invoked to claim considerable benefits for cross-border capital flows (Caves et al. 1993). But trade and claims for its benefits are extended to selling off natural resources, traditional knowledges and public services.

There is now a rich area of research in terms of the impacts of trade, probably most obviously in terms of environmental impacts – mainstream claims of increased efficiency (Alstine and Neumayer 2008) to be weighed against those of resource depletion, pollution havens, carbon and other emissions but also less well reported phenomena like species invasions (Buckman 2005). Economists recognize 'externalities' but questions of how we might, and whether we should, attach monetary values to damages wrought by trade remain germane. The impact in turn can influence future trajectories. The rainforest once logged for farmland becomes a different factor 'endowment'.

Capital, wage labour, landed property. Their interrelation

Without attempting a lengthy recapitulation of Marxist truisms, a genuinely critical investigation of trade needs to dig beneath apparently convivial exchange relations to examine them in relation to production and capitalism's unique expansionary dynamic and to see them as being always contested social processes. Social theory is never socially neutral.

Conceiving this level as prior to the nation state helps to decentre conventional thinking. As above, and as the growing global value chains literature makes clear, it is overwhelmingly corporations rather than states that actually buy and sell. Capitalism's enduring heterogeneity suggests many fruitful but under-developed avenues of enquiry. The unevenness may in part be predicated on the natural and general phenomena discussed above, but a geographical path dependence can create and deepen incidental peculiarities and sites of industrial specialization. These (then) have profound impacts on trade (Krugman 1990) but are themselves always potentially disrupted by capitalism's dynamism, for example the effects of technological change in production and transport and communications pulling in different directions. The rich literature of New Economic Geography still seldom ventures far beyond the methods or the subject matter of the mainstream, for example into examining ethnic and gendered divisions of labour, and how they become inextricably part of trades' construction, not merely its consequences. Trade and barriers to trade can themselves amplify and reify shades of geographical distinction, not only produced by, but contributing to, the constitution of national differences.

It is also corporations that trade in the sense of being the traders, the shipping companies and airlines. But at least since the demise of the East India and slaving companies, the traders themselves seldom receive attention outside the specialist journals. Yet the shipping companies and cargo airlines and those working for them are 'agents' in the most active sense, competing, co-operating and colluding (Hummels 2007), albeit not in conditions of their own choosing.

Remarkably, in terms of trade's consequences, orthodoxy, via Heckscher (1950) and Ohlin (1991) and Stolper and Samuelson (1941), discusses class in ways seldom visited by the ostensible critics. Amongst other things, these ideas have been developed in claims that increased income polarization within rich countries can be explained by trade. Greater openness increases the demand, and therefore the rewards, for capital and the work of the skilled and diminishes the demand for the work of the unskilled (whose jobs go to the lower-paid workers in countries where the unskilled are in relatively greater abundance) (Krugman 2008; Wood 1994). The theories tend to depoliticize inequality and, lacking any notion of exploitation, over-emphasize exchange relations and monetary rewards and thence trade in explaining inequality. The evidence from poorer countries is also harder to understand under the same rubric (Chusseau and Hellier 2013; Dunn 2014). But these ideas at least seem worth taking seriously. They contrast sharply with much of the critical political economy writing on inequality on which trade hardly seems to impinge (Stilwell, Chapter 2 in this volume). The international system imposes pressures and constraints on individuals, classes and other groups, within countries. In reclaiming these issues, a radical agenda might, of course, also go much further in looking at other dimensions of inequality and how trade interacts with other drivers of redistribution.

States

Even if an important aspect of a critical research agenda is to decentre the state as *the* essential unit of analysis, in practice, economic relations, including trade relations, are typically contested on the terrain of national political economies and cannot be understood adequately without also examining how and why states act. One striking aspect of mainstream international economics is the almost complete absence of any explicit ontology of the state. Typically, the state just *is*, a reified essence, a reprehensible incursion into market freedom or, for mercantilism and much of the Keynesian tradition, a rather benign champion of national interests. As above, conceiving states as coherent, unified actors leaves trade fundamentally unexamined. It is impossible here to venture into state theory, but the framework suggests getting behind and beyond the borders.

Again, time and space matter, with modern states shaped, for example, by the territories they inherit and their trading past. They become capitalist states, minimally in the sense of having a systematic bias towards the interests of the already socially and economically powerful. At the same time, policy is contested, with democratic and other pressures pulling in different directions producing outcomes, including outcomes for trade policy, determined in open-ended struggles. Rogowski's (1989) work, extending the Stolper–Samuelson theorem, may overstate the centrality of trade in overall policy formation but highlights how trade openness or closure can have a basis in material interests and contested urban–rural and class struggles. Contending forces couch their claims in universalist language but trade policy is misconceived as a matter of national interests, for good or ill.

There is, however, an irreducible, specific, state moment. Amongst other things, the social interests contesting trade policy include those of and within the state itself. The ability to raise revenue through import duties, for example, can be an important policy determinant. It seems reasonable to hypothesize that particular state forms may be more capable than others of breaking from existing trade patterns, redirecting national economies away from particular vested interests, for example in primary product dependency.

At the same time, as the Realist literature insists, states are also shaped by the inter-state system or 'world order', including the global trade regime (Cox 1981; Robinson 2008). Their trading relations can be thrust upon them by imperial power, international institutions or the demands of the world market. But even the most powerful states lack the teleology to discern objectively correct strategic ends, while even the weakest states strategize.

International relations

As above, both mainstream economic trade theory and much of the putatively radical criticism operates at the level of international relations. Like the other levels, the international has a distinct 'moment' of its own and there is much that can usefully be said. There may be potentially substantial gains from trade as Smith (1999) and Ricardo (1951) and their followers insist. Conversely, many of the insights into systemic asymmetries are eminently useful. It is entirely possible for exchanges to be unequal in a Marxist sense (Emmanuel 1972), although measuring this becomes an interesting research challenge in itself.

But the level of international relations, including international trade relations, can now be informed by the earlier ones with an appreciation of how the theories that treat this level as 'given' remain limited and limiting. Rival theories should be understood more as interesting hypotheses, worth investigating critically, than as abstract truths (Dunn 2017). Problems with the formal models and methods of neo-classical economics seem particularly clear. Modern marginalism relies (often implicitly) on mathematical methods that require assumptions of (something approximating to) an infinite number of infinitely small variables. This is problematic at economics' usual 'micro' level, but the world's two-hundred-odd nation states are more obviously neither similar nor, in many cases, small in relation to the whole. The US is not just a larger, wealthier version of Paraguay, and however many controls are poured into the regression analyses they are unlikely to capture the character of international diversity.

It also appears that a narrow focus on this level leads many professed radicals to reinstall methodological nationalism. Their concern too becomes that of the wealth of nations, if now also the poverty of others. Emmanuel is particularly emphatic that his 'subject is the "exploitation" of one nation by another, not the exploitation of man by man [sic]' (1972: 330). Where critical political economists are usually quick to unpick the asocial character of the mainstream, this seldom happens in trade theory, which often remains at the level of arguing about rival strategies' implications for national growth, without enquiring much further into the nature of nation states or the fundamental causes or 'meanings' of growth. Preoccupation with exchange relations tends to posit these as primary, or at least as determinant of, production relations (Brenner 1977). To repeat, this is not to dismiss the rival claims but to advocate a careful, socialized, evaluation.

International relations are also a domain of power, of money and finance, of foreign investment and human migration, all profoundly influencing trade practices. As Findlay and O'Rourke write, 'the greatest expansions of world trade have tended to come not from the bloodless tâtonnement of some fictional Walrasian auctioneer but from the barrel of a Maxim gun, the edge of a scimitar, or the ferocity of nomadic herdsmen' (2007: xviii). International debts require trade strategies to pay for them, with potentially lasting consequences. And, as Shaikh (1979, 1980) argues, even apparently temporary trade deficits create indebtedness, potentially meaning permanent economic contraction. I am unconvinced the evidence supports this, but it warrants more research. Currency seigniorage, currently falling on the US dollar, affords countries at least short-term advantages. But once these advantages are recognized as driven by state or class interests, rather than some putative general national interest, it is unsurprising to find the same process working in some tension with or even against the long-term interests of those national economies as territorial spaces. There are complex and contested connections between trade and foreign investment, too glibly understood by the mainstream under the same rubric. There are multiple dimensions and means of competition, few if any involving the gentle market adjustments depicted by the economic mainstream, but each requiring more research. As above, merchant capital can increase its profits by taking advantage of differences in costs, which differences it may help to undermine (Weeks and Dore 1979). Capital crosses borders but borders matter, not least in the way that trading firms can also prosper in the interstices between them.

The world market and crises

Finally, and very briefly, the world market imposes structural imperatives on individuals, firms and countries. For example, they must compete, perhaps gaining from trade, perhaps at others' expense. Trade matters, sometimes marginally and sometimes profoundly. Widening gaps between rich countries and poor have at least been accentuated over the last 200 years by entrenched trade specializations and locations within an international division of labour. Trade can also have a levelling effect, bringing distant and apparently discrete activities into comparison and competition and reducing everything to the law of value. There is no settled pattern as states, national economies, domestic social relations and human relations with the rest of nature remain inherently uneven. So trade simultaneously upsets established relations and creates countervailing pressures and new spaces of specialization and differentiation, and potentially of resistance. How all this plays out alongside other social and economic processes requires a more ambitious research agenda than either orthodox trade theory or nation-centric alternatives allow.

Trade's consequences are far-reaching. Amongst many other things, but neatly fitting Marx's schema as presented here, powerful arguments suggest that trade and trade imbalances contributed to each of the major economic crises of the last hundred years (Kindleberger 1996; Wolf 2010). It was also suggested above that radical ruptures might be required to overcome the lock-in effects that perpetuate trade patterns. Powerful vested interests have gained from the increased openness of recent decades and are unlikely to surrender their gains lightly.

Conclusions

Minimally, there is an enormous amount of potentially useful critical research to be done on trade, a terrain where mainstream economists have enjoyed too comfortable an occupation.

Re-conceiving trade as a social activity challenges what, even amongst too many critical scholars, remain national conceptions of society. People trade in the context of broader processes of international competition and co-operation, state practices, contested national political economies and the many 'non-economic' dimensions of social life. Marx's avowed method of political economy challenges methodological nationalism and more broadly directs attention to these connections and to how trade is situated analytically. It provides a potentially useful basis for a systematic engagement with existing theories but also for moving beyond criticism towards the construction of a more adequately critical political economy of trade.

References

Alstine, van J. and Neumayer, E. (2008) The environmental Kuznets curve, in Gallagher, K.P. (ed.) *Handbook on Trade and the Environment*, Cheltenham, UK and Northampton, MA, USA: Edward Elgar Publishing, pp. 49–59.
Arrow, K.J. (1994) Methodological individualism and social knowledge, *American Economic Review*, 84(2): 1–9.
Bartelson, J. (2009) Is there a global society? *International Political Sociology*, 3(1): 112–115.
Beckert, J. and Zafirovski, M. (eds) (2006) *International Encyclopedia of Economic Sociology*, London: Routledge.
Brenner, R. (1977) The origins of capitalist development: a critique of neo-Smithian Marxism, *New Left Review*, 104: 25–92.

Buckman, G. (2005) *Global Trade: Past Mistakes, Future Choices*, Halifax, Nova Scotia: Fernwood.

Caves, R.E., Frankel, J.A. and Jones, R.W. (1993) *World Trade and Payments*, 6th ed., New York: Harper Collins.

Chusseau, N. and Hellier, J. (2013) Inequality in emerging countries, in Hellier, J. and Chusseau, N. (eds) *Growing Income Inequalities: Economic Analyses*, Basingstoke: Palgrave Macmillan, pp. 48–75.

Cohen, R. and Kennedy, P. (2000) *Global Sociology*, Basingstoke: Palgrave.

Cox, R.W. (1981) Social forces, states and world orders, *Millennium: Journal of International Studies*, 10(2): 126–155.

Curtin, P.D. (1984) *Cross-Cultural Trade in World History*, Cambridge: Cambridge University Press.

Dale, G. (2010) *Karl Polanyi*, Cambridge: Polity Press.

Dowd, D. (2004) *Capitalism and Its Economics*, London: Pluto Press.

Dunn, B. (2014) Skills, credentials and their unequal reward in a heterogeneous global political economy, *Journal of Sociology*, 50(3): 349–367.

Dunn, B. (2017) Class, capital and the global unfree market: resituating theories of monopoly capitalism and unequal exchange, *Science & Society*, 81(3): 348–374.

Emmanuel, A. (1972) *Unequal Exchange: A Study of the Imperialism of Trade*, London: New Left Books.

Findlay, R. and O'Rourke, K.H. (2007) *Power and Plenty: Trade, War, and the World Economy in the Second Millennium*, Princeton, NJ: Princeton University Press.

Frank, A.G. (1978) *Dependent Accumulation and Under-Development*, London: Macmillan.

Gereffi, G. (2005) The global economy: organization, governance, and development, in Swedberg, N.J. and Smelser, R. (eds) *The Handbook of Economic Sociology*, 2nd ed., Princeton, NJ: Princeton University Press, pp. 160–182.

Gibson-Graham, J.K. (1996) *The End of Capitalism (As We Knew It)*, Cambridge, MA: Blackwell.

Guzzini, S. (1998) *Realism in International Relations and International Political Economy*, London: Routledge.

Heckscher, E. (1950) The effect of foreign trade on the distribution of income, in Haley, B.F. (ed.) *Readings in the Theory of International Trade*, London: George Allen & Unwin, pp. 272–300.

Hummels, D. (2007) Transportation costs and international trade in the second era of globalization, *Journal of Economic Perspectives*, 23(1): 131–154.

Jevons, W.S. (1957) *The Theory of Political Economy*, 5th ed., New York: Augustus M. Kelley.

Kindleberger, C.P. (1996) *Manias, Panics, and Crashes*, New York: John Wiley & Sons.

Krugman, P.R. (1990) *Rethinking International Trade*, Cambridge, MA: MIT Press.

Krugman, P.R. (2008) Trade and wages, reconsidered, *Brookings Papers on Economic Activity*, Spring: 103–154.

Krugman, P.R. and Obstfeld, M. (2003) *International Economics: Theory and Policy*, 6th ed., Boston, MA: Addison-Wesley.

MacLean, J. (2000) Philosophical roots of globalization and philosophical routes to globalization, in Germain, R.D. (ed.) *Globalization and Its Critics*, Basingstoke: MacMillan, pp. 3–66.

Marx, K. (1973) *Grundrisse*, New York: Random House.

McMichael, P. (2005) Global development and the corporate food regime, in Buttel, F.H. and McMichael, P. (eds) *New Directions in the Sociology of Global Development*

(Research in rural sociology and development, Vol. 11), Bingley: Emerald Group Publishing, pp. 265–300.

Murray, P. (1997) Redoubled empiricism: the place of social form and social causality in Marxian theory, in Moseley, F. and Campbell, M. (eds) *New Investigations of Marx's Method*, Atlantic Highlands, NJ: Humanities Press, pp. 38–66.

Ohlin, B. (1991) The theory of trade, in Flam, H. and Flanders, M.J. (eds) *Heckscher–Ohlin Trade Theory*, Cambridge, MA: MIT Press, pp. 76–214.

Polanyi, K. (2001) *The Great Transformation*, Boston, MA: Beacon Press.

Ricardo, D. (1951) *On the Principles of Political Economy and Taxation*, Cambridge: Cambridge University Press.

Robinson, M. (2008) Hybrid state: globalisation and the politics of state capacity, *Political Studies*, 56: 566–583.

Rogowski, R. (1989) *Commerce and Coalitions: How Trade Affects Domestic Political Alignments*, Princeton, NJ: Princeton University Press.

Rosenberg, J. (2010) Basic problems in the theory of uneven and combined development. Part II: Unevenness and political multiplicity, *Cambridge Review of International Affairs*, 23(1): 165–189.

Shaikh, A. (1979) Foreign trade and the law of value: part I, *Science & Society*, 43(3): 281–302.

Shaikh, A. (1980) Foreign trade and the law of value: part II, *Science & Society*, 44(1): 27–57.

Sikka, P. and Willmott, H. (2010) The dark side of transfer pricing: its role in tax avoidance and wealth retentiveness, *Critical Perspectives on Accounting*, 21(4): 342–356.

Simon, H.A. (1991) Organizations and markets, *Journal of Economic Perspectives*, 5(2): 25–44.

Skocpol, T. (1977) Wallerstein's world capitalist system: a theoretical and historical critique, *American Journal of Sociology*, 82: 1075–1090.

Smith, A. (1999) *The Wealth of Nations*, books IV–V, London: Penguin.

Stilwell, F. (2006) *Political Economy*, Oxford: Oxford University Press.

Stolper, W.F. and Samuelson, P.A. (1941) Protection and real wages, *Review of Economic Studies*, 9(1): 58–73.

Wallerstein, I. (1974) *The Modern World-System: Capitalist Agriculture and the Origins of the European World-Economy in the Sixteenth Century*, New York: Academic Press.

Weeks, J. and Dore, E. (1979) International exchange and the causes of backwardness, *Latin American Perspectives*, 6(2): 62–87.

Wolf, M. (2010) *Fixing Global Finance*, expanded and updated ed., New Haven, CT: Yale University Press.

Wood, A. (1994) *North–South Trade, Employment and Inequality: Changing Fortunes in a Skill-Driven World*, Oxford: Clarendon.

7 Sweatshop economics, the poverty of trade theory and the making of inequality across scales

Alessandra Mezzadri

1. Introduction: the relevance of fieldwork economics

In her renowned book *India Working* (2003), the development economist Barbara Harriss-White built the case for what she defines as 'fieldwork economics', that is, the study of economic systems and socio-economic relations based on concrete field-based observations. In fact, quite a few economists have directly or indirectly embraced this method of enquiry, particularly for the study of South Asia; famous examples are represented by Naila Kabeer's work on labour markets in Bangladesh or Jean Dreze's studies of poverty and inequality in India. However, mainstream economics remains largely disconnected from fieldwork as a methodology, as this is seen to be far more the domain of other social sciences, such as sociology, anthropology, geography or development studies.

This seems the case both in relation to macro, 'grand' economic theories and models, conceptualising change at a broader level of analysis, and in relation to microeconomic theories, more concerned instead with the concrete functioning of specific actors, markets, sectors, institutions, policies or domains. When it comes to issues concerning development, the former theories generally only invoke empirical evidence in the form of past historical data or trends – despite such data being problematic when used as a proxy to foresee changes in different geographical settings. Perhaps one of the most spectacular examples of failure in forecasts is represented by the so-called Kuznets's 'inverted-U' relationship, modelling the relationship between inequality and growth as one defined by an initial positive correlation, followed by an inverse relationship after a given turning point. In mainstream economics, it is still often referred to as a 'law', despite no longer even been followed by the very countries whose historical experiences inspired its theorisation in the first place, namely Germany, the UK and the US (Palma 2011).

Mainstream microeconomic theories, on the other hand, also suffer from their embedded methodological individualism, portraying economic behaviour as the necessary outcome of a set of pre-established hypotheses ahistorically applied across the board to a variety of settings and geographies. Hence, fieldwork has generally no role to play. In fact, even the rise to fame of Randomised Control Trials (RCTs) in microeconomics – through which Abhijit Banerjee and Esther Duflo landed the 2019 Nobel Prize – should not be misunderstood as a victory of field-based (mainstream) economics. While presented as fieldwork led, RCTs broadly depoliticise fieldwork, and turn into a sort of scientific experiment. They still suffer from the overstated claims of economic modelling (Deaton and Cartwright 2018), and despite their claim of developing 'economics for the poor' (namely *Poor Economics,* by Banerjee and Duflo 2011), they still severely downplay human agency and power relations (Kabeer 2019; Stevano 2019). They have numerous in-built biases conditioning results (e.g. Ravallion 2012; Akram-Lodhi 2014; Deaton and Cartwright 2018; Bédécarrats et al. 2019; see also the recent World Development *Symposium on Experimental Approaches,* 2020), and dubious ethical standards (Sinha 2018). If anything, RCTs twist the case for fieldwork-informed theorisation on its head. They do not show the relevance of fieldwork for economic analysis; rather, they make the case for economic analysis indicating which is the 'right' fieldwork and analysis to pursue. In this sense, they should be understood as the latest frontier of (mainstream) 'economic imperialism' (on the concept, see Lazear 2000).

The antipathy of mainstream economics for field-informed research is often articulated as due to its supposed subjective nature, lack of rigour and overly qualitative, unpredictable and 'unscientific' approach. Moreover, fieldwork-informed knowledge may also be undervalued based on its perceived disconnect with the 'big questions' and concerns characterising more abstract economic analysis. However, instead, 'fieldwork economics' can quite powerfully dispel many of the myths of mainstream economic thinking, and quite rigorously too. Below, I draw on my own experience as a long-term 'economic fieldworker' across global garment sweatshops to show the limits of mainstream theories of trade and debates on inequality. I aim to show that a lot can be learnt from *sweatshop economics.*

2.   The sweatshop against the mythology of comparative advantage

Nothing seems further from the neatness and scientific aspirations of mainstream economic thinking than the world of the sweatshop: chaotic, messy, flexible, mobile and unpredictable. I have been researching garment sweatshops for one and a half decades, and I still often remain surprised at its changing mechanisms for market adaptation and labour subordination. 'Steered' globally, regionally and locally by multiple actors (global buyers and retailers, regional traders and exporters, and local producers and contractors), the sweatshop is a remarkable joint enterprise, able to cope with the ever-changing features and vagaries of global demand and drawing into its orbit millions of workers worldwide (Mezzadri 2017). Despite the apparent sharp separation between the very concrete world of the sweatshop and the abstract world of economic theorising, *not only can we* put the two in conversation, but *we must* do so. In fact, the world of the sweatshop and its functioning mechanisms teach us key lessons in relation to the limits of key economic concepts and theories, namely comparative advantage and international trade models.

Interestingly enough, comparative advantage, one of the stickiest concepts in economics, was formulated by David Ricardo exactly based on the well-known example of cloth and wine produced, respectively, in England and Portugal. It cannot be unreasonable to examine the concept through the lens of how that cloth is turned into clothes. However, rather than confirming the theory of comparative advantage, the analysis of the sweatshop unsettles some of its core assumptions. The theory of comparative advantage works only based on a long list of rather unconvincing hypotheses (Schumacher 2013). The most problematic of all is probably the assumption that any country can produce any good, a significant fallacy of composition (Patnaik and Patnaik 2016) which does not account for the possibility of absolute cost advantage (Shaikh 1980). Besides erasing geographical differences and varying development levels at the very start of the analysis, this problematic hypothesis is further reinforced by assumptions on equal technology and perfect mobility of labour between sectors. Translated into the example provided by Ricardo, these assumptions would mean that wine and cloth may be produced by both England and Portugal, using the same techniques, and that the same labour deployed to produce wine could be deployed for cloth, at least inside each of the trading countries – as labour and capital mobility is only assumed to take place within national boundaries. Now, if one observes the functioning mechanisms of cloth and clothes production – the functioning mechanism of the sweatshop – one soon realises than even within such production in a single country there can be several production techniques not only co-existing, but also interplaying. Moreover, the labour deployed to produce cloth and to produce clothes may also be extraordinarily different, and it may be hardly mobile not just across economic sectors, but also in relation to sub-sectors.

The study of different typologies of sweatshops in India – large and medium factories and more informal workshops – indeed reveals that cloth and clothes can be manufactured through a great variety of techniques. Technology varies significantly based on factory size, on market segments, and also on the basis of factories' positioning in the export ladder and access to final markets. It varies based on the relative presence or absence of merchant capital and complex trading networks, and also on the basis of the technical organisation of production inside industrial units. The latter may include assembly-line work (the Taylorist organisation of production in batches, where each worker specialises in a single operation), group-systems (where a group of tailors are at work together to finish one garment) or what in India are called 'make-and-through' techniques (where each tailor stitches the whole garment). Given the widespread presence of subcontracting arrangements, all the above can co-exist in units connected to broader, highly differentiated and fragmented commodity chains. In short, trade theorists would benefit from knowledge of labour process theory, as this would have quickly disproven many of their initial key hypotheses.

The high differentiation of production techniques even within one single type of production, in a single country, is paralleled by the great differentiation of the typologies of labour deployed to produce clothes. Hardly a homogenous labour force, sweatshop workers change dramatically on the basis of geographical location, type of industrial unit or space of work, and type of activity performed. In India, a field-based analysis of sweatshops in distinct geographical locations reveals that workers may be male migrants (e.g. in northern smaller factories), women commuters (e.g. in southern larger factories), single home-based (women) workers (e.g. in ancillary activities in peri-urban/rural areas), or whole families/households (petty producers) deployed as disguised units of labour (Mezzadri 2017). These categories of labourers – or 'classes of labour' (Bernstein 2007) – cannot freely move within national and local boundaries, as the employment ladder is highly discriminatory and allocates tasks and rewards on the basis of social profile. In fact, different 'classes of labour' are likely to guarantee labour cost minimisation for distinct product cycles. For instance, male migrant labour, highly mobile, flexible and precarious, ensures cost minimisation within fragmented product cycles, while labour feminisation guarantees minimisation of costs within less seasonal and more stable product cycles (Mezzadri 2017). Indeed, the idea that anyone can work anywhere clashes with the reality of how labour mobilisation and deployment de facto takes place, in sweatshops and, I dare say, anywhere else. Labour markets have always been 'bearers of gender' (Elson 1999) as well as of other social institutions segmenting and compartmentalising the labour force. On the other hand, as argued by Karl Marx, and by generations of feminist political economists (e.g. Federici 2004; Fortunati 1981; Mies 1986; Picchio 1992; Bhattacharya 2017; Ferguson 2019) who have unpacked labour differentiation, labour is the most extraordinary, unique commodity and it is hardly surprising that its features escape the simplistic schema of comparative advantage.

If the concrete workings of the sweatshop, unveiled through field-based research, call into question Ricardo's theory of comparative advantage, they also unveil the limitations of models of international trade based on 'comparative factor advantage' or so-called 'natural endowments'. The Heckscher–Ohlin model in particular is greatly challenged by *sweatshop economics*. This model effectively aims at explaining the origins of comparative advantage, seen as linked to the relative abundance of specific factors of production in given settings (Schumacher 2013). Generally deployed in polarised examples of countries 'abundant' in either capital or labour (the world of classical political economy is here replaced by the far narrower one of neoclassical economics), the model implies that countries should specialise in the production of the good mainly utilising the factor of production either cheaper or more abundant nationally. In short, countries 'rich' or 'abundant' in cheap labour should specialise in labour-intensive productions and countries rich in capital – that is, literally rich – should focus instead on capital-intensive ones.

The great limitations of such models of international trade have already been widely acknowledged by heterodox economists. Ha-Joon Chang (2007, 2011) has convincingly demonstrated that countries that successfully climbed the development ladder have not done so merely by producing and trading based on their 'natural' comparative advantages and factor endowments. Instead, countries like South Korea have actively crafted comparative advantages in sectors commanding higher shares of value-added, a strategy often pursued through the deployment of protectionist measures and often also involving certain degrees of developmental state violence (see Chang 2009). The same analyses have also questioned how 'natural' the so-called natural advantages portrayed in these trade models really were. In fact, colonialism imposed patterns of production and trade. Many forms of commodity production were more the result of imperialist designs (Patnaik and Patnaik 2016) than the outcome of any natural advantage. Rubber production in Malaysia, for instance, an example quoted by Ha-Joon Chang (2007), was hardly the result of any natural endowment or advantage for the country. Plants were moved from Brazil by colonial powers, and plantations were organised on the basis of the infamous Kangani system, which mobilised armies of indentured workers from South Asia.

Contributing to these insightful analyses, *sweatshop economics* further develops this critique of models of international trade by deconstructing 'cheap labour' as a natural comparative advantage of any poorer nation. Analyses in praise of cheap labour as comparative advantage – epitomised by the work of economists like Paul Krugman (see Cawthorne and Kitching 2001) or Benjamin Powell (2014) – are detached from the concrete world of cheap labour. Field-based research on sweatshops, as on many other labour-intensive industries, reveals the endless and ruthless tactics through which labour must be subjugated and manufactured into a cheap commodity in countries pursuing low-road pathways to industrialisation. These tactics range from routine breaches in formal national and international labour laws and private labour standard regulations, to physical violence perpetrated against workers on shopfloors or beyond, by either employers or the state, or both. In 2013, the Rana Plaza disaster tragically epitomised the unacceptable features of the cheap labour model, which systematically exposes workers to lethal risks from working in unsafe buildings. In 2015, police shooting Cambodian workers mobilised to demand increases in wages in the streets of Phnom Penh further clarified the ways in which the cheap labour model is achieved (Mezzadri 2017). As I write this section, in December 2019, news of a factory fire killing over 40 workers in a Delhi garment workshop is featuring in the media (PTI New Delhi 2019). None of these instances speaks of a 'natural' comparative advantage in cheap labour. Rather, they show the poverty of economic theories, which naturalise power (and violence) and conflate it with necessary market outcomes, even when evidence suggests otherwise.

In fact, field-based accounts of the sweatshops reveal that even in the absence of industrial disasters or direct violence, a cheap labour force has to be made and remade, in factories, workshops and homes, a process entailing a cascade of labour recruiters, management agents and supervisors (e.g. Barrientos 2013; De Neve 2014) who need to mobilise, deploy and control labour, often moving significant floating populations from rural to urban areas. The complexity of these processes further deconstructs the mythology of labour being, in any way, shape or form, a natural comparative advantage of power economies. As argued by Jan Breman as early as 1995, as a critique of the then World Development Report (WDR) *Workers in an Integrating World* (World Bank 1995), within the schema of comparative advantage based on so-called natural endowments, labour was asked to surrender to capital (Breman 1995). And it was also re-imagined as being readily available for deployment, by whichever corporation needed it (De Neve 2005). The two subsequent WDRs focused on work, titled *Jobs* (World Bank 2013) and *The Changing Nature of Work* (World Bank 2019), are hardly progressive in the ways in which they essentially see workers as resources in a world organised in global production networks and led by technological innovations, side-lining instead considerations over the desirability of highly precarious jobs produced by international trade-led circuits (e.g. Anner et al. 2020).

Unfortunately, despite the many criticisms, comparative-factor-advantage international trade models still remain influential, and mainstream economic theory remains convinced of the possible effectiveness of the cheap labour model. The book by Benjamin Powell, *Out of Poverty: Sweatshops in the Global Economy*, which once again restates the case for the export-led cheap labour model as a way out of poverty, came out in 2014, just one year after the Rana Plaza disaster (Powell 2014). Arguably, one of the key reasons behind the resilience of ideas of specialisation within the international division of labour has little to do with production or trade per se, but all to do with inequality, how it is conceived and which policies are seen as useful to its fall. The poverty of mainstream trade theory is further confirmed by an analysis of how it conceives inequality and processes of convergence in the world economy. I show below how *sweatshop economics* can provide once again a useful corrective to misguided assumptions and conclusions.

3.   Convergence, interrupted: the fiction of productivity and the making of inequality across scales

Despite the many similarities between Ricardo's early conceptualisation of comparative advantage and later neoclassical models like Heckscher–Ohlin, one should be very aware of their differences, as these are crucial to understand the leading role trade has played in global policy since the rise of neoliberalism in the 1980s. As summarised by Anwar Shaikh (1980: 205), 'Poor Ricardo dared only claim that free trade is better; neoclassical theory can boldly claim that international inequality is best.' The real revolution led by neoclassical accounts in relation to trade is not about the beneficial effects of trading internationally per se, but its effects on global inequalities. While presented as a corollary to comparative-factor-advantage models, what is known as the Stolper–Samuelson theorem (Stolper and Samuelson 1941) is what has de facto placed trade at the centre of the inequality debate. According to this corollary, due to international trade-led specialisation, countries will eventually be able to move towards convergence. Countries engaging in trade based on their comparative factor advantage in cheap labour will increase the pool of labour deployed for labour-intensive production, and hence will see a rise in wages for their cheap labour force. Countries engaged in trade based on their advantage in capital-intensive production instead will see returns to capital declining. Eventually, these upward movements in the relative costs/prices of factors of production will lead to convergence. This is what Smith and Toye (1979) labelled as the 'happy story of international trade'.

These over-optimistic accounts have been subject to a great deal of criticism. Structuralist economists have highlighted how different price movements are strongly linked to terms of trade of different commodities – with primary commodities suffering from structural decline in prices. On this basis, and in a more radical framework, dependency theorists have theorised international trade as the key engine for underdevelopment, due to its reproduction of colonial patterns of dependence, greatly shaped by trade, and advocated for the de-linking of the Global South from a world economy created in the interests of their former colonial powers (Amin 1990; Patnaik and Patnaik 2016). Other heterodox critiques have shown that if one adopts an economic model where endowments are premised on skills differences rather than capital/labour intensity, then the final outcome of international trading becomes divergence instead. This is because specialisation would further magnify incentives for skill polarisation between, say, countries producing garments and countries producing cars, based on their comparative factor advantage (Wood 1994, 1995; Wood and Ridao-Cano 1996; Patnaik and Patnaik 2016).

Field-based *sweatshop economics* can arguably further disprove the Stolper– Samuelson thesis, based on the observation of wage formation on labour markets for labour-intensive production. As already highlighted in the previous section, a lot can be learnt from the labour process when it comes to the limits of comparative advantage theories. Many further insights are also gained by reflecting on wage formation. While models of international trade represent sectoral wages as homogenous, and formed on the basis of supply– demand movements, this is hardly the way in which local labour markets in developing regions work. In fact, this is hardly how any labour market works, as highlighted by decades of feminist scholarship on wage differentials and wage gaps (e.g. Elson 1999; Folbre 2018). The cheap labour model then, in particular, has been able to assert itself in the Global South thanks to processes of racialisation and gendering of the labour force, which vary based on locally defined systems of oppression and disadvantage, and where wage gaps are reproduced based on discourses devaluing the labour of given social groups (e.g. Salzinger 2003; Novo 2004; Caraway 2005; Wright 2006). At no point has wage formation ever been dependent on international markets or trading outcomes. Field-based evidence from India's sweatshop regime (Mezzadri 2017) once again provided me with key insights into this process. The labour force employed in garment-making in India is extremely diverse, on the basis of gender, geographical provenance, mobility and, obviously, caste. It is also extremely different based on spaces of work – factory/workshop/home – and tasks performed. All the above is linked to different recruitment patterns, wage levels and types of payments – for example, wage/piece rates. Wages may differ, within the same factory, on the basis of gender, geographical provenance or community of belonging for people engaging in exactly the same type of work. Wage formation has hardly any link to specialisation, and in any case the latter is a far more complex endeavour than trade models assume. For this reason, any expectation that specialisation may somehow lead to upward movements in wage levels for sweatshop workers is spectacularly wrong. Moreover, any assumption of this type should at least discuss the necessary mediating factors that could lead to this outcome. One obvious one would be the presence of trade unions or other labour representatives making sure that increases in productivity could turn into higher salaries. However, in India, this is hardly the case. While freedom of association is available to sweatshop workers, it is then de facto neutralised by the great differentiation of the labour force, its precarisation and its social segregation in different workspaces, activities and tasks. A survey of National Capital Region (NCR) workers carried out in 2013 indicated that almost two-thirds of the entire factory workforce was working in the same industrial unit for less than one year (Mezzadri and Srivastava 2015).

On the other hand, productivity itself is not necessarily a helpful indicator of potential wage movements in labour-intensive sectors. Like many other types of production, clothing is incorporated into complex global commodity chains, and the final consumer price is effectively decided by global buyers, retailers and giant domestic manufacturers. This price does not reflect productivity, but rather shifting business models increasingly placing a premium on fast consumption. A telling example of how prices cannot be seen as indicators of productivity is represented by the relatively recent case of the 'infamous' one-pound bikini, marketed by the UK brand Missguided as a promotional tool in 2019. The publicity stunt backfired spectacularly, with the buyer accused of unacceptable social practices of production and of fuelling 'modern slavery'. The case also showed the limits of linking increases in productivity to better social outcomes for workers. Crudely put, there would hardly ever be an international market large enough to guarantee that a final price of one pound could cover production costs including fair wages. One would need a final market several times the size of our planet. Considering that the global garment industry already produces 100 billion garments annually for a human race of roughly 7 billion (Remy et al. 2016), one would not see how a further market expansion would be possible.

This also provides a clear warning to those who insist that labour-intensive industrialisation via garment production may still be the way forward for other poor economies. In sectors like textile and clothing, prices do not signal productivity; rather, they are indicators of global inequality. The massive decline in clothing prices in the last decades has been accompanied by the spread of global outsourcing and by a wage squeeze for garment workers (Anner 2020). It has hardly been caused by rising productivity in manufacture, a point also revealing the limits of yet another economic theory, namely Baumol's cost disease.

Following from the analysis above, it should be noted how yet another contribution of field-based *sweatshop economics* to economic theories relates to the ways in which it informs debates on inequality. Often, within these economic debates, inequality is sub-categorised as either inter-country or intra-country. The debate on convergence, which international trade theory has aimed to contribute to (with the severe shortcoming discussed in the above sections), is firmly placed within the former sub-category. The international sphere is indeed a central arena to discuss inequality outcomes given that, as illustrated by Branko Milanovic (2016), despite having slowed down since the late 1990s, inequality between countries still accounts for the most significant component of global distribution – and remains higher than the inequality internal to many highly unequal countries across the world today. However, the latter is also crucial, being clearly on the rise in China, India and many other key populous nations. Intra-country inequality may well offset the benefits of a reduction in inter-country disparities in GDP. As argued by Thomas Piketty (2014), it also leads to patrimonial capitalism, which rewards rentierism as opposed to more productive investment. This is epitomised by the rising polarisation between the incomes of the haves and those of the have-nots, which suggests that inequality trends are better captured at the tails of the distribution, where we find, respectively, the rich and the poor, as median classes – the middle classes – seem to be able to command a pretty stable share of income worldwide (Palma 2011).

An analysis of the sweatshop and its working poverty clearly suggests the need to abandon compartmentalised understandings of inequality, and shows the way in which processes fuel both inter-country and intra-country inequality at once. The process of social regulation and segmentation of the labour force, in particular, which reproduces the cheap labour force of the sweatshop, is foundational to the regeneration of both global and national/local inequalities. These, in turn, are instrumentally deployed to compete in international markets. On the one hand, the social segmentation of labour markets and of the workforce reinforces an international division of labour mediated by global commodity chains subject to patterns of global governance, turning them into engines for the reproduction of global inequality – namely, global inequality or poverty chains (Selwyn 2019; Quentin and Campling 2018). Within this division of labour, labour is reproduced as cheap input for the production of a great variety of global goods. Rises in wages are possible, but only as a result of the tightening of labour markets or based on labour protests which finally are erupting in a number of key producing areas (e.g. Xu and Schmalz 2017 on China), and not on the basis of natural processes of convergence. On the other hand, the social segmentation of labour markets and of the workforce also regenerates domestic/local inequality. Hence, gender, caste, ethnicity, geographical provenance or mobility – social and structural differences deployed to divide, rule and manage workers inside the sweatshop – are at once domestic/local mechanisms of labour control, as well as transnational modes of exploitation for a workforce mobilised to reproduce comparative advantage. Through the field-based lens of *sweatshop economics*, the law of comparative advantage appears as a mere self-fulfilling prophecy shaping the economic world in its own image. Within this world, local, national and global inequalities are stitched together by highly differentiated and ruthless social processes of labouring. This is because all patterns of global, national and local competition in any type of commodity production are still ultimately based on the one most extraordinary commodity of all, namely labour, and hence the concrete study of labour and labouring should always remain central to economic analyses of commodities, markets and inequalities. Fieldwork accounts – here in the specific avatar of *sweatshop economics* – can significantly help avoid falling into the trap of the many fetishisms reproduced by bad theory.

4.   Conclusions

A lot has been written on trade theory and comparative advantage. The latter remains, to date, one of the stickiest concepts in economics not only for its simplistic formula for shared economic gains, but mainly due to its far broader development claims of eventually leading to a reduction of global inequality and to convergence. While touching upon some key well-known criticisms of classical and neoclassical trade theories and concepts, it has been suggested that field-based accounts – what Barbara Harriss-White (2003) has defined as fieldwork economics – are fundamental to counter the dominance of poor-economy theory, detached from concrete realities on the ground. Informed by years of field-based research on garment production and its sweatshops in India, the chapter has illustrated several ways in which *sweatshop economics* contributes to demolishing the mythology of comparative advantage and neoclassical trade theories. These include the study of labour processes, and of the social differentiation of labour markets and the workforce on the ground.

The extreme complexity of such processes of differentiation not only suggests the need to abandon assumptions of labour as homogenous between sectors or even within the same sector, but also provides key insights into wage formation and productivity. Wage formation is not led by international trade; it depends on the way in which competition is internalised locally through processes of labour mobilisation that bank on social oppression and structural differences to contain rises in labour costs. As such, the international convergence in wages proposed by mainstream trade models will hardly be achieved. Prices do not respond to productivity in the way the model presupposes. In fact, the spectacular fall in the price of garments (and many other labour-intensive goods) in the last three decades should be a warning against facile narratives centred on productivity.

Finally, *sweatshop economics* also further contributes to the inequality debate, which in the last years has mobilised many critical voices in economics. Field-based accounts from the sweatshop and its processes of labouring provide further lessons on how inequality is reproduced both inter-country and intra-country, at once, in the context of complex production and trade chains and networks. Notably, this last point also underlines the need to theorise economic relations without falling into the trap of methodological nationalism, while also avoiding abstract theorisations of a global economy disembedded from material processes taking place in specific geographical boundaries. A concrete way to escape both these traps when it comes to the study of production and trade is to re-centre the analysis on the concrete study of labour and labour markets. Starting from labour is necessary in order to demystify comparative advantage, de-fetishise relations of exchange, and show which processes lie beneath trade and how only these, in turn, can explain the reproduction, erosion or re-organisation of specific inequalities across the world economy.

Acknowledgements

Thanks to Christopher Cramer for comments on the initial draft and to the whole SOAS PED team with whom I co-teach on inequality and trade.

References

Akram-Lodhi, H. (2014) Poor economics: a radical rethinking of the way to fight global poverty, *Journal of Peasant Studies*, 41(3): 426–429.

Amin, S. (1990) *Delinking: Towards a Polycentric World*, London: Zed Books.

Anner, M. (2020) Squeezing workers' rights in global supply chains: purchasing practices in the Bangladesh garment export sector in comparative perspective, *Review of International Political Economy*, 27(2): 320–347.

Anner, M., Pons-Vignon, N. and Rani, U. (2019) For a future of work with dignity: a critique of the World Bank Development Report, *The Changing Nature of Work*, *Global Labour Journal*, 10(1): 2–18.

Banerjee, A.V. and Duflo, E. (2011) *Poor Economics: A Radical Rethinking of the Way to Fight Global Poverty*, New York: PublicAffairs.

Barrientos, S. (2013) Labour chains: analysing the role of labour contractors in global production networks, *Journal of Development Studies*, 49(8): 1058–1071.

Bédécarrats, F., Guérin, I. and Roubaud, F. (2019) All that glitters is not gold. The political economy of randomized evaluations in development, *Development and Change*, 50(3): 735–762.

Bernstein, H. (2007) Capital and labour from centre to margins, keynote address for conference on *Living on the Margins, Vulnerability, Exclusion and the State in the Informal Economy*, Cape Town, 26–28 March 2007.

Bhattacharya, T. (2017) *Social Reproduction Theory: Remapping Class, Recentering Oppression*, London: Pluto Press.

Breman, J. (1995) Labour, get lost: a late-capitalist manifesto, *Economic and Political Weekly*, 30(37): 2294–2300.

Caraway, T.L. (2005) The political economy of feminization: from 'cheap labor' to gendered discourses of work, *Politics & Gender*, 3: 399–429.

Cawthorne, P. and Kitching, G. (2001) Moral dilemmas and factual claims: some comments on Paul Krugman's defense of cheap labor, *Review of Social Economy*, 59(4): 455–466.

Chang, D. (2009) *Capitalist Development in Korea: Labour, Capital and the Myth of the Developmental State*, London and New York: Routledge.

Chang, H.J. (2007) *Kicking away the Ladder*, London: Anthem.

Chang, H.J. (2011) *23 Things They Don't Tell You about Capitalism*, London: Penguin.

De Neve, G. (2005) Weaving for IKEA in South India: subcontracting, labour markets and gender relations in a global value chain, in Assayag, J. and Fuller, C.J. (eds) *Globalizing India: Perspectives from Below*, London: Anthem, pp. 89–116.

De Neve, G. (2014) Entrapped entrepreneurship: labour contractors in the South Indian Garment Industry, *Modern Asian Studies*, 48(5): 1302–1333.

Deaton, A. and Cartwright, N. (2018) Understanding and misunderstanding randomized controlled trials, *Social Science & Medicine*, 2010: 2–21.

Elson, D. (1999) Labor markets as gendered institutions: equality, efficiency and empowerment issues, *World Development*, 27(3): 611–627.

Federici, S. (2004) *Caliban and the Witch: Women, the Body and Primitive Accumulation*, Brooklyn, NY: Autonomedia.

Ferguson, S. (2019) *Women and Work: Feminism, Labour, and Social Reproduction*, London: Pluto Press.

Folbre, N. (2018) The care penalty and gender inequality, in Averett, S.L., Argys, L.M. and Hoffman, S.D. (eds) *The Oxford Handbook of Women and the Economy*, Oxford: Oxford University Press, pp. 749–766.

Fortunati, L. (1981) *The Arcane of Reproduction: Housework, Prostitution, Labor and Capital*, Brooklyn, NY: Autonomedia. Originally published in Italian as L'Arcano de/la Reproduzione: Casalinghe, Prostitute, Operai e Capitale (Venezia: Marsilio Editori, 1981).

Harriss-White, B. (2003) *India Working: Essays on Society and the Economy*, Cambridge: Cambridge University Press.

Kabeer, N. (2019) Randomized Control Trials and qualitative evaluations of a multifaceted programme for women in extreme poverty: empirical findings and methodological reflections, *Journal of Human Development and Capabilities*, 20(2): 197–217.

Lazear, E.P. (2000) Economic imperialism, *Quarterly Journal of Economics*, 115(1): 99–146.

Mezzadri, A. (2017) *The Sweatshop Regime: Labouring Bodies, Exploitation, and Garments Made in India*, Cambridge: Cambridge University Press.

Mezzadri, A. and Srivastava, R. (2015) *Labour Regimes in the Indian Garment Sector: Capital–Labour Relations, Social Reproduction and Labour Standards in the National Capital Region (NCR)*, final ESRC report for the project 'Labour Conditions and the Working Poor in China and India', London: SOAS.

Mies, M. (1986) *Patriarchy and Accumulation on a World Scale: Women in the International Division of Labour*, London: Zed Books.

Milanovic, B. (2016) *Global Inequality: A New Approach for the Age of Globalization*, Cambridge, MA: Harvard University Press.

Novo, C. (2004) The making of vulnerabilities: indigenous day laborers in Mexico's neoliberal agriculture, *Identities: Global Studies in Culture and Power*, 11(2): 215–239.

Palma, G. (2011) Homogeneous middles vs. heterogeneous tails, and the end of the 'inverted-U': it's all about the share of the rich, *Development and Change*, 42(10): 87–153.

Patnaik, P. and Patnaik, U. (2016) *A Theory of Imperialism*, New York: Columbia University Press.

Picchio, A. (1992) *Social Reproduction: The Political Economy of the Labour Market*, Cambridge: Cambridge University Press.

Piketty, T. (2014) *Capital in the Twenty-first Century*, Cambridge, MA: Belknap Press of the Harvard University Press.

Powell, B. (2014) *Out of Poverty: Sweatshops in the Global Economy*, Cambridge: Cambridge University Press.

PTI New Delhi (2019) 43 killed as massive fire sweeps through north Delhi factory, *The Hindu BusinessLine*, available at https://www.thehindubusinessline.com/news/43-killed-as-massive-fire-breaks-out-in-factory-in-delhis-anaz-mandi/article30236413.ece#, accessed 10 June 2020.

Quentin, D. and Campling, L. (2018) Global inequality chains: integrating mechanisms of value distribution into analyses of global production, *Global Networks*, 18(1): 33–56.

Ravallion, M. (2012) Fighting poverty one experiment at a time: a review of Abhijit Banerjee and Esther Duflo's 'Poor Economics: A Radical Rethinking of the Way to Fight Global Poverty', *Journal of Economic Literature*, 50(1): 103–114.

Remy, N., Speelman, E. and Swartz, S. (2016) *Style that's Sustainable: A New Fast-Fashion Formula*, McKinsey report, available at https://www.mckinsey.com/business-functions/sustainability/our-insights/style-thats-sustainable-a-new-fast-fashion-formula, accessed 2 June 2020.

Salzinger, L. (2003) *Genders in Production*, Berkeley, CA: University of California Press.

Schumacher, R. (2013) Deconstructing the theory of comparative advantage, *World Economic Review*, 2: 83–105.

Selwyn, B. (2019) Poverty chain and global capitalism, *Competition & Change*, 23(1): 71–97.

Shaikh, A. (1980) The laws of international exchange, in Nell, E. (ed.) *Growth, Profits and Property: Essays in the Revival of Political Economy*, Cambridge: Cambridge University Press, pp. 204–235.

Sinha, D. (2018) Using experiments to tackle poverty: what it gets right, what it may not, Blog, available at https://www.asiavillenews.com/article/using-experiments-to-tackle-poverty-what-it-gets-right-what-it-may-not-17486, accessed 2 June 2020.

Smith, S. and Toye, J. (1979) Introduction: three stories about trade and poor economies, *Journal of Development Studies*, 15(3): 1–18.

Stevano, S. (2019) Small development questions are important, but they require big answers, *World Development*, 127. https://doi.org/10.1016/j.worlddev.2019.104826.

Stolper, W.F. and Samuelson, P.A. (1941) Protection and real wages, *Review of Economic Studies*, 9(1): 58–73.

Wood, A. (1994) *North–South Trade, Employment and Inequality: Changing Fortunes in a Skill-Driven World*, Oxford: Clarendon Press.

Wood, A. (1995) How trade hurt unskilled workers, *Journal of Economic Perspectives*, 9(3): 57–80.

Wood, A. and Ridao-Cano, C. (1996) *Skill, Trade and International Inequality*, IDS Working Paper 47, available at https://www.ids.ac.uk/ids/bookshop/wp/WP47.pdf, accessed 20 September 2015.

World Bank (1995) *Workers in an Integrating World*, Washington, DC: World Bank.

World Bank (2013) *Jobs*, Washington, DC: World Bank.

World Bank (2019) *The Changing Nature of Work*, Washington, DC: World Bank.

World Development (2020) *Symposium on Experimental Approaches in Development and Poverty Alleviation*, 127.

Wright, M. (2006) *Disposable Women and Other Myths of Global Capitalism*, New York: Routledge.

Xu, H. and Schmalz, S. (2017) Socializing labour protest: new forms of coalition building in South China, *Development and Change*, 48(5): 1031–1051.

8 Structure and agency: themes from experimental economics

Shaun P. Hargreaves Heap

1.   Introduction

The individual preferences that people reveal through their choices in laboratory experiments are often unstable. That is, people often confront what is the same decision problem from a rational choice perspective several times and they do not always select the same course of action. Moreover, this instability is not simply random noise at work. There are patterns to the instability. In this chapter I focus on one of these patterns: people's choices frequently vary with the social, institutional or historical context to a particular decision problem. This context can be manipulated in the lab or brought into the lab through the way subjects are selected without changing the decision problem. In this sense, individual preferences seem to be endogenous to this social, institutional or historical framing of the decision problem. There are many other insights from experimental economics, but I shall focus on this because it is readily understood in terms of the interplay between structure and action.

People in the lab do not *individually* choose the social/institutional/historical staging that frames the decision problem they encounter in the lab. The experimenter does this. These features are, as it were, inherited or given to the subjects in the experiment. They 'structure' the decision problem in much the same way that institutions and history help constitute the decisions problems that we face outside the lab. The subjects in the lab still have agency: they still make choices from within a given set of actions, just, as it were, and to paraphrase, 'we make our own history but not in circumstances of our own choosing'. It is in this way that laboratory experiments reveal a variety of 'structural' influences on individual decision-making.[1]

In this chapter, I shall consider two particular kinds of structural influence that have been revealed in experiments. I have selected them because they address what seem to me to be a set of key issues for contemporary politics. I should also say that they happen to be areas that I have worked on. I think I work on them, of course, because they are politically important. But, in the spirit of this chapter, I should recognise that the explanation may be rather more 'structural' in the sense that I may have come to think they are politically important because I work on them. I leave the reader to judge!

I take up the first in the next section: the influence of group identification on individual behaviour. Broadly, this influence from group identification is connected to the burgeoning field of identity politics, and such social identification has become a topic of widespread interest in economics (e.g. see Akerlof and Kranton 2000) and politics (see Kalin and Sambanis 2018). The first example of the influence of such identification I consider is the in-group bias. There are many experiments that reveal people behave differently in the same situation depending on whether they are interacting with a fellow member of their group or with someone who belongs to another. They are more pro-social in the former than the latter; that is, they reveal stronger social preferences in relation to fellow group members.

This aspect of social identification has become central in debates around migration, because migration is often thought to increase diversity in a society and so increase the incidence of between-group interactions. For example, a common line of argument of those arguing for tighter immigration control is that, otherwise, the growth of diversity depletes the social capital of trust and cooperation in a society because people trust and cooperate more readily with members of their own group (e.g. see Goodhart 2013; Kaufman 2018; Collier 2018). Or to put this slightly differently, it is claimed that societies face a fundamental choice between diversity and solidarity and this sets a challenge for social democrats. I consider what the experimental evidence reveals on this issue. It is more complicated.

The second example of the influence of group identification that I consider concerns how people vote. This is potentially important in understanding what is in many respects a key puzzle in contemporary political economy. One might expect that the growth of inequality since the mid-1980s in most democratic rich countries would have been more strongly checked through the operation of democratic politics. The point is that as inequality increases, the gap between the mean and median income typically grows and so the incentive of the median voter to vote for redistribution also increases. But this has not happened to any significant degree (see Scheidel 2017).

One possible explanation of this puzzle is that in diverse societies people have reason to vote on grounds of social identification as well as material self-interest. For instance, some white working-class people in the US may have voted for Trump in 2016 because they identified with his evident white rhetoric/racism and despite the fact that his proposed income tax cuts favoured the rich. Likewise, it is argued that many poor areas in the UK voted for BREXIT in 2016 through a cultural concern, again despite the fact that their regions were some of the largest net recipients of EU funds. They felt their cultural identities were undermined by membership of the EU and this weighed more heavily than their material self-interests when voting in the referendum (e.g. see Ford and Goodwin 2017). The prospects for redistributive politics depend plausibly, therefore, in part on understanding how diversity affects voting, and I also consider what experiments suggest on this in the next section. They point to the importance of a form of political inequality.

In section 3, I take up the second structural influence: that of the character of governance arrangements for a subject pool that contextualises their decision problem. People seem to behave differently depending either on how the details of what is apparently the same decision problem originated or on apparently inessential but nevertheless broadly understood governance features of the decision problem. For example, on the latter, it is well known that contributions to a public good rise when there is scope for anonymous chat between subjects in the lab. The existence (or otherwise) of chat opportunities is a part of the governance arrangement for the public goods problem in the lab. It is either available to the subjects or not when they make their decision over individual contributions to the public good, but, from the point of view of mainstream game theory, its presence should not affect behaviour because any discussion is 'cheap talk'. That is, since there is no way to hold people to account for what they say in such anonymous chat rooms, people can say what they like. It is so much 'hot air' that it will be sensibly and safely ignored by fellow subjects. This is the sense in which it is an inessential feature. 'Chat' nevertheless has a beneficial effect on public goods contributions in the lab, and so the experimental evidence seems to support the claims that deliberative procedures are conducive to the public good in ways that game theory does not recognise. This has long been the claim of those who argue for deliberative or participatory democracy as compared with a democracy that simply counts and weighs individual votes equally. This is potentially important for contemporary politics because it is well known that participation in elections has been in decline and this, in turn, has fuelled concern over whether democracy is itself in terminal decline (e.g. see Runciman 2018).

While my first example of the influence of governance arrangements concerns their democratic or otherwise character, my second focuses on whether the procedures governing the creation of a decision problem have been influenced by luck or effort.

In the final section, I change tack. The arguments in sections 2 and 3 develop an agenda in explanatory political economy around some of what we know about the interplay between structure and agency from experiments. In section 4, I conclude by briefly taking up what this evidence might mean for prescriptive analysis in political economy.

2.   The in-group bias

In Hargreaves Heap and Zizzo (2009), subjects play a Trust game. Subjects are randomly paired and one is assigned to the role of 1st mover, the other to the role of 2nd mover. The 1st mover has an endowment of 100 points and must decide how much to give to the 2nd mover in the knowledge that however much is given it will be multiplied by three and the 2nd mover must then decide how much of this multiplied sum to return to the 1st mover. When both subjects assume that each is selfishly rational, then we can expect that nothing will be given by the 1st mover. The 1st mover reasons that any gift will be kept by the selfishly rational 2nd mover and nothing will be returned. Since any gift detracts from their own return in these circumstances, the selfishly rational give nothing.

It is well known from experiments that people typically reveal a social preference (i.e. their preferences take account in some way of the interests of others) by giving around 50 per cent of the endowment and something like 30 per cent is returned. In the Hargreaves Heap and Zizzo experiment, we reproduced this typical result in our Baseline; and, in a group treatment, we additionally assigned subjects either to a 'red' group or a 'blue' group. In these group treatments, subjects knew their own group membership and the group membership of their partner; and they were sometimes paired with someone from their own group and sometimes with someone from the other group. Table 8.1 gives the aggregate results for the Baseline and all the group treatments in the experiment (there were several variants depending on frequency of interaction and other factors like how the other group was identified).

There is a clear in-group bias in the results. Furthermore, it arises through *negative* discrimination against outsiders and so suggests that group diversity

Table 8.1   Trust game giving rates

	Baseline	To own group	To other group
Giving rate	0.56	0.52	0.35

may lower the social capital of trust. To see this, notice that in the Baseline where there is no group differentiation, the level of 'giving' is 56 per cent, whereas in the group treatments, where there is group differentiation, the 'giving' rate is not significantly different from the 56 per cent Baseline with own group members, but it is statistically significantly lower at 35 per cent with other group members. Thus, on the basis of this experiment, we expect that, to the extent that there are interactions between groups in the diverse societies (with the lower trust levels), there will be lower levels of trust in the aggregate than there would be if the society was homogenous (i.e. not characterised by internal group differentiation, as in the Baseline).

This result is consistent with non-experimental evidence on trust and diversity (e.g. Putnam 2007) and it has fuelled a kind of conventional wisdom that, while diversity has advantages in terms of the generation of new ideas, it has a significant disadvantage in terms of the erosion of social capital (e.g. Goodhart 2013).

There is also some non-experimental evidence that reinforces this conventional wisdom because it points to a similar result with respect to the social capital of cooperativeness and diversity (see Knack and Keefer 1997), but it is patchier (e.g. see Putnam 2007, where there is no such corrosive effect of diversity on the cooperation). Interestingly, when Corr et al. (2015) used the same artificial group set up as Hargreaves Heap and Zizzo to examine the in-group bias in Trust and Prisoners' Dilemma games, they reproduced the result above for the Trust game but found a very different result for cooperation in the Prisoners' Dilemma game. Table 8.2 gives their results for the contributions to the public good in the Prisoners' Dilemma game as a proportion of subjects' endowment – this fraction is usually taken as the index of people's cooperativeness in such Prisoners' Dilemma/Public Goods games because it reflects their apparent inclination not to be guided by the selfish temptation to free-ride on the other's contribution.

Again, there is a clear in-group bias. But the nature of the bias is very different: it arises now from *positive* discrimination towards insiders. The own group contribution rate is notably higher with group differentiation than when the population is homogenous (0.4 versus 0.26). Furthermore, the contribution

Table 8.2   Public Goods game contribution rates

	Baseline	To own group	To other group
Contribution rate	0.26	0.40	0.26

rate with outsiders is no different with group differentiation than it would be in the homogenous population (0.26 in both). This is intriguing and potentially important because it runs completely against the 'diversity depletes social capital' conventional wisdom by suggesting the opposite: group diversity boosts cooperativeness (see also Balliet et al. 2014 for a summary of similar evidence). This is because, to the extent that there are within-group interactions in the diverse society, this experiment now suggests that the level of cooperativeness in the aggregate will be higher than in homogenous ones.

This is intriguing because it is not obvious why trust and cooperation should be affected so differently by group identification. It is doubly intriguing because it is also known from experiments that economic differentiation (i.e. economic inequality) appears to affect behaviour differently in Trust and Public Goods games too – only this time, economic differentiation harms cooperation. In Hargreaves Heap et al. (2013), we find that inequality has no effect on overall levels of trust. But in Hargreaves Heap et al. (2016), we find that economic inequality lowers cooperation in Public Goods games.

Three questions naturally arise. First, are these experimental results on the different apparent effects of group diversity on trust and cooperation robust? Second, if they are, why is social behaviour affected so differently in trust as compared with public goods interactions by heterogeneity within the population? Finally, why is group identity heterogeneity so different in its effects to that of the economic heterogeneity associated with inequality?

My second illustration of group identification picks up on the last question of the relation between economic and other kinds of social differentiation (i.e. questions of intersectionality, broadly understood). How is voting behaviour affected by the dual influence of inequality and group identification?

There is one experiment on a distribution decision in a direct democracy setting that provides support for the 'divide and rule' explanation of why the poor do not always vote for redistribution; that is, the poor are divided by their different social identifications. Klor and Shayo (2010) find that the poor who belong to a group that is richer on average than the other group tend to vote less for redistribution than would be the case if there were no groups. In this way heterogeneity may weaken redistribution because the poor are divided across different social groups. One interpretation of this result is that people who belong to a group care not only about their individual pay-offs but also those that their group enjoy. This works against redistribution when a person belongs to a rich group because redistribution in these circumstances will transfer resources to the other, poorer group (as well as making the 'poor' in general better-off).

I have an experiment that examines whether group identifications have the same effect in a representative democracy (see Hargreaves Heap et al. 2019). The representative nature of democracy introduces a couple of further mechanisms through which groups might influence voting behaviour. First, people may cast their vote so that a candidate from their own group is more likely to win the election. Second, they may value candidate character/sincerity and judge the character of the candidate by that candidate's group affiliation. We find evidence of both, and they combine to make a kind of political inequality a crucial determinant of the extent of redistribution in heterogeneous societies. It is not simply the case that heterogeneous populations are less likely to vote for redistribution for a given level of initial inequality; their willingness to vote for redistribution depends on the group identities of the candidates in the election. If the candidates both come from the richer group, then there is less redistribution than when both candidates come from the poorer group. This is the sense in which political inequality also matters for redistribution via the ballot box in heterogeneous societies.

Again, a question arises about the robustness of these results. If they prove robust, then this kind of political inequality may prove a key ingredient in the politics of redistribution in heterogeneous societies.

3.   Governance arrangements and historical origins

All societies make collective decisions over things like tax rates, expenditure programmes, regulations regarding health and safety, and so on. These collective decisions provide the framework within which people make individual decisions in markets, households and other social settings. Many smaller groups of people, like firms and other organisations, make similar collective decisions, for example over the price that they charge their customers. Again, the character of these rules of collective decision-making establishes a structure within which individuals within a firm or organisation make other individual decisions over how much effort and diligence to employ in the production of widgets.

There are many experiments that examine how the character of these collective governance arrangements affects individual behaviour in settings where the options are otherwise identical. For example, it is well known that when people have the opportunity to punish fellow players in a Public Goods game that cooperation typically rises (in rich countries) – see Fehr and Gächter (2002) and Herrmann et al. (2008). There are also experiments that examine whether it makes a difference if the institution of punishment was created through a democratic vote by the subjects in the experiment or was an exogenously given feature of the public goods decision problem ('as if' it arose by nature). It does. It seems we become more cooperative when the origin of the institution of punishment has been a process of democratic collective decision-making (see Dal Bó et al. 2010). There are similar experiments that examine the payment of taxes when tax rates that have been chosen via a ballot-box vote as compared with being given exogenously (e.g. see Feld and Tyran 2002). Most point to a similar pro-social boost from ballot-box democracy (although see Castillo et al. 2018 for a counter example). It is natural to interpret these results in terms of the way that voting lends legitimacy to the collective decision and so encourages greater compliance.

In Hargreaves Heap et al. (2020) we also consider whether democracy in making a collective decision (over a price in this instance that influences revenue for the group) spills over to affect behaviour in a subsequent public goods decision made by the same group of people through some legitimacy effect. In other words, does legitimacy from democratic inclusiveness in the arrangement for collective decision-making encourage greater pro-sociality among the group in other arenas. We introduce two novelties. One is that we have two dimensions for democratic inclusiveness in collective decision-making: a voting and a deliberating/participatory dimension. The other is that we contrast democratic inclusiveness in these senses with the case where one person within the group (and not nature) makes the collective decision. In this way, we contrast *social* processes for making a collective decision along a continuum of inclusive-to-dictatorial possibilities.

We find that the deliberative aspect of democratic inclusiveness has a powerful positive spillover effect on cooperation in the Public Goods game. There is no spillover from voting. Indeed, if anything, the spillover effect from deliberation is stronger when there is no voting and a 'dictator' makes the collective decision. This result is broadly consistent with Ellman and Pezanis-Christou

(2010), who contrast a dictator-like collective decision in either horizontal and vertically constituted organisations with and without deliberation.

We were surprised that inclusiveness via voting in collective decisions did not seem to produce a subsequent cooperative spillover through a legitimacy effect. Voting had a positive effect on the quality of the collective decision through the property of the 'wisdom of the crowd', but its seeming legitimacy in this respect did not encourage any further social identification with other members of the group to the benefit of cooperation. Nevertheless, this result boosts the claims of those who argue for deliberative versions of democracy. It also may help explain, since voting seems not to be valued in the sense that its presence or absence has no effect on group cohesion, why the participation in elections has been falling in many countries.

The questions that naturally arise are again whether these findings are robust and generalise to other kinds of subsequent decision-making in, for example, Trust games and Minimum Effort games. If they do, then the key questions will concern how the protocols for deliberation may affect the degree of the pro-social spillover. Do some kinds of protocols (e.g. those of an 'ideal speech situation' in Habermas 1984) for deliberation in collective decisions encourage closer social identification within the group?[2]

In these experiments, it is the institutional procedure responsible for the punishment regime/the pricing decisions/and so on that affects subsequent pro-sociality within the group in Public Goods games. These social preferences are endogenous to this governance institutional backdrop. There are other experiments where the procedural backdrop to a given decision problem also influences social preferences. I wish to focus on one set of these experiments where the character of the procedures has nothing to with their democratic inclusivity. It concerns the historical origins of the decision problem.

The decision problem in these experiments is a distributional one (see Cappelen et al. 2013). It is always the same distributional decision problem. For example, one person might have 200 and another person 600 experimental points and each must decide whether to redistribute any of the 600 to the person with the 200 (and typically in these experiments an impartial spectator is also asked to make the same decision). The treatment differences in these experiments relate to the historical process generating the 200 and the 600 for the two subjects. In one case both took a risky decision and one got lucky and the other did not. One could say in this case that the subsequent inequality was due entirely to the operation of luck when making a risky decision. In the other case, one decided not to take a risky decision and the other did (and their investment paid off). Here, the inequality was not simply a matter of luck; it arose in part from the decisions that each individual had made over whether to engage in risky decisions. It seems that people redistribute more in the first case than the second (see Cappelen et al. 2013). In other words, luck in the procedure determining the outcome as compared with individual volition encourages greater redistribution.

This is a very interesting result and it may help explain why the electorate in most rich countries have been especially supportive of public expenditure on health care because health outcomes are often determined by matters of luck. It may also explain why the welfare state is relatively small in the US because there is evidence that the US electorate are more inclined than those in other rich countries to think that an individual's income is driven by individual effort and skill rather than luck. Apart from obvious questions concerning whether the perception of the relative roles of luck and effort affects other types of behaviour, on which we have no experimental evidence, there is a key question that needs addressing about how people come to hold views on the relative contribution of each in determining outcomes.

4.   Prescriptive political economy when preferences are endogenous

Traditional welfare economics makes policy prescriptions on the basis of (Pareto) efficiency, that is, how well people's preferences are or might be satisfied. Once preferences cannot be taken as exogenous, the rationale for using efficiency to guide policy disappears. The extent of preference satisfaction, as usually understood, makes no sense as a criterion when a policy might change the preferences themselves. In such a context, policy is as much involved in the determination of what preferences we have as it is with their satisfaction. This additional consideration requires some other kind of language or discourse and it is singularly lacking in economics. This is a major gap created by the endogeneity of preferences and it needs filling.

One approach to this new problem is to posit or argue about the existence of, in effect, meta-preferences, that is, preferences over preferences. Even if such meta-preferences exist, the difficulty and challenge for policy is to know how we might discover what they are. In the absence of such knowledge, it seems we will need some way of talking, discussing and debating what people we would like to be. This is the approach taken, in effect, by Sandel (2012) when he argues that there should be limits to the institution of the market. In this, he is developing an argument based on a different kind of endogeneity of prefer-ences to the ones discussed above. He is concerned with the way that markets (as compared with non-market institutions like the family) affect the kinds of experiences that are possible. Some social preferences cannot be experienced in the market: they get crowded-out. This is sometimes a matter of definition as when friendship or love cannot be transacted via the market because the definition of both friendship and love have crucial non-instrumental com-ponents. But it is also sometimes a matter of human psychology, for example when a norm of respect for others is weakened in interactions mediated by the market (see Gneezy and Rustichini 2000). These 'crowding-outs' of social pref-erences in the market are well known, and I have not, for this reason, discussed them here as illustrations of the structural influence over decision-making and the endogeneity of preferences (see Bowles and Polania Reyes 2012 for a recent survey). Whatever the reason, Sandel (2012) wants to argue that we should value love and friendship and so we will have to limit the market. In this respect, it seems a version of an appeal to, or an argument that we should have, a meta-preference for the capacity to have friends and love people.

I do not wish to claim that, as a response to the endogeneity of preferences, there is anything wrong with such a developed but still consequential approach to prescriptive political economy (the consequences here are love and friend-ship).[3] But I do want to argue that the endogeneity of preferences is likely also to require a shift away from consequential reasoning of this kind. This is, in part, because the problem of endogeneity of preferences is not just confined to our social preferences. I have focused on these, but the problem is more general. We acquire preferences of all sorts during our lives. Indeed, this is why in liberal democratic societies we would like our preferences to be authentic. We would like to feel that our preferences are our own because in this way they identify our individuality. Of course, this concern with individual autonomy can be turned into an outcome and so preserve (notionally) the consequential approach, but I think this is to miss the point. We cannot know in advance in any detail what autonomy will consist of for a particular person. Autonomy is a state that does not depend on some set of final outcomes (like the experience of friendship or love); rather, it is a state that depends on the character of the route taken to it. For this reason we will need to talk in prescriptive political economy not only about the character of outcomes but also, and distinctly, about the character of procedures.

5.   Conclusion

I will conclude with an illustration of the distinction between outcomes and procedures, and the associated challenge it presents for prescriptive political economy. One type of argument for egalitarian institutions is that, in this way, our institutions respond to the fact that we have a preference for inequality aversion (e.g. as revealed in experiments, see Fehr, Naef and Schmidt 2006). We judge, as a result, institutions according to the inequality of outcomes that they produce because this determines the extent to which this preference for equality is satisfied. A different argument, however, in favour of egalitarian institutions is that they are a precondition for the shared project of promoting individual autonomy in liberal democratic societies. If individual autonomy is what matters, then it matters equally for all individuals by virtue of the fact that they are individuals. The rules, therefore, have to give everyone the same prospect of acquiring autonomy. Likewise, they could not encode scope for domination. This is a procedural sense of equality and it is unlikely to be well captured by a measure of the equality of the outcomes that the rules produce. This is because as individuals *qua* individuals, we will not respond to the rules in the same way. Procedurally equal rules will not produce equal outcomes among a group of individuals *qua* individuals. The challenge, then, is to know how to judge the egalitarian character of the rules.

Notes

1.   Here and elsewhere in this chapter, I shall implicitly assume when drawing the distinction between 'action' and 'structure', that 'action' is to be understood as the individual choice from a set of actions that yield a given set of consequences for the individual (and others when the choice is interactive). As such it will naturally, but need not exclusively, be associated with an instrumental or rational choice account of action.
2.   See Thompson (2008) for a review of the evidence.
3.   He is encouraging us to think about the choice of institutions based on the kind of people we will be in each in much the same way that the usual economic approach is to choose between market and non-market institutions for a particular interaction on the basis of the degree of preference satisfaction under each (e.g. Williamson 1985).

References

Akerlof, G. and Kranton, R. (2000) Economics and identity, *Quarterly Journal of Economics*, 115(3): 715–753.

Balliet, D., Wu, J. and De Dreu, C.K.W. (2014) Ingroup favoritism in cooperation: a meta-analysis, *Psychological Bulletin*, 140(6): 1556–1581.

Bowles, S. and Polania Reyes, S. (2012) Economic incentives and social preferences: substitutes or complements, *Journal of Economic Literature*, 50(2): 368–425.

Cappelen, A., Konow, J., Sorensen, E. and Tungodden, B. (2013) Just or luck: an experimental study of risk taking and fairness, *American Economic Review*, 103(4): 1398–1413.

Castillo, J., Xu, Z., Zhang, P. and Zhu, X. (2018) *The Effects of Centralized Power and Institutional Legitimacy on Collective Action*, Working Paper, SSRN https://papers .ssrn.com/sol3/papers.cfm?abstract_id=3127775.

Collier, P. (2018) *The Future of Capitalism: Facing the New Anxieties*, London: Penguin.

Corr, P., Hargreaves Heap, S., Seger, C. and Tsutsui, K. (2015) An experiment on individual parochial altruism revealing no connection between individual altruism and individual parochialism, *Frontiers in Psychology*, 6: 1261.

Dal Bó, P., Foster, A. and Putterman, L. (2010) Institutions and behavior: experimental evidence on the effects of democracy, *American Economic Review*, 100(5): 2205–2229.

Ellman, M. and Pezanis-Christou, P. (2010) Organizational structure, communication and group ethics, *American Economic Review*, 100(5): 2478–2491.

Feld, L. and Tyran, J.-R. (2002) Tax evasion and voting: an experimental analysis, *Kyklos*, 55: 197–221.

Fehr, E. and Gächter, S. (2002) Altruistic punishment in humans, *Nature*, 415: 137–140.

Fehr, E., Naef, M. and Schmidt, K.M. (2006) Inequality aversion, efficiency, and maximin preferences in simple distribution experiments: comment, *American Economic Review*, 96(5): 1912–1917.

Ford, R. and Goodwin, M. (2017) Britain after Brexit: a divided nation, *Journal of Democracy*, 28(1): 17–30.

Gneezy, U. and Rustichini, A. (2000) A fine is a price, *Journal of Legal Studies*, 29(1): 1–17.

Goodhart, D. (2013) *The British Dream: Successes and Failures of British Postwar Immigration*, London: Atlantic Books.

Habermas, J. (1984) *The Theory of Communicative Action: Reason and the Rationalization of Society*, Cambridge: Polity Press.

Hargreaves Heap, S., Manifold, E., Matakos, K. and Xefteris, D. (2019) *Group Identification and Redistribution in Democracies: An Experiment*, Working Paper.

Hargreaves Heap, S., Stodard, B. and Ramalingam, A. (2016) Endowment inequality in public goods games: a re-examination, *Economic Letters*, 146, September: 4–7.

Hargreaves Heap, S., Tan, J. and Zizzo, D. (2013) Trust, inequality and the market, *Theory and Decision*, 74: 311–333.

Hargreaves Heap, S., Tsutsui, K. and Zizzo, D. (2020) Vote and voice: an experiment on the effects of inclusive governance rules, *Social Choice and Welfare*, 54: 111–139.

Hargreaves Heap, S. and Zizzo, D. (2009) The value of groups, *American Economic Review*, 99: 295–323.

Herrmann, B., Thöni, C. and Gächter, S. (2008) Antisocial punishment across societies, *Science*, 319(5868): 1362–1367.

Kalin, M. and Sambanis, N. (2018) How to think about social identity, *Annual Review of Political Science*, 21: 239–257.

Kaufman, E. (2018) *Whiteshift: Populism, Immigration and the Future of White Majorities*, London: Penguin.

Klor, E. and Shayo, M. (2010) Social identity and preferences over redistribution, *Journal of Public Economics*, 94: 269–278.

Knack, S. and Keefer, P. (1997) Does social capital have an economic pay-off? A cross-country investigation, *Quarterly Journal of Economics*, 112(4): 1251–1288.

Putnam, R. (2007) *E Pluribus Unum*: diversity and community in the twenty-first century: the 2006 Johan Skytte Prize Lecture, *Scandinavian Political Studies*, 30(2): 137–174.

Runciman, D. (2018) *How Democracy Ends*, London: Profile Books.

Sandel, M. (2012) *What Money Can't Buy: The Moral Limits of Markets*, London: Penguin.

Scheidel, W. (2017) *The Great Leveller: Violence and the History of Inequality from the Stone Age to the Twenty First Century*, Princeton, NJ: Princeton University Press.

Thompson, D.F. (2008) Deliberative democratic theory and empirical political science, *Annual Review of Political Science*, 11: 497–520.

Williamson, O. (1985) *The Economic Institutions of Capitalism*, London: Macmillan.

9   Time, space, geographical scale and political economy

Andrew Herod

Introduction

The passage of time, the organisation of space and the geographical scale at which various human and natural processes are structured and unfold are three central elements of social and biological life. How we think about time, space and scale, however, has important implications for understanding political economy, as none of these concepts is unproblematic. To take but one example, whereas Isaac Newton saw time and space as forming an unchanging stage upon which interaction between, say, the Sun and planets takes place, for Albert Einstein both time and space are parts of the play, with heavenly actors shaping the form of space and the flow of time through their movement. Although both of these scientists were largely focused upon understanding the nature of the universe, their views on time and space have also shaped thinking in the social sciences, including political economy. Below, then, I outline how the manner in which we conceptualise time, space and geographical scale can have particular implications for understanding the political economy of human social organisation.

Time

The shift from a Newtonian view of the universe to an Einsteinian one is one of the most significant developments in human thought. In his 1687 work *Philosophae Naturalis Principia Mathematica*, Newton argued that time and space are absolute things existing separately from one another and independently of the social and natural objects inhabiting them. With regard to time, he saw this as passing at the same rate everywhere and infinitely divisible into smaller blocks. In such a view, time gives us a metric by which to quantify the duration of processes and the chronology of events but is otherwise external to social and natural objects and processes. So, rather than the unfolding of processes being used to delineate the passage of time, temporal units become the benchmarks by which the unfolding of processes is measured. The result is a somewhat mechanical view of time, one in which we imagine that it can be 'stopped' and perhaps even run in reverse so that we can understand processes and the origins of events and their ultimate outcomes. However, arbitrarily dividing processes into segments according to some external temporal yardstick ('How does process X play out per hour/day/month/year etc.?') for purposes of exposition risks conceptually disconnecting actions from their consequences to create what Karl Marx in the *Grundrisse* called 'chaotic conceptions', in which two or more objects that are functionally indissoluble are arbitrarily separated or in which two or more objects that can exist independently are put together conceptually in such a way that they appear, in fact, to be dependent upon one another.[1] Finally, because it is deemed an ultimate truth, time's organisation is also considered to be independent of the process of observation, a perspective that underlies philosophical approaches like positivism, which views 'fact' and 'value' as separable.[2]

By way of contrast, Einstein viewed time and space relationally, with the passage of time related to the speed at which an object travels through space – the faster something travels the slower time passes for it relative to its more sluggish surroundings and the more the space it occupies contracts, even as its mass increases.[3] Time and space, for him, are so intimately entwined that it is really only possible to talk of them as a single entity – time-space – and not as separate things. This means that for social scientists, adopting an Einsteinian view of time provides a way to see it not as external to objects and something by which simply to measure the unfolding of various natural or social processes but, instead, as a way to understand how the passage of time and the unfolding of such processes are deeply connected. This approach sees time as only having order in relation to these processes, rather than according to its own internal logic. As geographer David Harvey (1969: 418) put it, there is 'no absolute measure of time, only an infinite number of such measures, each associated with a particular set of processes'. The upshot of this Einsteinian view is at least three-fold.

First, in the Newtonian approach time itself can end up being viewed as somehow being causal with regard to processes' operation – the simple passage of time, in other words, becomes part of the explanation, a perspective which, *in extremis*, can lead to an analytical position in which all we really have to do to understand a process's dynamics is to let time proceed. By way of contrast, explanations adopting a more Einsteinian-influenced view of time see its passage as a manifestation of how particular processes play out – time, in other words, can never be considered causal because its passage is a function of the very processes which are under investigation.

Second, a Newtonian view of time can predispose analysis towards a teleological understanding of the future, one which is frequently incorporated into models involving transition upon which political economists have often relied for explanation – Rostow's (1959) stages of economic development or the Demographic Transition Model are good exemplars. In such a view all one has to do is figure out at what stage a society is at any given time and then run the script forward to see where it 'should' end up. Einstein's view of time, however, results in a much less linear view of how events might unfold. Hence, he argued that the relationship between 'now' and the 'past' and the 'future' is not always well defined, such that B might appear to follow A when viewed by one observer but to precede A when viewed by a different observer.[4] This is different from Newton's view in which the order of events is assumed to be seen in the same way by all observers, who are portrayed as witnessing them from a privileged 'God's-eye' position that places them outside time and space.[5] Einstein's interpretation, then, tends towards a position in which the future is imagined not to follow the present in some regimented linear fashion but as something that is much less deterministically connected to the present. This comports more with dialectical ways of thinking in which the future is only knowable to the extent to which various actors are involved in making it. In this regard, although he sometimes drifted into teleological thinking with his belief in the inevitability of the end of capitalism, Marx's faith in dialectics makes him what Neary and Rikowski (2002: 64) have called, in a different context, 'post-Newtonian' (we could also see Darwin in a similar light, given his argument that random mutation drives evolution). Whereas a Newtonian view, then, tends to view time as history, an Einsteinian one tends towards a view of time as process.

Third, as intimated above, Einstein rejected absolutist views that see time as constant for all objects and independent of them and their observers. Instead, in viewing space and time as 'forms of intuition, which can no more be divorced from consciousness than can our concepts of colour, shape, or size[, such that s]pace has no objective reality except as an order or arrangement of the objects we perceive in it, and time has no independent existence apart from the order of events by which we measure it' (Barnett 1949: 14), Einstein adopted a somewhat phenomenological position concerning existence, arguing that the positionality of any observer is integral to processes of observation and, so, of constructing 'reality'.[6] This view provides a mechanism to more closely link developments in time consciousness with material changes in the world around us than does Newton's. Such a perspective has import for political economists. Hence, Thrift (1996) examined how various social developments – such as the geographical spread of literacy – changed time consciousness in Middle Ages Europe whilst Kern (1983) detailed how material changes during the *fin de siècle* era changed people's perceptions of time. For his part, Togati (2001) has suggested that John Maynard Keynes was influenced by Einstein's rejection of notions of absolute time and space, a rejection reflected in his challenging the orthodoxy of 'rational man', whose preferences can be defined on *a priori* grounds (i.e., independent of time and context) (see also Galbraith 2001, who argued that Keynes sought to disestablish the 'absolute space' of classical markets). This, Togati (1998) suggests, makes Keynes's macroeconomic approach 'Einsteinian', in contrast to the Neoclassical Synthesis, which he views as 'Newtonian'.

Several other ways in which we think about time also have implications for political economy. Hence, evolutionary biologist and historian of science Stephen Jay Gould (1987) has suggested that the 'discovery of deep time' in the 19th century (i.e., that the Earth is very much older than the Bible and many contemporary scientists believed it to be) fundamentally changed people's conceptions of how long human society had had to progress to its current point of development. This shifted the *zeitgeist* from a view in which human history effectively equated to Earth history to one in which, using one particularly resonant image, if we were to imagine the Earth's age as represented by the distance from the king's nose to the tip of his outstretched middle finger, filing his nail would erase all of human history. This discovery of deep time meant that geological and biological processes could be seen to have played out over very much longer periods of time than previously imagined, a realisation that reshaped understandings of things like orogeny and speciation – if the Earth is seen as too young then certain processes will not have had sufficient time to play out and therefore would have to be excluded as possible explanations for why certain landscapes or flora and fauna look the way they do today. Gould (1987: 10–11) also submitted that we can imagine the passage of time in at least two ways – as 'time's arrow' (in which 'history is an irreversible sequence of unrepeatable events') and as 'time's cycle' (in which 'events have no meaning as distinct episodes with causal impact upon a contingent history', such that time has no direction). Following from Durkheim's (1915: 440) argument that 'it is the rhythm of social life which is at the basis of the category of time', how these different understandings of time reflect the ways in which societies are organised can tell us something about how societies understand themselves, with obvious implications for political economy. For instance, Gould suggests that time's arrow is the primary metaphor of Biblical history which, through processes of imperialism, has been exported to many societies that historically viewed time cyclically, in the process challenging indigenous knowledge systems and ways of being. Likewise, the linear concept of time 'has had profound effects on Western thought' and without it 'it would be difficult to conceive of the idea of progress' (Morris 1985: 11).

Two further matters are important for political economists to consider regarding time. First, different groups may come into conflict over what is considered to be the appropriate timeframe for organising or viewing particular activities. In this regard, Harvey (1990) gives the examples of how an economist and geologist might quibble over the suitable time horizon for a resource's exploitation, as well as how capitalists and workers might argue over how a fair day's wage should be measured. With regard to the former, the economist's timeframe is likely much shorter and defined by the rate of return in the marketplace whereas the geologist's is likely much longer and related to the speed at which natural processes play out (e.g., how quickly an aquifer may replenish itself). With regard to defining a fair day's wage, Harvey suggests that a capitalist likely sees it as the money a worker requires to cover his/her daily reproduction costs whilst for a worker this ignores the shortening of his/her life caused by working for the capitalist, which should be incorporated into any calculations of a fair wage. Second, there are particular institutions which shape how we come to accept certain views of time and these institutions have political agendas. For instance, the 1884 International Meridian Conference held to standardise world time zones not only reflected the power politics of the day – British naval power assured that world time would be based upon Greenwich – but also imposed a new temporal consciousness on the planet, even as some places chose to resist this.[7] We can but wonder how our worldview might be different had planetary time been co-ordinated not with London but with Washington DC, Paris or Berlin, capitals which also vied to serve as the centre of the new global time discipline. Equally, how might our understanding of temporality be different had the French revolutionaries' earlier efforts to decimalise time been accepted? For its part, the coming of capitalism brought with it the need for a new time consciousness – workers had to be brought together at specific times if factory production were to proceed, which required that new temporal understandings be inculcated in them. Such inculcation has often been conducted by various arms of the state (e.g., through the building of public clocks, through teaching school children the importance of 'being on time', and so forth), with obvious implications for the study of political economy.

Space

The distinction between Newtonian and Einsteinian ways of thinking about time is replicated in their thinking about space. Hence, for Newton space is absolute, simply a container for interaction that is unconnected to the objects inhabiting it. For Einstein, however, space is made by the movement of objects. These divergent views have implications for how political economists (and others) view space. Hence, Newtonian thinking has led to the adoption of a generally Euclidean view of space which sees it as flat, uniform, grid-like and described mathematically (think latitude and longitude), with distances between places measured in terms of fixed metrics like miles or kilometres. In such a view, space serves as a stage for social action but is separate from, and unchanged by, such action. It is pre-given and empty, merely the setting in which things happen, a blank canvas to be filled in by human and natural activities. As with time, in such approaches space is imagined to be infinitely divisible into ever-smaller pieces with little consideration for what this might mean for respecting the spatial integrity of processes that occur across and within it. By way of contrast, Einstein's views helped encourage the spread of non-Euclidean views of space, which see it as relativistic and not fixed.[8] In this regard he follows to a degree German philosopher Gottfried Leibniz's views that space is relational, that is to say that it is created through the relationships between things. Consequently, it cannot be empty in the way in which Newton assumed. What this means for political economy analysis is that space must be seen as a social product, one that is contestable between and amongst different social actors, each of whom has a vested interest in making spatial relationships between places and people in particular ways. As such, there is a politics to the production of space.

The politics of space has been manifested in social science thinking during the 20th century in at least three different ways. First, in the early 20th century the idea of environmental determinism, popular in social sciences like Geography and Anthropology and upon which many imperialists drew for understanding patterns of development in their colonies, saw space essentially as deterministic of social life – the colonies were underdeveloped, they argued, because of their unfavourable geographical locations (hot climates, lack of access to modern transportation, etc.). Such notions of environmental determinism have made something of a comeback in recent years, perhaps most notably in the form of Diamond's (1997) book *Guns, Germs, and Steel*, a book severely criticised by some geographers as promoting 'junk science' (Sluyter 2003).

Second, a 'spatial science' tradition emerged mid-century that saw geographical patterns of society as little more than reflections of the social relations of life – a corporation's geographical organisation, for example, was seen to be a spatial reflection simply of its social organisation. In this tradition many drew upon Newton's laws of gravitational attraction to explain things like migration patterns between various places or to determine the geographical breakpoint at which shoppers living closer to small cities would travel instead to larger ones (Reilly 1931).[9]

Third, by the late 20th century the idea of what Soja (1980) called the 'socio-spatial dialectic' had emerged, especially in Marxist-inspired work. Such an approach views space as both constituted by social practices but also constitutive thereof, such that – amending Marx – people make their own geographies but not under the conditions of their own choosing.[10] For instance, the building of the railways in 19th-century Europe led to what Marx in the *Grundrisse* called the 'annihilation of space by time' as places were brought closer together in terms of travel times, whilst this annihilation subsequently transformed the ways in which people in different places could interact. Drawing upon such ideas, Harvey (1982) showed how capital creates space in particular ways as a central element in its own self-reproduction. Following from this, other Marxist geographers explored how workers likewise struggle to shape the economic landscape to serve their own interests, an approach termed 'Labour Geography' (Herod 2001). The result is that conflicts between capitalists and workers are frequently over how the geography of capitalism should be constituted.

Another important development with implications for political economy came from the field of cartography. Maps are representations of space and, as such, can shape how we understand the world and behave in it. Frequently, maps have been seen as neutral things which more or less accurately (depending upon the skill of the individual cartographer) depict the Earth's surface. However, inspired by the work of people like Harley (1989), in the 1980s an approach viewing maps as texts and so deconstructable came to prominence. Such a 'critical cartography' argues both that maps reflect particular power relations – what gets included or left off a map reflects the interests of the maker – and that reading them is not a culturally neutral activity, for different societies (and groups within them) have different ways of seeing (Berger 1972). As such, maps can play an important role in creating different 'spatial imaginaries' which shape social behaviour in realms ranging from imperialism (how might indigenous peoples be 'mapped out' of landscapes [Brealey 1995]?) to international economics (how is a transnational corporation's spatial organisation visualised by its executives and what does this mean for how they behave?)

to natural resource use (how have changes in our understanding of 'wilderness' [Cronon 1995] shaped whether we see various 'empty spaces' as appropriate for exploitation?) and more.

Geographical scale

The term 'geographical scale' has two quite different meanings. On the one hand it is a technical term referring to the ratio between the size of something on the Earth's surface and how large it appears on a map. On the other it can refer to the spatial resolution at which certain processes are understood to occur or particular entities are spatially constituted. This second meaning allows us to circumscribe the spatial range of various practices, processes and organisations so as to be able to make certain statements about the world – 'process X is a local process whereas process Y is a global one', 'company A is organised regionally but company B is organised nationally', and so forth. However, the way in which we conceptualise such geographical scales is the subject of much dispute. Three sets of issues predominate.

The first relates to whether geographical scales are real or not – that is to say, whether they are the product of an investigator's mind or the product of material processes. This question speaks principally to philosophical divergences between idealists and materialists. The former have often drawn inspiration from Immanuel Kant (1894: 65, emphasis in original), who viewed space as an *a priori* form of intuition rather than as something created through natural and social processes, suggesting that '[s]*pace is not something objective* and real [but] *subjective* and ideal, arising ... from the nature of the mind'.[11] Drawing upon such thinking, the geographer John Fraser Hart (1982: 21–22) argued that scales like that of the region, an areal delineation frequently used to draw a boundary around particular spatial arenas of study, are mental fictions, 'subjective artistic devices ... shaped to fit the hand of the individual user'. In his view, there can be 'no universal rules for recognizing, delimiting, and describing' scales, a position that encourages viewing the absolute spaces of the Earth's surface as capable of being carved up into bigger or smaller areas more or less arbitrarily and without concern for whether they relate to any coherent structures 'on the ground'. For idealists, then, the world's scalar hierarchy is unconnected to social and political activity and merely reflects a convenient way for any researcher to divide the world up for purposes of analysis. By way of contrast, Marxist geographers have contended that geographical scales of social organisation are real things that emerge from various political processes. For instance, Smith (2008) argued that the urban scale is constituted by the spatial extent of daily labour markets (as measured by travel-to-work areas), the regional scale by the territorial division of labour based upon the structure of various industries (steel-making regions, automobile-manufacturing regions, textile-manufacturing regions, etc.), the national scale is the spatial resolution at which economies increasingly became organised during the 20th century (a scale of organisation recognised by Keynes in the *General Theory*, who took the national economy to be the implicit focus of his analysis), and the global scale as the scale to which collective capital seeks to universalise the wage labour form of production.[12] In an effort to show how workers may create scales of organisation as part of their political praxis, Herod (1997) detailed how dockers in the US succeeded in rescaling contract bargaining in their industry from a port-by-port basis to a regional and then national one.

Second, the different ways in which scales are described can shape how we understand the world to be organised geographically and so what we consider politically possible. Hence, an image that is frequently used to describe the relationships between scales like the local, the urban, the regional, the national and the global is that of a ladder. Indeed, the English word 'scale' comes from the Latin *scala*, meaning a ladder or staircase. In such an image, each scale can be thought of as a rung in a vertically configured framework, wherein the global scale is seen to be above other scales up which one must climb to become global – a firm may be imagined to start off as a local one and then become regional or national before ascending to a global scale of organisation. By way of contrast, if we view these various scales not as rungs on a ladder but as sets of concentric circles, with the local at the centre, surrounded by the other scales, then moving from the local to the global scale of organisation or praxis entails moving not upwards but outwards into ever-larger scales. In such a view, the global is not above other scales but it does envelop them and is bigger than them (for more on other ways of visualising the relationship between different scales, see Herod 2010). Imagining whether they must move upwards or outwards to become global, then, can shape the strategies workers adopt as they seek to make common cause with confederates in different parts of the world.

Finally, whereas approaches that view scales as ladder rungs or concentric circles are topographical, with each scale imagined to circumscribe different-sized units of territory (French Marxist Henri Lefebvre [1991: 351] described these units as 'space envelopes'), sociologist Bruno Latour (1996: 370) has argued for a topological approach, contending that the landscape's variegation cannot be truly captured by 'notions of levels, layers, territories, [and] spheres', areas of bounded space that precisely dovetail with one another, but that we must think of it as 'fibrous, thread-like, wiry, stringy, ropy, [and] capillary'. In such an approach, scales are seen in non-hierarchical terms, rather like a spider's web wherein each part is connected to every other part of the web, with some parts being closer in space than others – the local, then, may be understood as lying at the web's middle, linked to an ever-widening set of strands beyond it. This means that instead of conceptualising the economic landscape as organised into hierarchically ordered 'space envelopes', scales like the 'global' and the 'local' do not have area but are a lexicon for differentiating between shorter and less connected networks and longer and more connected ones.

Summary

Above, I have explored some of the ways in which time, space and geographical scale have been conceptualised. These varying views have important implications for political economy and understanding how the geography of capitalism is made. For instance, a Newtonian view of space does not allow for conflicts over the geographical arrangement of capitalism and its economic landscapes to be central foci of political praxis in the way in which a view which sees space as constitutive of, and constituted by, social action does. Likewise, understanding geographical scales to be the products of social processes and political struggles rather than figments of the imagination means that the scalar organisation of capitalism must be an object of political economic analysis rather than regarded as something which we just accept as pre-given. This means that, for instance, the relationship between the global, national and local scales of capitalism is fluid rather than fixed, constantly changing rather than invariant. Conflicts over how society is organised temporally, spatially and scalarly (and understood to be organised temporally, spatially and scalarly), then, are central to how it functions, whilst how we understand each of these three terms plays an important role in how we comprehend such conflicts, their causes and their consequences. Given that a central aspect of political economy is the study of social conflict, political economists must consider how different understandings of time, space and geographical scale affect their investigations of the situations they seek to comprehend.

Notes

1.   For more on chaotic conceptions and what they mean for understanding social processes, see Sayer (1984).
2.   For more on positivism as an epistemology, see Keat and Urry (1982).

3. Although Einstein indicated that these properties of time and space would only really become evident as an object's speed approaches that of light, in a famous 1971 experiment several atomic clocks flown around the globe on commercial airliners experienced small differences in the passage of time relative to one that remained on the ground (Hafele and Keating 1972). This experiment has had practical consequences with regard to the operation of GPS navigation technology – in order to provide accurate indications of a user's location, a GPS system must compensate for the fact that the satellites upon which this technology depends each experience time passing at a slightly different rate to that on Earth.

4. In a famous letter to the family of his colleague Michele Besso upon the latter's 1955 death, Einstein stated 'us physicists believe the separation between past, present, and future is only an illusion, although a convincing one'.

5. A God's-eye view presupposes that we can remove ourselves from our social context and survey the world as it 'really is' from some objective point of view, as if we were an omniscient being.

6. Mastrobisi (2018) argues that Einstein's view that time and space can only be understood from the privileged position of each individual observer (Einstein's *Beobachter*) was influenced by the German phenomenologist Edmund Husserl.

7. For instance, although time zones were introduced into the US in 1883, Detroit continued keeping local time until 1905, which caused Henry Ford such consternation that he used a watch with two dials, one showing Detroit time and another standard time!

8. Euclidean geometry only works for flat surfaces. It does not work in situations where an object's mass bends space *à la* Einstein.

9. Newton argued that the gravitational pull one body exerts upon another is a function of the bodies' relative sizes and the distance separating them. This was replicated in the field of Urban Geography, with interactions between cities viewed as a function of their relative sizes and how far apart they are from one another.

10. For more on Marxists' development of a spatialised political economy, see Sheppard, Chapter 11 in this volume.

11. Significantly, Weinert (2005) suggests that, though sceptical of *a priorism*, Einstein was in many ways a Kantian.

12. The argument that economies were becoming increasingly nationally organised (in part because of the protectionist measures employed during the Great Depression, which cut them off from broader global flows of goods) contrasted the dominant 19th-century view, based upon the operation of the Gold Standard, which saw them as internationally organised. This new view required the invention of fresh analytical tools to describe the (national) economy – the terms Gross National Product and Gross Domestic Product, for instance, were both developed in the 1930s and both take the nation-state's territorial boundaries as their point of reference.

References

Barnett, L. (1949) *The Universe and Dr. Einstein*, London: Victor Gollancz.
Berger, J. (1972) *Ways of Seeing*, London: Penguin.

Brealey, K.G. (1995) Mapping them 'out': Euro-Canadian cartography and the appropriation of the Nuxalk and Ts'ilhqot'in First Nations' territories, 1793–1916, *The Canadian Geographer/Le Géographe canadien*, 39(2): 140–156.

Cronon, W. (1995) The trouble with wilderness; or, getting back to the wrong nature, in Cronon, W. (ed.) *Uncommon Ground: Rethinking the Human Place in Nature*, New York: W.W. Norton & Company, pp. 69–90.

Diamond, J. (1997) *Guns, Germs, and Steel: The Fates of Human Societies*, New York: W.W. Norton & Company.

Durkheim, E. (1915) *The Elementary Forms of the Religious Life: A Study in Religious Sociology*, London: George Allen & Unwin.

Galbraith, J. (2001) Keynes, Einstein, and scientific revolution, *The American Prospect*, Winter, available at https://prospect.org/article/keynes-einstein-and-scientific-revolution, accessed 27 May 2020.

Gould, S.J. (1987) *Time's Arrow, Time's Cycle: Myth and Metaphor in the Discovery of Geological Time*, Cambridge, MA: Harvard University Press.

Hafele, J.C. and Keating, R.E. (1972) Around-the-world atomic clocks: observed relativistic time gains, *Science*, New Series, 177(4044): 168–170.

Harley, J.B. (1989) Deconstructing the map, *Cartographica*, 26(2): 1–20.

Hart, J.F. (1982) The highest form of the geographer's art, *Annals of the Association of American Geographers*, 72(1): 1–29.

Harvey, D. (1969) *Explanation in Geography*, New York: St Martin's Press.

Harvey, D. (1982) *The Limits to Capital*, Oxford: Basil Blackwell.

Harvey, D. (1990) Between space and time: reflections on the geographical imagination, *Annals of the Association of American Geographers*, 80(3): 418–434.

Herod, A. (1997) Labor's spatial praxis and the geography of contract bargaining in the US east coast longshore industry, 1953–1989, *Political Geography*, 16(2): 145–169.

Herod, A. (2001) *Labor Geographies: Workers and the Landscapes of Capitalism*, New York: Guilford Press.

Herod, A. (2010) *Scale*, London: Routledge.

Kant, I. (1894) *Kant's Inaugural Dissertation of 1770*, New York: Columbia College.

Keat, R. and Urry, J. (1982) *Social Theory as Science*, 2nd ed., London: Routledge & Kegan Paul.

Kern, S. (1983) *The Culture of Time and Space, 1880–1918*, Cambridge, MA: Harvard University Press.

Latour, B. (1996) On actor-network theory: a few clarifications, *Soziale Welt*, 47: 369–381.

Lefebvre, H. (1991) *The Production of Space*, Oxford: Basil Blackwell.

Mastrobisi, G.J. (2018) Phenomenology and relativity: Husserl, Weyl, Einstein, and the concept of essence, *Revista da Abordagem Gestáltica – Phenomenological Studies*, 24(3): 350–357.

Morris, R. (1985) *Time's Arrows: Scientific Attitudes toward Time*, New York: Simon & Schuster.

Neary, M. and Rikowski, G. (2002) Time and speed in the social universe of capital, in Crow, G. and Heath, S. (eds) *Social Conceptions of Time: Structure and Process in Work and Everyday Life*, Basingstoke: Palgrave, pp. 53–65.

Reilly, W.J. (1931) *The Law of Retail Gravitation*, New York: Knickerbocker Press.

Rostow, W.W. (1959) The stages of economic growth, *Economic History Review*, New Series, 12(1): 1–16.

Sayer, A. (1984) *Method in Social Science: A Realist Approach*, London: Hutchinson.

Sluyter, A. (2003) Neo-environmental determinism, intellectual damage control, and nature/society science, *Antipode*, 35(4): 813–817.

Smith, N. (2008) *Uneven Development: Nature, Capital and the Production of Space*, 3rd ed., Athens, GA: University of Georgia Press.

Soja, E.W. (1980) The socio-spatial dialectic, *Annals of the Association of American Geographers*, 70(2): 207–225.

Thrift, N. (1996) *Vivos voco*: ringing the changes in the historical geography of time consciousness, in Thrift, N., *Spatial Formations*, London: Sage, pp. 169–212.

Togati, T.D. (1998) *Keynes and the Neoclassical Synthesis: Einsteinian versus Newtonian Macroeconomics*, London: Routledge.

Togati, T.D. (2001) Keynes as the Einstein of economic theory, *History of Political Economy*, 33(1): 117–138.

Weinert, F. (2005) Einstein and Kant, *Philosophy*, 80(314): 585–593.

10 Uncertainty, the modern financial market and the real economy

Fernando Ferrari Filho and Fábio Henrique Bittes Terra

1.   Introduction

As is generally recognized, Keynes's primary legacy consists in demonstrating the logic of a monetary economy. In such an economy, fluctuations in effective demand and employment occur because, in a world in which the future is uncertain and unknown, individuals may prefer to retain money, postponing consumption and investment. In Keynes's words, in a monetary production economy

> money plays a part of its own and affects motives and decisions and is, in short, one of the operative factors in the situation, so that the course of events cannot be predicted, either in the long period or in the short, without a knowledge of money between the first state and the last. (Keynes 1973: 408–409)

Thus, one central question in the Keynesian theory concerns the relationship between uncertainty, money and unemployment. Working in this direction, Post-Keynesian theory recovers this fundamental Keynesian insight: fluctuations in effective demand and in employment are related to the liquidity preference of individuals seeking safeguards against uncertainty. It is for this reason that Post-Keynesians develop a theoretical structure in which the Keynesian revolution is studied within the context of a monetary theory of production (Carvalho 1992). Minsky (1975), for instance, explains how economic cycles are conditioned and aggravated by financial cycles, so that 'financial relations are major determinants of the behaviour of a capitalist economy' (Minsky 1975: 6).

Taking into consideration Minsky's idea, this chapter aims at exploring the relationship between the financial market and investment decisions, and, as a consequence, the expansion of economic activity. To achieve this objective, first it presents the main characteristics of agents' asset portfolio composition based on the concepts of risk and uncertainty. More specifically, it shows that, on the one hand, according to mainstream economics, risk is a situation where agents take decisions relying on numerical probabilities of all outcomes that are related to that decision. Thus, economists who follow this theoretical approach argue that the efficient market theory (EMT) applies to the financial market.[1] On the other hand, Keynes and Post-Keynesians reject the EMT because the future is dominated by fundamental uncertainty. According to them, because uncertainty exists, agents have heterogeneous expectations. Thus, their decisions involve either the accumulation of wealth or the possession of liquidity. Second, in a context of fundamental uncertainty, the organization of the financial market faces a severe trade-off between liquidity and speculation. Bearing this in mind, the chapter shows how the financial market affects (boosting or slumping) economic activity. In other words, it describes the modus operandi of a monetary theory of production.

After this Introduction, the chapter is divided as follows: section 2 presents the idea of risk and explores the notion of uncertainty; section 3 shows the relationship between the financial market and the real economy; and the last section summarizes.

2.   Financial market: risk *vis-à-vis* uncertainty

One key feature of the Keynesian revolution was the insertion of uncertainty, and its counterpart expectations, in the realm of economic theory. Before Keynes's *The General Theory of Employment, Interest and Money* (hereafter GT), in which expectations play a major role in economic dynamics, uncertainty was not a variable that the economic mainstream took into account. However, after Keynes, uncertainty and expectations were no longer disregarded, although modern mainstream economics views them, from a Post-Keynesian point of view, as a matter of risk, not of uncertainty.

The distinction between risk and uncertainty is due to Knight (1921) and Keynes (1921, 1973, 1976). Risk means that the outcome of a decision resides within a closed and known set; therefore, it is possible to estimate the probability of a particular result and there is no uncertainty. For instance, '[t]he game of roulette is not subject, in this sense, to uncertainty ... Or ... the expectation of life is only slightly uncertain. Even the weather is only moderately uncertain' (Keynes 1973: 113).

Although the mainstream models try to address uncertainty and expectations, what they are really concerned with is risk. One of the pillars of EMT is the Rational Expectations Hypothesis. It establishes that agents are capable of knowing the distribution of events in space and time, and so do not make mistakes when anticipating some future possible outcomes of their present actions. As Davidson (1994) states, ergodicity prevails within the Rational Expectations Hypothesis.[2]

Keynes (1921, 1973) and the Post-Keynesians do not equate risk and uncertainty. Uncertainty is the impossibility of calculating and knowing the future outcomes of a decision. As Keynes (1973: 113–114) describes it,

> by 'uncertain' knowledge, let me explain, I do not mean merely to distinguish what is known for certain from what is only probable … The sense in which I am using the term is that in which the prospect of a European war is uncertain, or the price of copper and the rate of interest twenty years hence … About these matters there is no scientific basis on which to form any calculable probability whatever. We simply do not know.

The first venture Keynes made in the realm of uncertainty was his 1921 *A Treatise on Probability* (Ferrari Filho and Terra 2016). In this book he developed an epistemological theory aimed at arguing that reasoning on premises that first looked right and then proved wrong does not make an agent irrational. Keynes argues that the idea that led to the wrong conclusion was rational and that the agent reached an incorrect decision because of uncertainty: 'But is it certain that Newton and Huyghens were only reasonable when their theories were true, and that their mistakes were the fruit of a disordered fancy?' (Keynes 1921: 284).

Keynes (1921) establishes that the first step in obtaining knowledge is direct acquaintance. This means that using their natural skills, agents can become acquainted with meanings, experiences and feelings and these abilities enable them to collect data that they assume to be known. These data are direct knowledge, the second step in acquiring knowledge. Human reasoning uses it to form what Keynes (1921) called indirect knowledge (the third and final step in acquiring knowledge), an idea about something that does not actually exist, an expectation.

As the set of direct knowledge does not include the reasoned indirect knowledge, the latter is always uncertain. Thus, the set of direct knowledge can never have the future outcome of a decision, because any outcome exists only when the decision has been taken. So the data available for making a decision are always incomplete, making uncertainty fundamental: there will always be some relevant data missing when someone decides something.

For Ferrari Filho and Terra (2016), uncertainty has two aspects. The epistemological one derives from Keynes (1921). It depends on human beings' incapacity to reason over all the relevant data upon which they make their decisions. Human beings have a limited capacity for reasoning and so it is impossible to estimate all the possible future scenarios. Based on Davidson (1994, 2002), the other aspect of uncertainty is environmental. The environment is unable to offer sufficient data to back a forecast of possible results. The past cannot furnish the data to form a perfect idea of the future, because events do not tend to settle around average values in time or in space – that is, non-ergodicity overrules. We (Ferrari Filho and Terra 2016) argue that both uncertainties reinforce one another and form the nature of uncertainty in Post-Keynesian theory.

According to Dequech (2000), two types of uncertainty exist. On the one hand, there is the fundamental uncertainty, the uncertainty described above that derives from both individuals being epistemologically incapable of accessing and assessing all the relevant data to take a decision and the environment not supplying all the data necessary for a perfect decision. On the other hand, some results come about within a finite set; nevertheless, the range of values the finite set can take on is immense, and the values it assumes change greatly over time. This uncertainty is called ambiguity by Dequech (2000), while Lavoie (2014) calls it probability uncertainty.

As uncertainty is an ineradicable feature, agents create various institutions to deal with it, like laws, norms and culture. When it comes to the economic system, money is the insurance against uncertainty and the negative expectations that may come along with it when future outlooks are doubtful. This is the essence of Keynes's (2007) liquidity preference theory. Whenever they distrust their expectations, agents desire to keep their wealth in its most secure and liquid form, namely money, saving it as a store of value.

In Keynes's (1973, 2007) monetary economy of production, accumulation of wealth is the logic of the economic system. However, this accumulation depends on individuals getting yield on interest-bearing financial investments or profiting from productive investments. The latter are based on individuals buying capital goods in the present because of their positive expectations of future returns. These capital goods are illiquid and it is impossible for them to guarantee a fixed income. In turn, financial assets have a number of demandants in well-organized secondary markets so that they are liquid. Also, their deals can contract a fixed income, making it clear to individuals what their gains will be.

Hence, when individuals are deciding how to accumulate wealth over time, they consider a broad range of purchasable financial and real assets. Given uncertainty, the decision as to what to buy depends very much on agents' expectations. Positive and confident outlooks motivate them to buy capital goods whereas doubtful and diffident approaches stimulate the acquisition of liquid financial assets.

The first step in a decision-making process is whether to hold money precautionarily or not. If the decision is to put money into movement, the speculative demand for money comes into play, and the second step that individuals take is to analyse the returns offered by liquid financial assets, ranging from the more secure fixed income ones to riskier securities paying variable returns. In the second step individuals have entered the domain of the speculative demand for money. They bet on knowing better than the other agents what the market conditions are going to be in the future. This is the sphere of speculation, as Keynes (2007) defines it, the area where agents try to profit without taking a shot in the dark in which uncertainty wraps future outcomes.

Individuals only buy illiquid capital goods, the third step of an investment decision, whose returns are always unpredictable, after pricing the conditions of the financial markets. To fulfil their desire to accumulate wealth by purchasing capital goods and engaging in entrepreneurial activity, individuals must have a good degree of confidence in their expectations. However, jobs and income creation in monetary economies of production are determined by investments in capital goods. Thus, the harder it proves to undertake investments, the lower will be the GDP growth and the higher the unemployment level.

Hard as it is to have a sustainable dynamics of productive investment because of its illiquidity and the high level of uncertainty that surrounds it, there is another element that has aggravated the purchase of capital goods, namely the intense development of assets in the connected, deregulated and globalized modern financial markets. A large range of financial assets prolongs the decision-making process when it comes to purchasing capital goods.

As Carvalho (2015a) argues, the habitual behaviour of individuals is to prefer the safety of liquidity. This defensive behaviour, as Carvalho (2015a) calls it, gained a huge potential with the burgeoning of a vast series of financial assets supplied in the modern deregulated financial markets. The outcomes of this financialized economy are, on the one hand, more hindrances to sustaining an economic dynamic that guarantees stable jobs and a regular creation of income. On the other hand, the collapse of the economic system into financial crisis has never been so common, as exemplified by the 2001 Nasdaq crisis, the 2007–2008 subprime crisis, and the post-2017 debate on how to manage the central banks' balance without causing any economic instability and loosening monetary policy.

Financial assets have several risks, yet they can offer gains in the short term, and they are very liquid as most of them have well-organized secondary markets, a feature capital goods cannot enjoy. Thus, uncertainty has increasingly been leading to seeking safety in financial assets. However, various factors of the modern financial markets, such as leverage, price volatility and short-term speculation, have increased uncertainty in the financial market, and this is very different from the risk according to EMT, which has it that agents learn over time and stop making mistakes. They cannot learn. Also, their defensive behaviour tends to make them feel more fear than excitement, and so they stay as close as they can to liquidity. Thus, speculation tends frequently and rapidly to oscillate only between money and financial assets. But, as Keynes (1976) states, agents' preference for liquidity can largely affect productive investments, and so they are not neutral in relation to the real economy.

The link between the financial market and real economy is explored in the next section.

3.   The financial market and the real economy in a Keynesian perspective

In the 1930s, Keynes developed his monetary theory of production, also called entrepreneur economy, in which the principle of effective demand (PED) is essential. It determines the employment and output levels and is strictly related to the non-neutrality of money, in both the short and the long terms. Keynes explains the relationship between effective demand and the non-neutrality of money as follows: 'Money is *par excellence* the means of remuneration in an entrepreneur economy which lends itself to fluctuations in effective demand' (Keynes 1979: 86). In other words, in Keynes's monetary theory of production, money is the starting and end point of the economic process. The following quotations make this clear:

> the entrepreneur is guided, not by the amount of product he will gain, but by the alternative opportunities for using money having regard to the spot and forward price structure taken as a whole. (Keynes 1979: 83)

> [the monetary theory of production describes] an economy in which money plays a part of its own and affects motives and decisions and is, in short, one of the operative factors in the situation, so that the course of events cannot be predicted, either in the long period or in the short, without a knowledge of the behaviour of money between the first and the last. (Keynes 1973: 408–409)

Implicitly, the quotations above show that the reason for fluctuations in effective demand is holding money, because of uncertainty about the future. More specifically, considering that, within fundamental uncertainty, entrepreneurs and households do not know the future outcomes of their current decisions, they can decide either to retain money or buy liquid financial assets. Thus, the concept of the non-neutrality of money has to do with the decision process of agents in the light of fundamental uncertainty.

Moreover, in a monetary theory of production, the financial market has an active role in the economic process. Arestis and Terra (2017: 48) present the following reasons for this:

> First, besides the central bank, banks ... are the other grand players of the financial markets; partly due to their capacity to create money, partly because they are the greatest intermediaries from which the agents can have access to the financial system. Second, the fact that banks grant finance without the requirement of previous savings explains the endogenous nature of money, which is of fundamental importance to monetary policy.

To sum up, according to the monetary theory of production, the capitalist system is an economy where 'expenditure [mainly investment] creates its own income' (Keynes 1979: 81). In this economy, insufficiency of effective demand occurs because agents, in conditions of fundamental uncertainty, prefer to hold money or other liquid assets instead of acquiring goods produced by labour. Thus, the liquidity preference inhibits economic agents' spending decisions and affects the economic activity.

How does Keynes develop his monetary theory of production? Implicitly, he develops his theory in *A Treatise on Money* (*Treatise*), published in 1930, and in his 1936 GT.

In the first volume of his *Treatise*, Keynes formulates an 'asset choice theory' which aims at

> describing, not merely the characteristics of static equilibrium, but also those of disequilibrium, and to discover the dynamical laws of governing the passage of a monetary system from one position of equilibrium to another ... [and] also describ[ing] the salient features of modern banking and monetary systems. (Keynes 1976: v)

Keynes's 'asset choice theory' aims to show how, in a context of uncertainty in which agents' expectations always change, the financial market works in terms of stimulating (or not stimulating) the economic activity. That is, Keynes presents an institutional framework of the financial market as the main cause of disruption in the real economy.[3]

To develop his idea, Keynes divides the economic system into two categories: industrial and financial circulations. According to Keynes (1976: 243, original italics):

> By *Industry* we mean the business of maintaining the normal process of current output, distribution and exchange and paying the factors of production their incomes ... By *Finance*, on the other hand, we mean the business of holding and exchanging existing titles to wealth ... including Stock Exchange and Money Market transactions, speculation and the process of conveying current savings and profits into the hands of entrepreneurs.

More specifically, the industrial circulation refers to the volume of money held by individuals and firms in order to expand consumption and investment. The latter is the amount of wealth held by agents with the purposes of saving and financial speculation.

Given these definitions, Keynes explains the causality between the two economic spheres: the industrial circulation is determined by the investments of firms and households; the financial market provides bank loans (credit) to undertake the real sector transactions. Therefore, Keynes shows that banks (or the financial market as a whole) play an institutional role in the economy, because their deposits/liabilities fund the real economy. According to him, given that the outcomes of a monetary economy are inherently uncertain, when the financial market becomes more prudent – that is, banks decide to revise their lending behaviour to firms – the main result is that industrial circulation of capital is discouraged and, in this situation, 'a state of unemployment may be expected to ensue, and to continue' (Keynes 1976: 206). Thus, as Keynes (1976: 254) explains:

> changes in the financial situation are capable of causing changes in the value of money in two ways. They have the effect of altering the quantity of money available for the Industrial Circulation; and they may have the effect of altering the attractiveness of Investment …; whereas if [the financial market] refuses to increase the volume of Bank-money, it may so diminish the amount of money available for Industry, or so enhance the rate of interest at which it is available, as to have an immediately deflationary tendency.

To conclude, the main idea of the *Treatise* is that money and the financial market (what Keynes called the financial circulation of capital) are important in order to understand the development of the real economy and the fluctuations in the levels of prices and employment (i.e., they affect the industrial circulation of capital).

In the GT, Keynes develops the idea of the PED, emphasizing the idea of the non-neutrality of money.[4] According to the PED, the insufficiency of effective demand occurs because agents, in conditions of uncertainty, prefer to hold money or other liquid assets (liquidity preference) instead of taking investment decisions. As a result, economic crises come about because money is an alternative form of wealth. Thus, given that uncertainty is the reason for retaining money, the greater the uncertainty surrounding the expectations of agents, the more they are likely to postpone spending decisions and, consequently, the greater proves the liquidity preference.

Chapters 11 and 12 of the GT show, implicitly, how the speculative behaviour of agents (households, firms and banks) contributes to stimulate their liquidity preference, as well as connecting the financial market and the real economy.

Initially, it needs to be pointed out that speculation is essentially an 'activity of forecasting the psychology of the market' (Keynes 2007: 158). In an entrepreneur economy, the organization of the financial market bears a severe trade-off between liquidity and speculation: on the one hand, the financial market encourages the development of productive activities, providing liquidity to consumers and entrepreneurs; on the other hand, it increases the possibility of speculative gains, which involves the ability to buy and readily resell financial assets for cash. Furthermore, the latter facilitates the use of financial assets to finance investments as soon as they can encourage savers to provide the necessary funding that stimulates investors to spend their monetary resources on new investment projects.

In Chapter 11 Keynes shows that the volume of investment involves two types of risk: the entrepreneur's and lender's risks:

> The first one … arises out of doubts in his own mind as to the probability of his actually earning the prospective yield for which he hopes … [the] second type of risk [is related to] the possible insufficiency of the margin of security … (Keynes 2007: 144)

This brings out Keynes's idea that there are close connections between the financial market and the real economy. One of these connections is the impact of speculation on productive activity, and especially on investment.

More specifically, as speculators dominate the financial market, its stability requires a larger number of speculators with different opinions (bull and bear expectations). Although the liquidity of the financial market often facilitates the course of a new investment, it can sometimes impede it, because '[i]n the absence of security markets, there is no object in frequently attempting to revalue an investment to which we are committed' (Keynes 2007: 151).

What is the problem with this connection? It arises when speculation predominates over the economic activity. As Keynes (2007: 159) states:

> the position is serious when enterprise becomes the bubble on a whirlpool of speculation. When the capital development of a country becomes a by-product of the activities of a casino, the job is likely to be ill-done.

Reflecting on Keynes's idea in the 2000s, in a context where the global economy is increasingly deregulated and integrated, the financial market has become a great casino and, therefore, speculation has proved disruptive. Thus, the institutional design of the financial market developed between the 1970s and the 1990s determined its potential as an environment where speculation can easily flourish.

One of the keys of the Post-Keynesian approach is to understand the modus operandi of a system of borrowing and lending based upon margins of safety. In other words, the idea is to show that, in a context of fundamental uncertainty about the future, borrowers (households and firms) and lenders (mainly banks) take precautions (margins of safety) to mitigate the systemic risk they are exposed to.

Working in this direction, Minsky (2008), for instance, based on Keynes's GT, elaborates his 'financial fragility hypothesis' (FFH). The idea is to explain how economic cycles are conditioned and aggravated by financial cycles. Thus, he develops a 'financial theory of investment' to show that capitalist economies have a system of borrowing and lending based upon margins of safety.

Carvalho (2015b) summarizes Minsky's theory in two theorems: first, according to the FFH, the economy has stable and unstable financing regimes; second, stability is destabilizing. Going into the second one, Minsky argues that the existence of a prolonged period of economic prosperity leads to '[t]he economic instability … [that] is the result of the fragile financial system that emerge[s] from cumulative changes in financial relations and institutions' (Minsky 2008: 5). Minsky's FFH can be explained as follows:

1. From Keynes (2007), the first step in the entrepreneur's decision-making process is estimation of the internal rate of return of investment plans, or in other words the marginal efficiency of capital. If the return rate of a capital asset is greater than the minimum acceptable rate of return offered by other assets, particularly low-risk and fixed-income financial assets, an investment is usually made.
2. Funding is fundamental for investments and, in general, firms can issue equities and/or borrow money not only by selling bonds, but by contracting loans from banks. Unlike sharing equities, borrowing entails liabilities that firms pay back only if they collect their planned revenues.
3. From the relation between the expected revenues and the financial obligations of an economic unit, Minsky defined three financial positions, corresponding to different degrees of fragility: (a) the *Hedge* financing position is the safest. This unit has a reasonable safety margin between returns and financial payments; (b) the *Speculative* financing position is the intermediate financial fragility stance. It entails that revenues cover financial commitments only partly and, as a result, the firms in this position need to roll over their liabilities/debts; and (c) the *Ponzi* financing position is the one in which the unit fails to raise sufficient revenue to cover either the interest or the principal payments, as well as to pay its operating costs. Thus, in this situation, the unit crisis is inevitable.

Given that, a question arises: how do *Ponzi* units come about? Considering that economies are inherently cyclic, alternating booms and recessions, in a phase of economic prosperity revenues and production grow and capital gains increase. Thus, based on the conventional reasoning that the good current conditions will recur in the future, entrepreneurs are encouraged to develop new business plans and raise funds to carry them out. Meanwhile, the banks' revenues also rise, and they are ready to meet the entrepreneurs' loan demand. The economy thus leans into a higher-risk overall stance, moving from *Hedge* to *Speculative*. Furthermore, units become leveraged, modifying banks' risk assessments. Thus, credit becomes tighter, new investments are not made, revenues no longer grow, and *Speculative* units turn rapidly and involuntarily into *Ponzi* positions, intensifying the possibility of an economic crisis. Carvalho (2015b: 107) summarizes this idea: '[l]everage, thus, grows during prosperity phases, intensifying and accelerating growth and prosperity itself. However, increasing leverage means also increasing fragility. With lower and lower margins of safety, lenders become more and more exposed to shocks that could be small and fundamentally harmless under ordinary circumstances.'

Concluding this section, the Post-Keynesians, and in particular Minsky, show that *Speculative* and *Ponzi* booms occur when prolonged stability is experienced, and finance and speculation dominate enterprise, as the following quotations point out:

> increasing fragility is a natural result of the way the system operates. (Carvalho 2015b: 108)

> Our economy is unstable because of capitalist finance. (Minsky 2008: 244)

4.   Final remarks

The main goal of the chapter was to show, in a Keynesian perspective, the relationship between the financial market and the real economy.

To achieve this goal, first, we considered the difference between risk and uncertainty. Section 2, on the one hand, showed that EMT understands uncertainty as risk and so the mainstream economists believe that the future can be predictable and known. On the other hand, Keynes and the Post-Keynesians see risk as a very particular case, linked to almost no economic transaction. Uncertainty is an indelible feature of reality and it looms very large over the economic system. In this respect, for instance, the frequent financial and exchange rate crises that have occurred in the global economy since the 1970s, when the financial markets became deregulated and integrated, confirm that it is not risk that prevails, but uncertainty.

Second, after defining Keynes's monetary theory of production, in which money and financial assets play an important role in the economic system, section 3 showed that the relationship between the financial market and the real economy is inherently unstable. Based on Keynes's 'theory of the cycle' and Minsky's 'financial theory of investment', it was shown that 'stability is destabilizing'. In other words, booms and busts occur because agents (entrepreneurs and consumers) engage in high-risk leverage and lending practices, but they rapidly abandon them when their expectations turn to negative future scenarios, driving the economy into a slump.

Notes

1. It is worth mentioning that according to the conventional approach (or EMT) financial risk can be classified as three types: market, credit and liquidity risk.
2. The EMT has its foundation in the ergodic axiom, which means that the expected value of an objective probability can always be estimated from observed data that provide reliable information on the conditional probability function that will govern future outcomes. For additional details, see: Davidson (2002).
3. It is important to mention that in *A Tract on Monetary Reform* (Keynes 1971), published in 1923, Keynes shows that changes in money supply (i.e., financial system deposits) could not only explain the fluctuations in the price levels but also the production and employment levels, at least in the short term.
4. In Chapter 17 of the GT, Keynes showed that money is not neutral because it differs from other assets due to the following properties: first, the elasticity of money production is zero – that is, money is not produced by the quantity of labour the private sector employs in the productive process. Second, the substitution-elasticity of money is also zero, so it is not substituted by any other asset when its price changes. Third, the carrying cost of money is near zero.

References

Arestis, P. and Terra, F.H.B. (2017) Monetary policy in the Post Keynesian theoretical framework, *Brazilian Journal of Political Economy*, 37(146): 45–64.

Carvalho, F.J.C. (1992) *Mr Keynes and the Post Keynesians*, Aldershot, UK and Brookfield, VT, USA: Edward Elgar Publishing.

Carvalho, F.J.C. (2015a) Keynes on expectations, uncertainty and defensive behaviour, *Brazilian Keynesian Review*, 1(1): 44–54.

Carvalho, F.J.C. (2015b) *Liquidity Preference and Monetary Economies*, New York: Routledge.

Davidson, P. (1994) *Post Keynesian Macroeconomic Theory*, Aldershot, UK and Brookfield, VT, USA: Edward Elgar Publishing.

Davidson, P. (2002) *Financial Markets, Money and the Real World*, Cheltenham, UK and Northampton, MA, USA: Edward Elgar Publishing.

Dequech, D. (2000) Fundamental uncertainty and ambiguity, *Eastern Economic Journal*, 26(1): 41–60.

Ferrari Filho, F. and Terra, F.H.B. (2016) Reflexões sobre o método em Keynes, *Brazilian Journal of Political Economy*, 36(1): 70–90.

Keynes, J.M. (1921) *Treatise on Probability*, London: Macmillan.

Keynes, J.M. (1971) *A Tract on Monetary Reform*, London: Macmillan.

Keynes, J.M. (1973) *The General Theory and After: Preparation*, Cambridge: Cambridge University Press.
Keynes, J.M. (1976) *A Treatise on Money: The Pure Theory of Money*, New York: AMS Press.
Keynes, J.M. (1979) *The General Theory and After: A Supplement*, Cambridge: Cambridge University Press.
Keynes, J.M. (2007) *The General Theory of Employment, Interest and Money*, London: Palgrave Macmillan.
Knight, F. (1921) *Risk, Uncertainty and Profit*, University of Illinois at Urbana-Champaign's Academy for Entrepreneurial Leadership Historical Research Reference in Entrepreneurship, available at https://ssrn.com/abstract=1496192, accessed 2 August 2019.
Lavoie, M. (2014) *Post Keynesian Theory: New Foundations*, Cheltenham, UK and Northampton, MA, USA: Edward Elgar Publishing.
Minsky, H. (1975) Financial resources in a fragile financial environment, *Challenge*, 18(3): 6–13.
Minsky, H. (2008) *Stabilizing an Unstable Economy*, New York: McGraw-Hill.

11 The capitalist *space* economy: uneven geographical development, value and more-than-capitalist contestations

Eric Sheppard

Introduction

While Marx paid occasional attention to geographical aspects of the capitalist economy (such as town and country relations and the annihilation of space by time), it was never central to formulating the theory laid out in *Kapital*, *Die Grundrisse* and *Theories of Surplus Value*. Time is central—the basis for measuring exploitation and the dimension of crisis—but space is an afterthought. Over the past 35 years, however, Marxist geographers—first and foremost David Harvey—and their fellow-travelers have sought to recuperate Marxist theory from this neglect (e.g., Harvey 1982, 2005, 2006b, 2010, 2014; Liossatos 1980, 1983, 1988; Massey 1984; Scott 1988; Sheppard 2016; Sheppard and Barnes 2015 [1990]; Storper and Walker 1989; Webber and Rigby 1996). A substantial theoretical and empirical literature has emerged within which the consensus has emerged, notwithstanding profound internecine disagreements, that Geography *matters*. Capitalism in the wild (Callon 1998) is inescapably geographical, and paying careful attention to its geographical nature reveals insights about capitalism that are otherwise occluded. In this brief chapter, I offer one take on this.

Thinking geographically about capitalism (Sheppard 2015) means, first, taking its spatialities seriously (like time) as having a causal effect, thereby shaping capitalism's spatial evolution. For geographers, the concept of spatialities references various ways of conceptualizing spatial relations. By now there is a long list of such mid-range spatial concepts, which I restrict here to an over-lapping and dialectically co-constitutive triad: place/territory, geographical scale and networks of connectivity. These cannot be reduced to an exogenous backdrop shaping the conditions of possibility within which capitalism takes shape, as economists tendentially assume. Spatialities are *produced*, through societal (and biophysical) processes. But these seemingly dependent, con-structed spaces also have causal effect on the trajectory of political economic processes (cf. Herod, Chapter 9 in this volume). Ed Soja (1980) dubbed this the socio-spatial dialectic: political economic processes and spatialities are both co-constitutive of one another, and continually subject to reconstitution through these relations (Plummer and Sheppard 2006).

Thinking geographically is not just about space, however. Reflecting Geography's interdisciplinary nature as a discipline, this also means attending to how eco-nomic, political, cultural and biophysical processes are co-constitutive of one another. For a geographer, the economy can never be studied in isolation; nor is it plausible to claim that other processes are dominated by, or reducible to, economic processes (econocentrism). In what follows, given word limitations I focus primarily on the implications of taking space seriously, returning to this second aspect of thinking geographically towards the end.

Spatialities of capitalist production

Marx highlighted the importance of temporality for realizing profits on capital-ist production: profit rates depend on the length of the production period—the lag between advancing capital and realizing profits, and on the turnover time of capital. Labor costs, productivity and exploitation are measured in hours, and the rate of profit per annum. Thus the manipulation of time is central to profit-maximizing strategies.

Yet space is also central. Capitalists must purchase fixed and variable capital inputs from firms located elsewhere, implying that the cost of non-labor inputs depends on transportation costs, and indirectly on the geographical organization of production (where firms locate—itself a strategic decision for each firm). Workers also must be hired from somewhere, with costs depending on their location and other factors (e.g., skill, gendered and racial formations, local labor relations, intersectional identities). To realize profits, firms must then ship their commoditized output to spatially distributed markets of firms and/or households, with capitalists incurring transportation costs and facing uncertainties about whether they can sell in unfamiliar markets at prices that realize a competitive profit rate. In turn, these revenues must be returned across space to the firm, to be advanced for the next period of production (in the same location, or elsewhere). Connectivities shape the space economy: they entail costs in exchange (and labor) value terms that affect rates of profit (and exploitation).

Place also matters to commodity production. Consider the place of production, where class politics is grounded. Marx captured nicely the political difference between labor markets—places where workers are "free" to negotiate a labor contract—and the places workers are hired to work in. Entering the latter:

> the money-owner now strides in front as capitalist; the possessor of labor-power follows as his laborer. The one with an air of importance, smirking, intent on business; the other, timid and holding back, like one who is bringing his own hide to market and has nothing to expect but—a hiding. (Marx 1967 [1867]: 176)

Individual and collective resistance to such a hiding makes places of production key starting points for class struggle; being gathered in the same place with shared grievances provides a strong incentive for collective action. Consider also territorial economies: territorially delimited places (cities, sub-national regions, nation-states) with distinct mixes of technologies and economic activities, governance systems, work cultures and relational assets that enable/ constrain capitalist innovation, labor relations, income distributions and economic growth (Markusen 1980; Dunford 1988; Scott 1988; Webber 1996, 1997; Rigby and Essletzbichler 1997; Storper 1997; Peck and Theodore 2007).

Third, geographical scale matters (Herod, Chapter 9 in this volume). Class struggle is all about how localized conflicts, for example between workers and capitalists in places of production, jump scale to become national- or international-scale labor movements with the potential to shape broader geographies of capitalist production. Herod (2001) terms this labor geographies. Systems of governance, shaped by capitalist lobbying, labor politics and democratic politics, also are multi-scalar. But beyond this, governance processes operating at different scales relationally affect one another. Global institutions such as the World Bank or the World Trade Organization (WTO) reach down to shape capitalist production and labor relations in sub-national regions and cities. In the opposite direction, the actions of firms (like those of labor) have larger-scale, even global, consequences (shaping, e.g., transnational trade agreements or global warming). Thus geographical scale operates relationally:

causality moves upward and downward, shaping events at, and the very nature of, different geographical scales (Brenner 2004; Leitner and Miller 2007).

Finally, place, connectivity and scale are mutually constitutive. As Doreen Massey (1991, 2005) has emphasized, what happens in a territorial economy is shaped by how people and entities in that region are differentially and unevenly connected with other places—unequally empowering that region's residents. By the same token, the networks linking capitalist enterprises together, ranging from the internal networks of transnational corporations to more loosely organized global production networks (Coe and Yeung 2015; Dicken 2015; Dicken et al. 2001) and networked markets, enable capitalist firms to operate at and shape global-scale processes—just as they are shaped by such processes.

Accessibility as commodity

A prime vector of connectivity is transportation, essential for enabling firms to acquire inputs and ship commodities (also enabling labor migration, mobility and commuting). The transportation sector includes fixed capital infrastructure (publicly and privately produced roads, railroads, shipping and airline routes and nodes, etc.), firms producing the means of transportation (cars, ships, etc.) and firms offering transportation services. In both mainstream and Marxist economic theory, transportation infrastructure characteristically is reduced to a transactions cost that differentially elevates the price of commodities and labor, depending on location and the accessibility of firms and workers to one another. Yet this overlooks how accessibility is itself a commodity, produced by capitalist firms in the expectation of realizing a profit and subsidized by state investments in infrastructure. This implies that accessibility is endogenous to a capitalist space economy, not an exogenous cost of doing business. Higher accessibility (faster/cheaper transportation) reduces costs and accelerates the turnover of capital, making it a valued input to all capitalist production—undermining claims that the labor invested in circulation is unproductive.

Crucially, accessibility's role in an inter-sectoral capitalist economy makes it a very special, indispensable commodity, like labor or energy. Representing the capitalist space economy as both multi-sectoral and multi-regional (spatializing Marx's scheme of reproduction, cf. Morishima 1973), the transportation sector not only is produced using inputs from other sectors (plus labor), but is a direct input to all sectors. Even if we assume constant production technologies, transportation inputs are endogenously determined, implying that the overall inter-regional technology matrix also is endogenous.

Incorporating the production of accessibility in this way has two important implications. First, since it reduces turnover time, for capitalism it is collectively beneficial to raise the speed and productivity of transportation. Second, whenever firms seek to enhance their productivity and profitability, reducing material or labor inputs per unit of output or relocating, this will increase transportation requirements for some regions/sectors even as it decreases these for others, altering the price of accessibility (for details, see Sheppard and Barnes 2015 [1990]). The effects of these changes on overall profitability are unpredictable, but vital. For example, in a geographically differentiated economy it is impossible for economic analysts (let alone capitalists or workers) to predict whether cost-reducing technical change enhances the average profit rate, even when real wages remain constant (cf. Okishio 1961). With some transportation requirements increasing, individuals' cost-reducing strategies may have the unintended consequence of *lowering* overall profit rates.

Put otherwise, capitalism's spatiality increases the likelihood that individual capitalists' profit-enhancing strategies result in undesirable, unintended consequences. Adding temporality into the mix, the dynamical complexity of a capitalist space economy only compounds the instabilities of capitalism (Bergmann et al. 2009; Bergmann 2012).

The question of Value

Treating the production of the accessibility commodity as endogenous undermines core propositions in both mainstream and Marxist economic theory. With respect to the latter, it goes to the heart of Value itself. First, is the question of what abstraction means in a *space* economy. Marx's calculations of Value abstract from the heterogeneity of everyday commodity production and exchange; they are calculated for the economy as a whole. But what does "as a whole" mean? It is reasonable to presume that Marx, like his contemporaries, had a national territorial economy in mind—although conceivably it could be globalized capitalism. Yet even if we (heroically) assume that rates of profit (and exploitation) are equal across sectors and locations, Value for the same commodity/economic sector will vary from one region to another. Even if technologies are the same in every region, the Value of accessibility must be factored into the Value of all commodities, raising questions also about the validity of claims made on the basis of Marx's aspatial Value theory (Sheppard 2004).

This raises the interminable debates about the transformation problem. In a spaceless economy, with the technological matrix of an economy assumed to be fixed, it is well known that Values and prices of production can be calculated through parallel inversions of this matrix (Morishima 1973). There is an ongoing debate, of course, about whether and how best to transform the one into the other, accompanied by robust empirical evidence that Value and equilibrium prices of production are closely correlated (Cockshott 2005; Wright 2016; Tsoulfidis and Tsaliki 2019). In a capitalist *space* economy, however, where some entries in the technological matrix are always endogenous, Values and prices of production can no longer be separately calculated; they are (dialectically) inter-related (Sheppard and Barnes 1986).

Value, prices of production and wages also will vary across space, varying systematically across the uneven geographical space that makes up a national territory. On the same grounds they vary between national economies. This greatly complicates questions of class identity and conflict. Participants in the economy identify with where they live not just with their social identity (intersectionally shaped by economic class, gender, race, sexuality, etc.). This has enabled elites to appeal to geographical identity (nation, region, city) to persuade other classes to collaborate with them in the name of increasing local prosperity in competition against other places (Logan and Molotch 2007 [1987] coined these urban growth coalitions). In places where real wages are above the average, this can create labor aristocracies (Bettelheim 1972) whose purchasing power is elevated by importing cheaply produced commodities from other regions with low real wages (Herod 2003; Hudson and Sadler 1986).

Spatialities of governance and policy mobility

Particularly in the past two decades, geographical political economy also has focused on the role of the state (indeed, of governance more generally) as inescapably significant in shaping a capitalist space economy. Drawing on regulation theory (Dunford 1990; Jessop 1990), and more recently the varieties of capitalism literature, scholars have sought to trace and account for shifts in discourses and state–market relations and associated regulatory norms across time, space and scale. With respect to time, the focus has been on the shift from Fordist to post-Fordist and particularly to neoliberal norms (Peck and Tickell 2002; Sheppard and Leitner 2010; Peck and Theodore 2019). With respect to space, scholars have sought to tease out how and why neoliberalism has evolved differently in distinct national contexts. As Jamie Peck (2010) has argued, no territorial economy should be seen as quintessentially neoliberal: in the wild, neoliberal norms articulate with preexisting conjunctures to create hybrid forms—a process he has dubbed neoliberalization. With respect to scale, research has teased out how global norms, such as those propagated by the Bretton Woods institutions, reach down to shape national and sub-national territorial economies. Scholars also have explored whether and how municipal-scale political economies have sought to challenge larger-scale pressures (Tickell and Peck 1992; Goldfrank and Schrank 2009).

A closely related literature examines the practices incentivized by governance norms. Noting that governance institutions and ideologies—particularly those behind the Washington and post-Washington consensus—have become skilled at mobilizing policy initiatives to advance their agenda, scholars have traced how policies move across scale and space, and documented their local impact (Peck and Theodore 2015; McCann 2011; Roy 2010). This research examines how policies are shaped by ideologies and institutions, and the complexities of their diffusion: policies mutate through space and time as they move between places and across scales and encounter local contestation and resistance.

Vectors of uneven geographical development

The pervasiveness and persistence of uneven geographical development is one of the most robust empirical features of capitalist space economies in the wild: at scales ranging from the globe to the metropolitan region, prosperous territories—a geographical core—co-evolve with impoverished territories—a geographical periphery. Geographical political economy offers a two-fold explanation for why uneven geographical development is a shifting but ubiquitous feature. Convergence towards a hypothesized equilibrium in which income and wealth equalize across space, as predicted by neoclassical regional economic theory, is the exception, not the rule. Rather, processes of capitalist commodity production, commodity trade and economic growth generate and reproduce persistent inequality.

Neil Smith (1984: 197–198) theorized what he saw as a continual seesaw movement of investment capital between territorial capitalist economies:

> Capital moves to where the rate of profit is highest (or at least high), ... synchronized with the rhythm of accumulation and crisis. The mobility of capital brings about the development of areas with a high rate of profit and the underdevelopment of those areas where a low rate of profit pertains .... At the opposite pole ... the lack of capital ... leads to high unemployment rates, low wages, and reduced levels of workers' organization. Thus the underdevelopment of specific areas leads, in time, to precisely those conditions that make an area highly profitable and hence susceptible to rapid development .... That is, capital attempts to seesaw from a developed to an underdeveloped area, then at a later point back to the first area which is by now underdeveloped, and so forth.

In his seminal Marxist account of the capitalist space economy, Harvey (1982) attributes seesawing to the exhaustion of opportunities for profit-making in places already subject to intensified capitalist investment. This happens as infrastructure becomes outdated, workers organize, new industries emerge, relational assets underwriting local innovation (Storper 1997) deteriorate, and other locations become more advantageous. "The building of a geographical landscape favourable to capital accumulation in one era becomes ... a fetter on capital accumulation in the next. Capital therefore has to devalue much of the fixed capital in the existing geographical landscape in order to build a wholly new landscape in a different image" (Harvey 2014: 155). "Like a plague of locusts, capital would descend on a place, devour everything of value, and then move on" (Peck 2017: 7). The result, Harvey famously argues, is a third cut to capitalist crisis: a "spatial fix" of devaluation here combined with relocation of capital accumulation to elsewhere. As Smith (1984: 6) noted, these processes can be observed across a "number of geographical scales". Examples would include the relocation of capitalist production from central cities to suburban or exurban locations, from the American manufacturing belt to right-to-work states in the US south, or from European and white settler colonies to China, Brazil or South Africa. It is also important to acknowledge that the result is not the irreversible polarization between fixed core and peripheral locations suggested by the likes of Andre Gunder Frank (1979): peripheral territories occasionally become cores, and vice versa, but the landscape is always characterized by cores and peripheries.

This theorization of uneven geographical development focuses on changes in place, whereby ongoing capital accumulation undermines opportunities to realize competitive profit rates, in the broader context of other locations whose more favorable conditions of possibility may make relocation worthwhile. But a second dynamic also is at work, driven by unequal and asymmetric connectivities between territorial economies. Doreen Massey has been a key thinker in drawing attention to this, through her relational theorization of space (Massey 1991, 1993, 2005). Challenging methodological territorialism (Brenner 1999)—the presumption that territories can be treated as homogenous and autonomous units of analysis—Massey shows how the conditions of possibility in a territory (a place, region or nation) are shaped by how it is connected with elsewhere (across space and scale). Beyond this, she questions the coherence of any territorial economy (and indeed its meaningfulness as a unit of analysis), arguing that its various residents will be differentially (dis)empowered by their particular connections with elsewhere—generating intra-territorial inequalities. Importantly, she also teases out the gendered aspects of these relations (Massey 1994).

In mainstream spatial and development economics, the default presumption is that such connectivities are mutually beneficial (Milanovic 2016). The free trade doctrine preaches that specialization and trade flatten the geographical playing field: a rising tide that lift all boats (Sheppard 2005). Transnational production networks, unfettered by state regulation of corporate investment strategies, are presented as creating opportunities for home and host countries alike. Globalized financial markets are imagined to equalize opportunities to raise funding, and make money, everywhere. Globalization is imagined to accelerate the diffusion of cutting-edge technologies to disadvantaged places. The free movement of people seeking work could likewise benefit all bodies and places—if states would only countenance this. Cyberspace is seen as flattening the world.

If this were the case then it would indeed be possible, at least in principle, to imagine a capitalist path to development that would enable all places to prosper as long as those lagging behind imitate those in front (Rostow 1960). Gillian Hart (2002) has dubbed this Development—a capitalist prescription of prosperity for all bodies and places willing to play the capitalist game. This has been propagated by international financial institutions and their fellow travelers since the Bretton Woods conference. Geographical political economists show, however, that such connectivities are not a mutually beneficial tide lifting all boats. They are asymmetric and inequalizing, creating wealth here through, inter alia, impoverishment elsewhere. While this is not a new idea (having been the central claim of dependency and world-systems theory), geographical political economists tease out the logic through which this happens at all scales, in the really existing, already unequal space economy (as opposed to the flat world theorized by geographical and development economists, Sheppard 2018). The rich tradition of international trade theory legitimizing the free trade doctrine does not hold up in a capitalist space economy, and is not consistent with the empirical experience of unequal exchange (Sheppard 2012). Global production networks empower corporations and their headquarters' locations, globalized finance markets enable the powerful to borrow money at low rates and launder it through tax havens, and patents cluster strongly in space reinforcing the prosperity of technologically privileged cities (Coe and Yeung 2015; Wójcik 2013; Balland et al. 2015). It logically follows that catching up is a fool's errand in the really existing multi-scalar capitalist space economy—opening space to consider the necessity of more-than-capitalist alternatives.

Capitalism's raggedy fringes

If uneven geographical development constitutionally impoverishes some places and bodies so as to enrich others, this fundamentally challenges claims that variants on capitalism, taken together, should be the default, least-worst political economic prescription for living well. The challenges discussed above, internal to the operation of a capitalist *space* economy, are further compounded if we turn to the second aspect of thinking geographically: conceptualizing political economy as co-evolving with cultural and biophysical processes. In Karl Polanyi's terms, humans and nature are fictitious commodities (Polanyi 2001 [1944]): notwithstanding ongoing attempts to commodify culture and "nature" to subsidize capitalist production—for example, accumulation by dispossession (Harvey 2006a)—commodification is always incomplete. Humans and the more-than-human world possess agency that is not reducible to economic logics, implying that culture and "nature" continually exceed capitalist logics—constituting a more-than-capitalist world.

Marxist analyses of capitalism certainly acknowledge such outsides: Marx emphasized the importance of materiality—how human actions are shaped by more-than-human processes, and by pre-capitalist social formations. Harold Wolpe (1980) and others have discussed how capitalism co-exists and co-evolves with other modes of production—particularly in formerly colonized or quasi-colonized territorial economies. Yet the presumption has been that these outsides are *constitutive* of capitalism: that capitalism is more than capable of absorbing such outsides through the ever-inventive commodification of Earth and everyday life. The influence of Harvey's notion of accumulation by dispossession is a case in point, as is Jason Moore's sophisticated and historically nuanced analysis of the capitalocene (Harvey 2006a; Moore 2015). In this view, in the end capitalism founders—if at all—on irresoluble internal "foundational" contradictions (Harvey 2014).

If capitalism is unable to deliver, however, on its promise of opportunity and prosperity for all bodies and places conforming with its norms—supplemented by capitalist state-organized governmentality and biopolitics—then it is only rational for impoverished communities to experiment with alternatives. Further, such alternatives should be taken seriously, not just as ways of resisting capitalism but also as spaces within which alternatives can be crafted that destabilize capitalism from the outside—spaces of contestation (Leitner et al. 2007). Harvey (1995) has been somewhat dismissive of what he terms militant particularism, but others are more optimistic about the possibility of local social movements pursuing spatial strategies that can destabilize globalizing capitalism (Featherstone et al. 2012; Routledge 2017). Within the heartlands of neoliberalizing capitalism, the paradigm-shifting scholarship of J.K. Gibson-Graham and colleagues in the community economies collaborative has established empirically that what they term non-capitalist economic practices are quite pervasive (Gibson-Graham 1996, 2006; Gibson-Graham et al. 2013: https://communityeconomies.org/). More broadly, they argue that these are habitually overlooked by Marxists, who suffer from what Fred Block (2018) dubs capitalism as an illusion. Gibson-Graham calls this capitalocentrism: the presumption that sooner or later the logic of capital rules.

Such potentially destabilizing alternatives are widespread. The World Social Forum ecosystem is organized around one "no" (to capitalism) and many more-than-capitalist "yeses": other worlds are possible (Santos 2008). Informality, economic practices operating beyond the "rule of law" of capitalist formal state–market relations, are more common across the post-colony than are those that fall within it (Sheppard 2019). Informality is not just a way for marginalized populations to survive, but is also regularly resorted to by the middle classes and economic and political elites seeking to evade the rule of law—a reminder that more-than-capitalist alternatives can be exploitative as well as emancipatory. Beyond this are state-led more-than-capitalist experiments, such as those of Latin America's "pink tide" of progressive regimes in the early 2000s, or China's current Belt and Road Initiative (Liu and Dunford 2016). Finally, in these days of out-of-control global warming it does not seem a stretch to conclude that biophysical processes not only exceed capitalist attempts to commodify nature (e.g., carbon trading, full cost pricing, environmental services) but pose an existential crisis for capitalism itself (Klein 2015; Moore 2015).

Conclusion

Since the early 1980s, geographical political economy has flourished as a sub-field of political economy, and heterodox economics more generally, bringing geographical perspectives to Marxian analyses of capitalism. The overarching conclusion is that Geography *matters*; that thinking geographically challenges some taken-for-granted arguments about capitalism (Massey and Allen 1989). On the one hand, examining how capitalist political economic processes produce geographies—spatialities—that themselves modify those processes, this research identifies additional contradictions, instabilities and unpredictabilities that further undermine the coherence of capitalist commodity production, exchange, profit realization and the distribution of the surplus. Put more technically, the capitalist space economy is an out-of-equilibrium complex dynamical system in which space-time is itself endogenous (Prigogine 1996; Rosser 2000; DeLanda 2006; Sheppard 2008). Uneven geographical development under capitalism—exacerbated by neoliberalization—enriches some bodies and places through the impoverishment of others, implying that capitalism fails both socially and spatially to deliver on the promise of prosperity for all who abide by its norms. More deeply, a spatialized theorization of capitalism poses hard questions for Marxian theory.

The second aspect of thinking geographically—conceptualizing capitalism as co-evolving with cultural and more-than-human processes that consistently exceed attempts to absorb them into capitalism through commodification and marketization—suggests the additional insight that capitalism's outsides are also capable of destabilizing its insides. If capitalism cannot deliver on its promise then stageist conceptions of capitalist development are bankrupt, implying that those bodies and places experiencing underdevelopment are compelled to experiment with more-than-capitalist alternatives (whose spatialities affect their success). Taking these seriously reveal capitalism as much less hegemonic, and more vulnerable, than it seems.

References

Balland, P-A., Rigby, D. and Boschma, R. (2015) The technological resilience of US cities, *Cambridge Journal of Regions, Economy and Society*, 8(2): 167–184.
Bergmann, L. (2012) A coevolutionary approach to the capitalist space economy, *Environment and Planning A*, 44(3): 518–537.

Bergmann, L., Sheppard, E. and Plummer, P. (2009) Capitalism beyond harmonious equilibrium: mathematics as if human agency mattered, *Environment and Planning A*, 41(2): 265–283.

Bettelheim, C. (1972) Appendix I: theoretical comments, in Emmanuel, A.G. (ed.) *Unequal Exchange: A Study of the Imperialism of Trade*, New York: Monthly Review Press, pp. 287–289.

Block, F. (2018) *Capitalism: Future of an Illusion*, Berkeley, CA: University of California Press.

Brenner, N. (1999) Beyond state-centrism? Space, territoriality, and geographical scale in globalization studies, *Theory and Society*, 28(1): 39–78.

Brenner, N. (2004) *New State Spaces: Urban Governance and the Rescaling of Statehood*, Oxford: Oxford University Press.

Callon, M. (1998) *The Laws of the Markets*, Oxford: Blackwell.

Cockshott, W.P. (2005) Robust correlations between prices and labour values: a comment, *Cambridge Journal of Economics*, 29(2): 309–316.

Coe, N. and Yeung, H.W-c. (2015) *Global Production Networks: Theorizing Economic Development in an Interconnected World*, Oxford: Oxford University Press.

DeLanda, M. (2006) *A New Philosophy of Society: Assemblage Theory and Social Complexity*, London: Continuum.

Dicken, P. (2015) *Global Shift: Mapping the Changing Contours of the World Economy*, New York: Guilford Press.

Dicken, P., Kelly, P.F., Olds, K. and Yeung, H.W-c. (2001) Chains and networks, territories and scales: towards a relational framework for analysing the global economy, *Global Networks*, 1(2): 89–112.

Dunford, M.F. (1988) *Capital, the State, and Regional Development*, London: Pion.

Dunford, M. (1990) Theories of regulation, *Environment and Planning D: Society and Space*, 8: 297–322.

Featherstone, D., Ince, A., Mackinnon, D., Strauss, K. and Cumbers, A. (2012) Progressive localism and the construction of political alternatives, *Transactions of the Insititute of British Geographers*, NS, 37(1): 177–182.

Frank, A.G. (1979) *Dependent Accumulation and Underdevelopment*, New York: Monthly Review Press.

Gibson-Graham, J.K. (1996) *The End of Capitalism (As We Knew It)*, Oxford: Blackwell.

Gibson-Graham, J.K. (2006) *A Postcapitalist Politics*, Minneapolis, MN: University of Minnesota Press.

Gibson-Graham, J.K., Cameron, J. and Healy, S. (2013) *Take Back the Economy, Any Time, Any Place*, Minneapolis, MN: University of Minnesota Press.

Goldfrank, B. and Schrank, A. (2009) Municipal neoliberalism and municipal socialism: urban political economy in Latin America, *International Journal of Urban and Regional Research*, 33(2): 443–462.

Hart, G. (2002) Geography and development: development/s beyond neoliberalism? Power, culture, political economy, *Progress in Human Geography*, 26(6): 812–822.

Harvey, D. (1982) *The Limits to Capital*, Oxford: Basil Blackwell.

Harvey, D. (1995) Militant particularism and global ambition: the conceptual politics of place, space, and environment in the work of Raymond Williams, *Social Text*, 42: 69–98.

Harvey, D. (2005) *Spaces of Neoliberalization: Towards a Theory of Uneven Geographical Development*, Wiesbaden: Fritz Steiner Verlag.

Harvey, D. (2006a) *A Brief History of Neoliberalism*, Oxford: Oxford University Press.

Harvey, D. (2006b) *Spaces of Global Capitalism: A Theory of Uneven Geographical Development*, London: Verso.

Harvey, D. (2010) *The Enigma of Capital*, Oxford: Oxford University Press.

Harvey, D. (2014) *Seventeen Contradictions and the End of Capitalism*, Oxford: Oxford University Press.

Herod, A. (2001) *Labor Geographies: Workers and the Landscapes of Capitalism*, New York: Guilford Press.

Herod, A. (2003) Geographies of labor internationalism, *Social Science History*, 27(4): 501–523.

Hudson, R. and Sadler, D. (1986) Contesting works closures in Western Europe's old industrial regions: defending place or betraying class?, in Scott, A.J. and Storper, M. (eds) *Production, Work, Territory: The Geographical Anatomy of Industrial Capitalism*, London: Allen & Unwin, pp. 172–193.

Jessop, B. (1990) Regulation theories in retrospect and prospect, *Economy and Society*, 19(2): 153–216.

Klein, N. (2015) *This Changes Everything: Capitalism vs. the Climate*, Simon & Schuster.

Leitner, H. and Miller, B. (2007) Scale and the limitations of ontological debate: a commentary on Marston, Jones and Woodward, *Transactions of the Institute of British Geographers*, 32(1): 116–125.

Leitner, H., Sheppard, E., Sziarto, K.M. and Maringanti, A. (2007) Contesting urban futures: decentering neoliberalism, in Leitner, H., Peck, J. and Sheppard, E. (eds) *Contesting Neoliberalism: Urban Frontiers*, New York: Guilford Press, pp. 1–25.

Liossatos, P. (1980) Unequal exchange and regional disparities, *Papers in Regional Science*, 45(1): 87–103.

Liossatos, P. (1983) Commodity production and interregional transfers of value, in Moulaert, F. and Salinas, P.W. (eds) *Regional Analysis and the New International Division of Labor*, Berlin: Springer, pp. 57–75.

Liossatos, P. (1988) Value and competition in a spatial context: a Marxian model, *Papers of the Regional Science Association*, 45: 87–103.

Liu, W. and Dunford, M. (2016) Inclusive globalization: unpacking China's Belt and Road Initiative, *Area Development and Policy*, 1(3): 323–340.

Logan, J. and Molotch, H.L. (2007 [1987]) *Urban Fortunes: The Political Economy of Place*, Los Angeles, CA: University of California Press.

Markusen, A. (1980) *Regions and Regionalism: A Marxist View*, Working paper no. 326, University of California, Berkeley, Institute of Urban and Regional Development.

Marx, K. (1967 [1867]) *Capital: A Critique of Political Economy*, Vol. 1, New York: International Publishers.

Massey, D. (1984) *Spatial Divisions of Labour: Social Structure and the Geography of Production*, London: Methuen.

Massey, D. (1991) A global sense of place, *Marxism Today*, June: 24–29.

Massey, D. (1993) Power-geometry and progressive sense of place, in Bird, J., Curtis, B., Putnam, T., Robertson, G. and Tickner, L. (eds) *Mapping the Futures: Local Cultures, Global Change*, London: Routledge, pp. 280–288.

Massey, D. (1994) *Space, Place and Gender*, Minneapolis, MN: University of Minnesota Press.

Massey, D. (2005) *For Space*, London: SAGE.

Massey, D. and Allen, J. (1989) *Geography Matters!*, Cambridge: Cambridge University Press in association with the Open University.

McCann, E. (2011) Urban policy mobilities and global circuits of knowledge: toward a research agenda, *Annals of the Association of American Geographers*, 101(1): 107–130.

Milanovic, B. (2016) *Global Inequality: A New Approach for the Age of Globalization*, Cambridge, MA: Harvard University Press.

Moore, J.W. (2015) *Capitalism in the Web of Life: Ecology and the Accumulation of Capital*, London: Verso.

Morishima, M. (1973) *Marx's Economics: A Dual Theory of Value and Growth*, Cambridge: Cambridge University Press.

Okishio, N. (1961) Technical change and the rate of profit, *Kobe University Economic Review*, 7: 85–99.

Peck, J. (2010) *Constructions of Neoliberal Reason*, Oxford: Oxford University Press.

Peck, J. (2017) Uneven regional development, in Richardson, D., Castree, N., Goodchild, M.F., Kobayashi, A., Liu, W. and Marston, R.A. (eds) *International Encyclopedia of Geography: People, the Earth, Environment and Technology*, Oxford: Wiley-Blackwell, 13 pp.

Peck, J. and Theodore, N. (2007) Variegated capitalism, *Progress in Human Geography*, 31(6): 731–772.

Peck, J. and Theodore, N. (2015) *Fast Policy: Experimental Statecraft at the Thresholds of Neoliberalism*, Minneapolis, MN: University of Minnesota Press.

Peck, J. and Theodore, N. (2019) Still neoliberalism?, *South Atlantic Quarterly*, 118(2): 245–265.

Peck, J. and Tickell, A. (2002) Neoliberalizing space, in Brenner, N. and Theodore, N. (eds) *Spaces of Neoliberalism: Urban Restructuring in North America and Western Europe*, Oxford: Blackwell, pp. 34–57.

Plummer, P.S. and Sheppard, E. (2006) Geography matters: agency, structures and dynamics, *Journal of Economic Geography*, 6(5): 619–637.

Polanyi, K. (2001 [1944]) *The Great Transformation: The Political and Economic Origins of Our Time*, Boston, MA: Beacon Press.

Prigogine, I. (1996) *The End of Certainty: Time, Chaos and the New Laws of Nature*, New York: The Free Press.

Rigby, D. and Essletzbichler, J. (1997) Evolution, process variety, and regional trajectories of technical change in U.S. manufacturing, *Economic Geography*, 73: 269–285.

Rosser, J.B. Jr (2000) Aspects of dialectics and non-linear dynamics, *Cambridge Journal of Economics*, 24: 311–324.

Rostow, W.W. (1960) *The Stages of Economic Growth: A Non-Communist Manifesto*, Cambridge: Cambridge University Press.

Routledge, P. (2017) *Space Invaders: Radical Geographies of Protest*, London: Pluto Press.

Roy, A. (2010) *Poverty Capital*, New York: Wiley-Blackwell.

Santos, B.d.S. (2008) *Another Knowledge Is Possible: Beyond Northern Epistemologies*, London: Verso.

Scott, A.J. (1988) *New Industrial Spaces: Flexible Production Organization and Regional Development in North America and Western Europe*, London: Pion.

Sheppard, E. (2004) The spatiality of limits to capital, *Antipode*, 36(3): 470–479.

Sheppard, E. (2005) Free trade: the very idea! From Manchester boosterism to global management, *Transactions of the Institute of British Geographers*, 30(2): 151–172.

Sheppard, E. (2008) Geographic dialectics?, *Environment and Planning A*, 40: 2603–2612.

Sheppard, E. (2012) Trade, globalization and uneven development: entanglements of geographical political economy, *Progress in Human Geography*, 36(1): 44–71.

Sheppard, E. (2015) Thinking geographically: globalizing capitalism, and beyond, *Annals of the Association of American Geographers*, 105(6): 1113–1134.

Sheppard, E. (2016) *Limits to Globalization: Disruptive Geographies of Capitalist Development*, Oxford: Oxford University Press.

Sheppard, E. (2018) Heterodoxy as orthodoxy: prolegomenon for a geographical political economy, in Clark, G., Feldman, M., Gertler, M. and Wójcik, D. (eds) *The New Oxford Handbook of Economic Geography*, Oxford: Oxford University Press, pp. 159–178.

Sheppard, E. (2019) Globalizing capitalism's raggedy fringes: thinking through Jakarta, *Area Development and Policy*, 4(1): 1–27.

Sheppard, E. and Barnes, T.J. (1986) Instabilities in the geography of capitalist production: collective vs. individual profit maximization, *Annals of the Association of American Geographers*, 76: 493–507.

Sheppard, E. and Barnes, T.J. (2015 [1990]) *The Capitalist Space Economy: Geographical Analysis after Marx, Ricardo and Sraffa*, London: Routledge.

Sheppard, E. and Leitner, H. (2010) Quo vadis neoliberalism? The remaking of global capitalist governance after the Washington Consensus, *Geoforum*, 41(2): 185–194.

Smith, N. (1984) *Uneven Development: Nature, Capital and the Production of Space*, Oxford: Basil Blackwell.

Soja, E.W. (1980) The socio-spatial dialectic, *Annals of the Association of American Geographers*, 70: 207–225.

Storper, M. (1997) *The Regional World: Territorial Development in a Global Economy*, New York: Guilford Press.

Storper, M. and Walker, R. (1989) *The Capitalist Imperative: Territory, Technology and Industrial Growth*, Oxford: Basil Blackwell.

Tickell, A. and Peck, J. (1992) Accumulation, regulation and the geographies of post-Fordism: missing links in regulationist research, *Progress in Human Geography*, 16: 190–218.

Tsoulfidis, L. and Tsaliki, P. (2019) Classical political economy and the evolution of post-war capitalism, in *Classical Political Economics and Modern Capitalism*, Cham: Springer, pp. 405–437.

Webber, M. (1996) Profitability and growth in multiregion systems: theory and a model, *Economic Geography*, 72(3): 335–352.

Webber, M. (1997) Profitability and growth in multiregional systems: prologue to a historical geography, *Economic Geography*, 73(4): 405–426.

Webber, M. and Rigby, D. (1996) *The Golden Age Illusion: Rethinking Postwar Capitalism*, New York: Guilford Press.

Wójcik, D. (2013) Where governance fails: advanced business services and the offshore world, *Progress in Human Geography*, 37(3): 330–347.

Wolpe, H. (1980) *The Articulation of Modes of Production: Essays from Economy and Society*, London: Routledge.

Wright, I. (2016) *The Law of Value: A Contribution to the Classical Approach to Economic Analysis*, Milton Keynes: The Open University.

12 Reclaiming local contexts: disrupting the virtual economy

Sabine U. O'Hara

Introduction

Attempts to alter the mainstream economic paradigm and account for the social and environmental context of markets have had limited success. Both ecological economics and feminist economics have offered alternative valuation frameworks to include non-market value and acknowledge the growing material destruction resulting from a market-based paradigm. Yet progress has been slow. Markets and neo-liberal valuation frameworks remain firmly embedded in economic policies and success measures. The growing move to virtual markets seems to exacerbate disruptions to social, cultural, and environmental context systems that maintain stability, resilience, and health.

The consequences are increasingly noticeable and include changing weather patterns, unprecedented floods, droughts, heat waves, and wildfires as well as social unrest despite rising life expectancies and incomes, with 50 percent of the world population now considered a part of the middle class or above.

This chapter examines the underlying causes of these trends and argues that they reflect the growing dematerialization of economic transactions, and life overall. It further argues that a strategy to reverse these trends is the re-localization of economies, a process which is emerging around the world. The process of re-embedding local economies also reintroduces ecosystems services and civic connections into depleted context systems.

Virtuality and the loss of context

The year was 1992. A few years earlier I had moved from my native Germany to the United States. It was a hot summer day and I was on my way to run a few errands at a recently expanded shopping mall. As I entered the mall a wave of cold air hit me. This was a familiar experience by now. Every shopping mall was air-conditioned here. Maybe it was my involvement in preparations for the so-called Rio Earth Summit – the UN Conference on Environment and Development – at the time, but this particular wave of cold air on a hot summer day seemed to have a sense of intentionality about it and the thought struck me that maybe cooling public spaces was not simply about keeping people comfortable, but about isolating them from the reality of heat and its impact on their local communities.

There is certainly nothing romantic about a heat wave or a cold spell, and cooling and heating systems can be lifesavers. But there is also something to be said for experiencing the changes of the seasons and those emanating from longer-term climate trends and shorter-term fluctuations in weather patterns. Sensing nature is important. New research on nature deficit syndrome, for example, is raising awareness of the importance of human–nature connections. Biases against sensing nature and our physical/biological bodies have been well documented by feminist scholars. They have also given rise to positive connotations associated with technology that isolates us from nature and sanitizes our physical/biological bodies (Griffin 2016; Harding and O'Barr 1987).

Food is one of the expressions of our growing disconnect from nature. Urban dwellers, especially the younger demographic, no longer know where their food comes from. Lack of access to fresh, unprocessed food is also an expression of discriminatory practices. In the United States full-service grocery stores are conspicuously absent from low-income minority neighborhoods. The intentional practice of dismantling decentralized networks of small grocery stores in urban minority communities is well documented as are its resultant adverse health outcomes and higher opportunity costs of food access (Reese 2019; Bell and Standish 2009). In Washington DC, for example, the rise of suburban grocery chains led to the demise of the District Grocery Store Cooperatives (Crowe et al. 2018). It was exacerbated by marketing studies that associated *suburban* with White, middle class, and quality of life, and *urban* with African American, low-income, and drugs (Pawasarat and Quinn 2001).

Recreation too is becoming increasingly disconnected from nature. It no longer takes place outdoors, but in front of a screen. Video games have become a sport in itself, and while all age groups have dramatically increased the amount of time they spend engaged in gaming, the 26–35-year-old age group is leading the way (Anderton 2019). Those committed to some level of physical activity can play golf, tennis, table tennis, or squash in front of the screen. Almost all on-line games limit social contact except possibly for interaction with a virtual community of fellow players who may never meet in person.

Shopping too has given way to the computer screen. Amazon, the most prominent example of the growing virtual marketplace, went from $89 billion in sales and a net loss of $241 million to $232 billion in sales and a net income of $10 billion in just five years. Victor Gruen, the architect credited with inventing the shopping mall, became disillusioned with his well-intentioned invention toward the end of his life. He had envisioned the mall as a social focal point in the artificial and community-deprived environment of suburbia. Yet the failure of the mall is mild in light of the new virtuality. Sandburn writes: "But for all its flaws, the mall did manage to bring people together in ways that, in the era of personal devices, even Gruen might appreciate" (2017). Virtuality has led to even greater social isolation than suburbia, along with the continued disconnect from the social/cultural and physical/environmental context that sustains all markets.

Losing social-physical contexts

The growing isolation associated with expanding virtual markets is but one issue; labor implications are another. As one-third of US malls have closed their doors, 450,000 jobs have been eliminated and only half of them have been replaced by jobs in the virtual economy. These new jobs are not only fewer but different. Services traditionally performed in-house have been outsourced to contracting firms and freelancers. Many job functions, including clerical, financial, procurement, and logistics services, can be provided on-line from almost anywhere (Autor et al. 2017). A growing segment of the new labor force works in low-wage jobs without traditional benefits while their new workplace is often rife with safety violations. At Amazon, for example, the pressure to fill orders and meet efficiency goals runs up against the physical limits of workers who need rest and care. The response to the physical, mental, and emotional needs of workers has not been improved workplace conditions, but the replacement of labor with robots. Amazon, for example, prides itself in improving its safety record through increased reliance on robotics rather than respect for the regenerative and restorative needs of its workers.

The pressures associated with the replacement of biological and ecological systems through mechanical and virtual ones have implications for social and civic engagement as well. Its net result is the erosion of social support systems and growing pressures to work two or three jobs to make ends meet (O'Hara 1997, 1998, 2004, 2014). Feminist scholars have long called attention to the biases against biological and ecological functions associated with the leaking and fluctuating cycles of the female body (Price and Shildrick 1999). The continued de-contextualization of work in the virtual economy now renders even the less cyclical male body as unreliable, and replaces him with the time-independent mechanical and digital bodies of robots.

Despite these concerns, there is some good news on the economic development front. Recent studies document progress in both income and life expectancy globally (Kharas and Fengler 2019). The double impact of a growing middle class and growing life expectancy is considered remarkable progress. A larger middle class may also imply more satisfaction, at least among those who are its recent arrivals (Kahneman and Deaton 2010). There is, however, little evidence to suggest that a growing middle class will lead to more democratic governance or better public services. Governments may instead find themselves unable to meet the expectations of a growing middle class for universal health care, public education, affordable housing, and environmental protection. Some of the resulting discontent may already be evident despite improved conditions. The *Washington Post* described 2019 as "the year of the street protester" (Diehl 2019). These protests may articulate at least in part a discontent with abstract improvements that neglect the concrete social/cultural and environmental/ physical contexts that shape people's lives and livelihoods.

Power and the loss of markets

Ironically, the continuing de-contextualization of markets has also led to a growing departure from market structures associated with the best ideals of the market. Markets at their best are decentralized, have a large number of players, and have distributed power. This is not what the marketplace of the virtual economy looks like. It is characterized by the so-called "superstar firm". These firms conduct business outside of the constraints of local or regional time and space. Economic transactions of production, distribution, and consumption take place around the clock and around the globe. Manufacturers and retailers, regardless of their location, can sell their wares on the digital platforms of superstar firms, and consumers can buy anytime and anywhere.

Amazon is a particularly compelling example of a superstar firm. It owns the digital platforms that shape the virtual marketplace within which it operates. It uses artificial intelligence and social media to not only facilitate exchange in its marketplace, but to create the marketplace itself and its demand. Superstar firms demand commissions and fees from manufacturers and retailers whose products they sell. The algorithms Amazon uses for its marketing purposes allow it to promote products it selects for increased demand. These same products may generate lucrative commissions and fees. Market power for the virtual superstar firm is therefore associated with both vertical and horizontal integration by controlling supply chains and functions across the array of services associated with the production, distribution, and consumption of products and services (Duhigg 2019).

Superstar firms also operate outside the bounds of regional and national laws that govern labor, procurement, data, technology, and commerce. In the United States just one regulation has been crafted to curtail the monopolistic power of superstar firms. The European Union has been more active in taking steps to regulate the virtual economy and ensure the transparency and accountability needed for a more competitive marketplace (European Commission 2011; Erixon 2019). In his book, *The Great Reversal*, economist Thomas Philippon documents the decline of competition in US markets and the growing power of a small number of firms (2019). The result has been negative for US workers and consumers alike. Since enforcement of existing antitrust regulations has been lax, and the expansion of regulations of the virtual marketplace has been slow, virtual markets look more and more like the monopoly markets of early capitalism. To be sure, the picture is complex. While Amazon squeezes its third-party vendors and sweeps workplace safety violations aside, it also supports the use of public transportation by its workforce and prides itself in green practices that improve environmental conditions. The power of superstar firms and virtual markets may therefore have somewhat ambiguous consequences. It may provide unprecedented consumer access, yet also unprecedented growth in conspicuous consumption, and unprecedented power to undermine regulatory frameworks.

As I have argued previously, the loss of the face-to-face communication of a traditional marketplace also results in the loss of differentiated expressions of value associated with a particular product, service, culture, and context (O'Hara 1997, 1998). The personalization of the digital marketplace as a place of diverse and decentralized expressions of value has been realized partially at best. Niche products, specialized customer service, and diversified market access are limited in scope. As human interaction is reduced to consumption and production rather than multifaceted expressions of needs and aspirations, the resulting expressions of isolation and discontent may well end up on the streets and may account for growing expressions of unrest even in light of higher incomes and life expectancies.

Material realities of decontextualized economies

The growing virtual economy is of course not virtual. It feeds on the material reality of workers, communities, and millions of organisms that process, buffer, and absorb the emissions and waste by-products of virtuality. As the economist Nicolai Georgescu-Roegen pointed out decades ago, what matters is not only the flow of inputs, outputs, and waste associated with the production and consumption of goods and services, but the very process of their conversion (Georgescu-Roegen 1984; see also Daly 1991; Gowdy and O'Hara 1997). There is no sustainable rate at which non-renewables can be processed; and there is no sustainable rate of substitution without material and energy consequences. All conversion uses energy and the process of conversion itself creates entropy regardless of the material flows involved. Attention must therefore focus on what conversion and distribution process minimizes energy and thus entropy; and what conversion and distribution process places the least amount of pressure on the adsorptive, buffering, and regulating capacities of the ecosphere and human communities (O'Hara 2016, 2014, 2010). This is nowhere more evident than in the support needs of the virtual economy. The around-the-clock and around-the-globe access it demands relies on enormous amounts of energy to feed millions of servers that store data about supply chains, on-demand orders, customer demographics, and personal pictures of babies and pets. What is virtual is therefore merely the facilitation of a material process of increased production and consumption that shifts attention squarely back to the core questions of economics: what? how? for whom? and how much?

The Intergovernmental Panel on Climate Change (IPCC) found that large-scale discontinuities in the Earth's systems which ensure the stability of regulatory cycles that impact hydrological, carbon, and climate systems are nearing a tipping point (Lenton et al. 2019; PIK 2017). William Rees writes:

> A cascade of data shows that the human enterprise is in ecological overshoot, consuming nature's goods and services faster than ecosystems can regenerate and

dumping (often toxic) wastes beyond nature's processing/recycling capacity. In short, we are currently "financing" economic growth by liquidating the biophysical systems upon which humanity ultimately depends. (2020)

How long will adjustments in population growth and conspicuous consumption take that reduce the speed at which we are nearing the tipping point of Earth's regulating systems? And who will make the needed adjustment? Will women, children, the elderly, and minorities again be the ones left to adjust to the environmental and social implications of a tipping point scenario? As feminist scholars and ecological economists have argued, marginalized populations have always carried a disproportional share of the burden of overused and undervalued ecosystems and communities (O'Hara 2010; Mellor 1992). If the strategy we hope to adopt is less growth, no growth or de-growth, are those at the top of the consumption pyramid ready to adopt it? The harm to democratic institutions associated with the unconstrained use of personal data in the virtual commons does not paint an optimistic picture. It suggests that the marginalization of those whose voices have gone long unheard will continue. Change will therefore have to come from intentional policies that reverse the default outcomes of de-contextualization and level the playing field.

Reclaiming local contexts

In light of the continued disappearance of social and environmental contexts and the disparate burdens it allots, it may seem that all is lost. Yet there are some hopeful signs. Communities are reclaiming their local economies and contexts. This is especially evident in the food sector. In the United States, the country that leads the world in market concentration, superstar agribusinesses, and over-processed food, local food initiatives are cropping up everywhere. According to the United States Department of Agriculture (USDA), farmers markets have almost doubled in the last ten years. The face-to-face interaction they offer makes room for expressions of value beyond those captured in prices. While they constitute only a small aspect of the re-localized food economy, they can be important catalysts for scalability. Food systems are webs of activity, resources, and people that cut across sectors, and represent a multitude of organizational arrangements (Chase and Grubinger 2014).

In an effort to support the re-localization of the food economy, the University of the District of Columbia (UDC) and its College of Agriculture, Urban Sustainability and Environmental Sciences (CAUSES) launched its Urban Food Hubs initiative. The objective of the Hubs is to improve the quality of life and economic opportunity of DC neighborhoods by improving food and water security and health outcomes, creating jobs, alleviating disparities, and reconnecting people to nature. According to the USDA, Food Hubs represent an effort to scale small local food businesses by pooling resources to reduce costs and aggregate production, distribution, and marketing services (Barham et al. 2012). The UDC model expands this definition to include four integrated components: food production, processing, distribution, and closing the loop through waste and water management.

While all UDC-CAUSES Urban Food Hubs include these four components, their specific characteristics may vary based on the physical, environmental, social, and cultural context where a Hub is located (O'Hara 2015, 2017). This adaptive approach enables the Urban Food Hubs to incorporate community goals and resources unique to their locations. The creative tension between consistency and local adaptability is an important consideration for local sustainability and resilience initiatives beyond the food system.

All four components of the Urban Food Hubs model offer opportunities for local business start-ups. Food production may take place on roofs, in raised beds, in small greenhouses and decommissioned factory buildings, but also in soil-less hydroponic and aquaponic systems. Food processing may take the form of catering businesses, and hot sauce, pesto, and smoothies produced in incubator kitchens and food trucks; food distribution may happen through farmers markets, direct marketing to local restaurants and ethnic food stores, or through community-supported agriculture networks that supply weekly deliveries of fresh food rather than selling by the pound; and an array of activities including composting food waste and selling the compost for soil enhancement, capturing water run-off and reusing it for drip irrigation, installing rain gardens and green roofs to reduce stormwater run-off, and generating energy in bio-digesters comprise the fourth component of the Food Hubs. Each component offers opportunities to turn negative externalities into positives.

Local food economies can thus serve as the motor to revitalize communities. In his book *Food Town USA*, Mark Winne documents the benefits of local food economies even in mid-sized cities that are not associated with the food celebrity status of metro areas like New York or Seattle (2019). This challenges the widely accepted base theory model of economic development, which places primary importance on producing goods and services that satisfy *external* demand. Demand that is *internal* to a region can play an important role in fueling a local economy. Considerable benefits can accrue when it becomes attractive for residents and businesses to spend their money at home and dollars no longer leak outside of a region.

The recirculating aquaponics and hydroponics systems of the UDC-CAUSES Urban Food Hubs also illustrate the opportunity for cutting-edge technological innovation. A unique aerator developed for urban locations enhances the recirculating water with dissolved oxygen by utilizing the molecular spin of the water molecules rather than compressor systems. The technology uses less than half the energy of other soil-less systems and less than 10 percent of the water of conventional agriculture (Kakovitch and O'Hara 2014).

Some vegetable varieties grown in the soil-less systems have also exhibited higher nutrient density and thus higher nutritional value than the same varieties grown in soil. Awareness of the connections between water, energy, health, and food triggers an important reassessment of the value of food. Food systems are not simply linear supply chains where the greatest benefit is the lowest price of food; they are complex systems with multiple social and environmental impacts. Cheap food produced in industrial-scale farms may therefore not be cheap at all, but may come at the expense of ecosystems and human health that carries enormous social costs.

Daniel Baker describes another example of a local food economy that benefitted from technological innovation. Panela, also known as jiggery, is an artisanal block sugar that predates white sugar and is produced by small sugarcane farmers. India produces more block sugar than any country in the world, and Columbia has the world's highest per capita output in panela. Traditional production methods consume vast amounts of firewood. By introducing a new evaporator that utilizes bagasse, the waste fiber that remains after the sugarcane is crushed to extract juice, it was possible to reduce the use of firewood by more than 80 percent and to reduce the time demand of evaporation by 40 percent. Small producers can therefore save time and lower their production costs (Baker 2017; O'Hara and Baker 2020). The new bagasse evaporators are also built locally with available skills and materials. In Columbia, for example, local metal shops fabricate the evaporators in partnership with a technical high school. The collaboration ensures that skilled labor will be available to build the evaporators. Since the new technology can be produced locally, it adds to the already significant employment impact of panela sugar production. In Colombia it supports 120,000 permanent jobs, and directly or indirectly engages 350,000 individuals in the supply chain of panela sugar (Gilbert and Pinzon 2014; Rodriguez et al. 2007).

As these examples illustrate, local economies can strengthen not only human networks, but also human–non-human connections. Farmers in Central America, for example, linked human economic goals to non-human conservation goals by reasserting traditional methods of shade coffee production.

Coffee grown under shade trees supports greater biodiversity, and shade coffee farms tend to be owned by smallholder farmers (Jha et al. 2014; Méndez et al. 2010). Between 2000 and 2009 Costa Rica alone saw a 50 percent decline in its shade coffee areas (Jha et al. 2014). The growing interest in specialty coffees with environmental certifications has helped reverse this trend and supports local efforts to maintain and reintroduce shade coffee production among small local growers. The potential to increase investment in these types of projects can be further enhanced through the use of payments for ecosystems services. This may include the sale of carbon credits to avoid deforestation and stormwater credits to reduce the risk of flooding. Scaling such initiatives can facilitate change at multiple levels. While initial efforts to re-localize markets may be personal and highly local, the potential for larger regional and trans-regional efforts may be considerable, especially when they are supported by incentive policies.

Another attribute of local economies that also connects them through larger networks are alternative models of ownership. Many local economy networks assert the value of shared goods, services, resources, and space and challenge the private property ownership model that is one of the hallmarks of markets. Participation in the sharing economy is defined through user access rather than ownership. This allows for the use of excess capacity in owned goods and services. When access to goods and services is shared more effectively, their value increases for individual users as well as for the community at large. For example, private vehicles go unused for 95 percent of their lifetime. Car-sharing models capture the benefits of the unused time without appro- priating the resources required to produce additional cars. Estimates suggest that one shared car replaces 15 owned ones and delivers the benefits of a car at significantly lower cost (Ross 2019; Prieto et al. 2017). As individuals provide access to their spare bedrooms, the need for hotel rooms is reduced and an additional income stream accrues to the homeowners. This has reduced travel costs associated with overnight stays by an average of 30 to 60 percent world- wide (Yaraghi and Ravi 2016). More recent additions to the sharing economy include furniture and carpet leasing. These services offer a full range of product installation, cleaning, maintenance, and eventually removal and recycling. Sharing services also include co-working services that provide shared work- space and equipment, and peer-to-peer lending platforms that provide access to capital at lower rates than those offered through traditional lending services.

Growth in the sharing economy has been substantial. By 2016 the market was valued at $26 billion, with new services and sharing platforms emerging almost daily. Bike-sharing services doubled from 2014 to 2018, and the number of shared bikes has increased almost twenty-fold during the same time from

950,000 in 2014 to 18.2 million in 2018. Car sharing grew from a local network to a global service available in over 1,000 cities. In 2015 an estimated 7 million users participated in car sharing, up from 350,000 in 2006, and projections indicate a usership of 36 million by 2025. Revenue totaled $1 billion in 2013 and over $5 billion five years later. Car- and bike-sharing programs can be organized as commercial businesses, cooperatives, public sector initiatives, and ad hoc user groups. Many programs started as community groups, but most are private sector businesses today.

The collaborative peer-to-peer and business-to-business interactions of sharing economies often take place via an on-line platform that manages access via smartphones and mapping apps. These on-line platforms represent aspects of the virtual economy at its best. Sharing economies grew out of the open-source community that seeks a more democratized marketplace. Sharing economies can also facilitate the re-localization of economic activity into its social and environmental context while connecting multiple local networks into sharing and learning communities.

Re-localizing economic activity can also bring local expertize into focus. Expert knowledge is useful, yet may not be sufficient and may even create distortions if it becomes too generalized or abstract. Local experts are therefore needed to provide details about local social, cultural, and environmental characteristics, assets, and barriers. One of the barriers to local participation is the specialized language associated with economic development expertise. Economic development goals tend to use the particular shorthand of growth rates, percentages, and benchmarks. This language, and the viewpoint it encodes, often excludes local participants who have valid and important knowledge to contribute. When goals are stated in plain language and strategies to move toward the goals are clearly articulated, it becomes easier to communicate a shared vision of successful outcomes and to identify a set of indicators that measure progress toward the shared vision.

An approach to level the playing field and assert the knowledge of local experts is the Five Pillars model of development (O'Hara 2019; O'Hara and Vazquez 2007). The Five Pillar categories identify community assets in education, health, social and cultural amenities, environmental quality, and access to information and transportation. Indicators within each of the five categories can determine a measure of the assets, while the categories themselves serve as a structuring element for a community vision developed in focus groups that write a shared story of successful development outcomes in the future. This structured storytelling approach invites a wider range of participants into the development and planning process. A story paints a picture in our minds, and most people can see that picture when a story is told. To make the picture that the story paints a reality may still require numbers to help draw a road map to get from the current state to the outcome that the story helps visualize. The indicators of the Five Pillar categories can also serve to measure the gaps between the vision of a successful development future and the present state. The approach thus serves as a way to both tell the story and measure progress toward making it a reality.

These examples illustrate emerging local economies that bring the concrete social, cultural, environmental, and physical context of local communities back into focus. From production networks to sharing resources, goods, and services, to green technology and local planning initiatives, these efforts paint a hopeful picture. They also suggest that the influence of fields like ecological economics and feminist economics may assert itself slowly but surely at the local and regional level even as their acceptance in national and global policy arenas is slow.

Conclusions

Attempts to alter the mainstream economic paradigm and to account for the social, cultural, and environmental context of economic activity beyond what is captured in markets have had limited success. In fact, markets and neo-liberal valuation frameworks seem to have grown in influence. The expansion of the virtual economy has further accelerated the dis-embedding of economic activity. At the same time, effective policies that counteract the negative externalities of an increasingly contextless virtual economy have declined. Existing antitrust policies have not been fully applied to the growing virtual economy and new policies have been slow to emerge, especially in the United States.

The consequences of this accelerating dis-embedding process are well documented. As the virtual economy feeds on the physical and social realities of real people, communities, and ecosystems, the outcome has been the continual undermining of social and environmental systems manifesting itself in changing weather patterns, unprecedented floods, droughts, heat waves, and wildfires, but also in growing social unrest especially among young people, despite rising average life expectancies and income levels.

This suggests that Earth's social and environmental context systems will not be rendered invisible without resistance. Communities around the world are showing signs of re-localizing and re-contextualizing their economies. These local efforts take the form of decentralized, local food systems, green infra-structure and green technology initiatives, sharing economies that shift from private property ownership to shared usership, and local financing models that range from informal networks to formal micro-financing arrangements. These models reintroduce human to human and human to non-human connections and have the potential to reintroduce ecosystems services and civic connec-tions into depleted environmental and social contexts.

The growing expressions of unrest that have been documented around the world may therefore be a hopeful sign. They may be the visible expression of local calls for re-embedding economic activity into the physical, environ-mental, social, and cultural realities that sustain it in the first place. As these local initiatives continue to expand, they may eventually touch each other and create a visible network that signals the reversal of the dis-embedding process of economic activity. Municipalities across the United States, for example, have reiterated their commitment to the Paris climate accords, even as the Federal government has rescinded theirs. This does by no means imply that concerted efforts at national and global policy change are less important or should let up. Local communities deserve and demand the support of national and global initiatives. Yet the emergence of a global network of sustainable and resilient communities may have to be more local than global as its effectiveness may depend first and foremost on local communities and people reclaiming their own local context.

References

Anderton, K. (2019) Research report shows how much time we spend gaming, Forbes. com, available at https://www.forbes.com/sites/kevinanderton/2019/03/21/research -report-shows-how-much-time-we-spend-gaming-infographic/#2c9de5e13e07, accessed November 2019.

Autor, D., Dorn, D., Katz, L.F., Patterson, C. and Van Reenen, J. (2017) *The Fall of Labor Share and the Rise of the Superstar Firms*, NBER Working Paper No. 23396.

Baker, D. (2017) Ecological panela production in Honduras: a lighter footprint for non-centrifugal sugar, *Cogent Food & Agriculture*, 3: 1372684.

Barham, J., Tropp, D., Enterline, K., Farbman, J., Fisk, J. and Kiraly, S. (2012) *Regional Food Hub Resource Guide*, Washington, DC: USDA, available at https://www .ams.usda.gov/sites/default/files/media/Regional%20Food%20Hub%20Resource %20Guide.pdf, accessed November 2019.

Bell, J. and Standish, M. (2009) Building healthy communities through equitable food access, *Community Development Investment Review*, 5: 75–87.

Chase, L. and Grubinger, V. (2014) *Food, Farms and Community: Exploring Food Systems*, Durham, NH: University of Hampshire Press.

Crowe, J., Lacey, C. and Columbus, Y. (2018) Barriers to food security and community stress in an urban food desert, *Urban Science*, 2(2): 46.

Daly, H. (1991) Sustainable development: from concept and theory to operational principles, in Davis, K. and Bernstein, M. (eds) *Resources, Environment, and Population: Present Knowledge and Future Operation*, New York: Oxford University Press, pp. 25–43.

Diehl, J. (2019) From Hong Kong to Chile, 2019 is the year of the street protester, *Washington Post*, 9 December, available at https://www.washingtonpost.com/opinions/global-opinions/from-hong-kong-to-chile-2019-is-the-year-of-the-street-protester-but-why/2019/10/27/9f79f4c6-f667-11e9-8cf0-4cc99f74d127_story.html, accessed January 2020.

Duhigg, C. (2019) The unstoppable machine, *New Yorker*, 21 October: 42–59.

Erixon, O. (2019) *Standing Up for Competition: Market Concentration, Regulation, and Europe's Quest for a New Industrial Policy*, ECIPE occasional paper, available at https://ecipe.org/publications/standing-up-for-competition/, accessed November 2019.

European Commission (2011) Consumer rights: 10 ways the new EU consumer rights directive will give people stronger rights when they shop online, available at https://ec.europa.eu/commission/presscorner/detail/en/MEMO_11_450, accessed November 2019.

Georgescu-Roegen, N. (1984) Feasible recipes versus viable technologies, *Atlantic Economic Journal*, 12: 21–31.

Gilbert, A.J. and Pinzon, L. (2014) *Colombia – Sugar Annual: Sugar Production Recovers to Normal Level*. GAIN Report, Washington, DC: USDA Foreign Agricultural Service, available at http://www.thefarmsite.com/reports/contents/ColombiaSugar9April2014.pdf, accessed November 2019.

Gowdy, J. and O'Hara, S. (1997) Weak sustainability and viable technologies, Special Issue: Nicholas Georgescu-Roegen, *Ecological Economics*, 22(3): 239–247.

Griffin, S. (2016) *Woman and Nature: The Roaring Inside of Her*, 2nd ed., New York: Crossroads Books.

Harding, S. and O'Barr, J. (1987) *Sex and Scientific Inquiry*, Chicago and London: University of Chicago Press.

Jha, S., Bacon, C. Philpott, S., Méndez, E., Läderach, P. and Rice, R. (2014) Shade coffee: update on a disappearing refuge for biodiversity, *Bioscience*, 64: 416–428.

Kahneman, D. and Deaton, A. (2010) High income improves evaluation of life but not emotional well-being, *Proceedings of the National Academy of Science (PNAS)*, 107(38): 16489–16493.

Kakovitch, T. and O'Hara, S. (2014) *Physics and the New Economy*, Amherst, MA: HRD Press.

Kharas, H. and Fengler, W. (2019) Double tipping points in 2019: when the world became mostly rich and largely old, Brookings Institution, 9 October, available at https://www.brookings.edu/blog/future-development/2019/10/09/double-tipping-points-in-2019-when-the-world-became-mostly-rich-and-largely-old/, accessed 10 December 2019.

Lenton, T., Rockström, J., Gaffney, O., Rahmstorf, S., Richardson, K., Steffen, W. and Schellnhuber, H-J. (2019) Climate tipping points – too risky to bet against, *Nature*, 27 November, available at https://www.nature.com/articles/d41586-019-03595-0, accessed 10 December 2019.

Mellor, M. (1992) Eco-feminism and eco-socialism: dilemmas of essentialism and materialism, *Capitalism, Nature, Socialism*, 3(2): 43–62.

Méndez, V.E., Bacon, C.M., Olson, M., Morris, K.S. and Shattuck, A. (2010) Agrobiodiversity and shade coffee smallholder livelihoods: a review and synthesis of ten years of research in Central America, *Professional Geographer*, 62: 357–376.

O'Hara, S. (1997) Toward a sustaining production theory, *Ecological Economics*, 20(2): 141–154.

O'Hara, S. (1998) Sustaining production: material and institutional considerations, *International Journal of Environment and Pollution*, Special Issue: Environmental Sustainability: The Challenges Ahead, 9(2/3): 287–304.

O'Hara, S. (2004) Economics in context, in Jochimsen, M., Kesting, S. and Knobloch, U. (eds) *Lebensweltökonomie*, Bielefeld: Kleiner Verlag, pp. 103–128.

O'Hara, S. (2010) Feminist ecological economics in theory and practice, in Salleh, A. (ed.) *Eco-Sufficiency and Global Justice: Women Write Political Ecology*, London and Melbourne: Pluto Press/Spinifex, pp. 180–196.

O'Hara, S. (2014) Everything needs care: toward a relevant contextual view of the economy, in Bjørnholt, M. and McKay, A. (eds) *Counting on Marilyn Waring: New Advances in Feminist Economics*, Bradford, ON: Demeter Press, pp. 37–55.

O'Hara, S. (2015) Food security: the Urban Food Hubs solution, *Solutions*, January–February: 42–53.

O'Hara, S. (2016) Production in context: the concept of sustaining production, in Farley, J. and Malghan, D. (eds) *Beyond Uneconomic Growth, Volume 2: A Festschrift in Honour of Herman Daly*, Burlington, VT: University of Vermont, pp. 75–106.

O'Hara, S. (2017) The Urban Food Hubs Solution: building capacity in urban communities, *Metropolitan Universities Journal*, 28(1): 69–93.

O'Hara, S. (2019) The Five Pillars of economic development: a storytelling approach to sustainable economic empowerment and development for underserved DC neighborhoods, available at https://www.fivepillarsdc.org, accessed December 2019.

O'Hara, S. and Baker, D. (2020) Local economies: leading the way to an eco-logical economy, in Costanza, R., Erickson, J., Farley, J. and Kubiszewski, I. (eds) *Sustainable Wellbeing Futures: A Research and Action Agenda for Ecological Economics*, Cheltenham, UK and Northampton, MA, USA: Edgar Elgar Publishing, pp. 374–386.

O'Hara, S. and Vazquez, J. (2007) *The Five Pillars of Economic Development: A Study of Best Practices for the Roanoke Valley*, Salem, VA: Roanoke College.

Pawasarat, J. and Quinn, L. (2001) *Exposing Urban Legends: The Real Purchasing Power of Central City Neighborhoods*, The Brookings Institution Center on Urban and Metropolitan Policy, available at https://www.brookings.edu/wp-content/uploads/2016/06/pawasarat.pdf, accessed 11 November 2019.

Philippon, T. (2019) *The Great Reversal: How America Gave up on Free Markets*, Cambridge, MA: Harvard University Press.

PIK – Potsdam Institute fuer Klimaforschung (2017) Tipping elements – the Achilles heels of the Earth system, available at https://www.pik-potsdam.de/services/infodesk/tipping-elements/kippelemente, accessed 15 October 2019.

Price, J. and Shildrick, M. (1999) *Feminist Theory and the Body*, London: Taylor & Francis.

Prieto, M., Baltas, G. and Stan, V. (2017) Car sharing adoption intention in urban areas: what are the key sociodemographic drivers? *Transportation Research Part A: Policy and Practice*, 101, July: 218–227.

Rees, W. (2020) Ecological economics for humanity's plague phase, *Ecological Economics*, 169: 106519.

Reese, A. (2019) *Black Food Geographies: Race, Self-Reliance, and Food Access in the Nation's Capital*, Chapel Hill, NC: University of North Carolina Press.

Rodriguez, G., Garcia, H., Diaz, Z.R. and Santacoloma, P. (2007) *Panela Production as a Strategy for Diversifying Incomes in Rural Area of Latin America*, Rome: FAO, available at http://www.fao.org/docrep/016/ap307e/ap307e.pdf, accessed 31 December 2019.

Ross, M. (2019) Everything you need to know about car sharing, *The Zebra*, 5 February, available at https://www.thezebra.com/stories/car-sharing/, accessed 15 November 2019.

Sandburn, J. (2017) Why the death of malls is about more than shopping, *Time*, 20 July.

Winne, M. (2019) *Food Town USA: Seven Unlikely Cities that Are Changing the Way We Eat*, Washington, DC: Island Press.

Yaraghi, N. and Ravi, S. (2016) *The Current and Future State of the Sharing Economy*, Governance Studies at Brookings, Impact Series No. 032017.

13 Urban political economy

Franklin Obeng-Odoom[1]

The commodification of land

Collectively owned land systems enable urban residents to build, farm or utilise urban land for any other purpose. Emphasising the individual *possession* and collective *ownership* of urban land, traditional custodians of land interpret, establish and enforce these and other customary norms in the use and ownership of land. Commodifying urban land, for example through the formal registration of land, triggers cascading processes of land decollectivisation. Extracting exchange value from use value in this way entails attempting to free land from its social bonds. Mainstream urban economists recommend different strategies for doing so (e.g., de Soto 2000; World Bank 2003). For state land, the dictum is for occupants to be registered as private leaseholders. Customary land can be registered as a group commodity that can be subdivided, while individual land can be formalised as transferable property.

This process of differentiated marketisation is deemed a panacea. Not only does marketisation reduce the cost of transacting in land, but it also facilitates free choice. Land commodification, proponents claim, enables both the demand and the supply of land which, otherwise, can be both expensive and price inelastic. By creating a land market, banks can more easily finance the provision of housing by offering secondary mortgages become the main path to home ownership. For banks and real estate investors, too, the transaction cost of marketing housing declines with the marketisation of land, as marketising land minimises the time and cost involved in ascertaining and exchanging ownership. This process is expected to bring down the cost of housing for others, too. Landlords can expect more rent from formalising their land. Urban residents' individual freedom is guaranteed (Turner 1977). This housing market, the argument goes, is therefore efficient. Not only does it ensure a win-win outcome for everyone, but it also does so at least cost (Haila

2016; Obeng-Odoom 2016a). Yet, political economists have raised many questions about these claims (Dunn 2009, 2014; Ouma 2020). They show the fundamental and long-term crises in neoclassical and new institutional schools of economics.

This chapter, therefore, develops an alternative path. Georgist urban political economic analysis. It investigates how land rent is systematically created through monopoly, speculation and growthism. At the heart of this process is transforming land from its use to exchange value. Landlords tend to appropriate socially-created rent. They work in cahoots with banks, the state and a range of property development professionals. Rather than alleviating homelessness, this housing pathway creates uncertainty and wealth concentration. This orthodoxy produces homelessness, too.

These arguments are developed in three sections. After this section introducing 'The commodification of land', the second section, 'Social problems', focuses on Accra, Ghana, to offer a Georgist explanation for why land commodification creates social problems. The third section, 'The right to land and the good society', then proposes a Georgist alternative remedial economic policy. Together, these three sections highlight methodological issues which emphasise the importance and urgent need for political economists to give greater attention to Georgist political economy. It is one way to overcome the fundamental problems of urban economics and develop an alternative urban political economy.

Social problems

Mainstream urban economics advocates the commodification of land. According to its practitioners, land collectivisation is fundamentally responsible for the corrosive problems that characterise cities and regions (Stilwell 1995; Obeng-Odoom 2016a). Together with landed interests, cities around the world have privatised their land. Yet, many social problems today arise from the commodification of land. A school of thought in its own right, Georgist political economy, which emphasises land economics, has been recognised as providing a formidable alternative to orthodoxy (Stilwell and Jordan 2004). Demonstrating its continuing relevance can be done in many ways. One is to analyse the urban-economic transformation of Accra, the capital city of Ghana, and Africa's leading 'globalizing city' (Grant 2009). It is a useful case study because in this city many have expressed significant interest in the promises and prospects of commodifying land (Ehwi et al. 2019). Indeed, the annual demand for the registration of land rose about tenfold between 1988 and 2013 and outstripped supply by an average factor of four (Abusah 2004; Ehwi and Asante 2016).

One reason for this widespread interest is that formally registered land is usually valued at 10 per cent higher than non-titled land (Obeng-Odoom and McDermont 2018). Another is the perceived security that formalisation is supposed to confer (Obeng-Odoom and Stilwell 2013; Ehwi et al. 2019). A third is statutory: in Accra, designated as a 'registration area', it is compulsory for newly purchased land to be registered (Ehwi and Asante 2016). Prestige and a certain desire for modernity (Obeng-Odoom et al. 2014) constitute additional incentives. The widespread and sustained promotion of registration complicates the situation. Not only is titling advocated as the passport for accessing housing finance for potential homeowners, it is also marketed to property developers as such (Ehwi et al. 2019). Whether these representations are borne out by social reality, however, needs more careful assessment.

Insecurity of tenure in Accra, if narrowly conceived as the absence of conflict about land (Obeng-Odoom and Stilwell 2013), is becoming more, not less, widespread (Obeng-Odoom 2014).The attempt to mark out collectively held land as privately-owned individual land has been associated with growing conflict (Obeng-Odoom 2016b). As the courts of Ghana have not automatically ruled in favour of registered land when determining questions of land ownership, financialising land through registration has created even more uncertainty (Obeng-Odoom and McDermott 2018). It follows that individual choices cannot be the primary basis for policy, especially when it is well known in both theory (Bourdieu 2005) and practice (Obeng-Odoom 2011b, 2016c) that such so-called *free* choices are *socially* constructed.

The number of transactions in Accra's 'luxury real estate' has, however, been substantial. 'There are more than 85,000 transactions per year in luxury real estate alone, with an estimated value of USD 1.7 billion.' 'With approximately 30,000 new expatriates expected over the next 10 to 15 years, demand for luxury residential real estate is expected to increase' (Ghana Home Loans PLC 2015: 19). Within this class of housing, also called 'luxury real estate', the number of gated communities increased from 24 to 63 between 2004 and 2011 (Obeng-Odoom et al. 2014: 550). The exchange value of these gated properties is on the rise, too. Two-bedroom houses in the gated neighbourhoods of the Airport Residential Area which sold for some $96,000 in 2004, could only be purchased for $290,000 in 2011 (Obeng-Odoom 2011a). A fortified space for the wealthy classes of the city, gated estates vary in their degrees of luxury and value over space and time (Obeng-Odoom 2018a).

Rental values in Accra in non-gated estates have been increasing, too. In 2008 alone, they increased by 180 per cent (Owusu-Ansah et al. 2018). This exponential growth in land price affects the housing situation of the 67 per cent of residents who are renters, and, hence, might face the possibility of paying an estimated rent of $5,000 per month instead of the prevailing $4 paid as rent by those in the lower-income brackets (Obeng-Odoom 2011a). This dynamic has been a long-term trend.

Between the 1950s and the 1990s, the value of land in some parts of the city increased by over 300 per cent (Obeng-Odoom et al. 2014: 554). Lower middle-income groups have been evicted to poor and marginalised neighbourhoods. In turn, they have experienced a substantial decline in the quality of their housing. They also spend more of their income and time to commute. Pressure on the poor to pay more rent has increased. Landlords seek to cash in on the new low-income renters who compete for housing.

The moderately rich have had to seek new types of gated communities. Located at the urban frontier, this asset class increases rental values in the urban core. Gating contributes to urban ecological crisis, too. Residents have to commute over longer periods and distances in private cars. They are usually fuelled by dirty oil (Obeng-Odoom et al. 2014; Obeng-Odoom 2018a, 2018b). Biodiversity also declines, as property developers remove urban green spaces to provide exclusive housing (Obeng-Odoom 2018a) raise additional questions. How can these two trends be explained consistently?

Most people in Accra are crowded on, and transact in, small parcels of urban land. Only a small class of absentee landowners is involved in large-scale, high-value land transactions (Grant 2009; Obeng-Odoom 2013). So, the transformation in urban land can be understood as restructuring urban society in favour of the wealthy. As in other cities in the world, they make a living through rents (Haila 1988, 2016). These speculators, many of them based in the Global North, finance the purchase of land in the Global South. They hold onto this land, build on it speculatively in what is often called 'development looking for consumers', and then sell it when they find willing and able buyers.

Major transnational real estate companies, located in London, New York and Chicago, have become particularly vibrant in buying land in the Global South (Liberti 2013; Watson 2014; Leon 2015; Ouma 2020). This urban land development is usually designed by international architects with little or no consultation with local planners and citizens. Their business is building speculatively (Watson 2014). In Accra, Rendeavour Company, whose shareholders live in the US, New Zealand, Norway and Britain, have built Appolonia City, regarded as an 'urban oasis' (Lutter 2018). This descriptor calls attention to the exclusive nature of this wealthy suburb.

At the local level, a smorgasbord of institutions collaborate to facilitate this speculation (Obeng-Odoom 2011a; Arku et al. 2012; Akaabre et al. 2018). Although it is held in mainstream urban economics that private banks mainly give credit to finance 'real' urban development through industrialisation, in practice, they create money to finance speculative urban development by lending against landed property. While the literature on 'financialisation' is growing (see Bonizzi 2013; Aalbers 2020), much less research has been done on the transformation of land. Research on land and finance has long been sketched theoretically in the literature (e.g., Haila 1988, 2016). Historically specific, this financialisation ought to be untangled both contextually and empirically (Bourdieu 2005; Ryan-Collins 2017).

A useful starting point is to consider the trends in the asset/debt profile of Ghana Home Loans (GHL). It is the largest single mortgagor in Ghana. Not only does it hold 50 per cent of existing mortgages in Ghana, but it also generates 75 per cent of all new mortgage facilities with very rapid growth in the 2010s (Ghana Home Loans PLC 2015). So, analysing the trends in the size of its assets/debtors can shed some light on the mortgage market. With the potential to become owners through foreclosure, GHL is often interested in maintaining the value of land. So, it sets higher interest rates. Although such rates can deter borrowing, GHL, as a monopolist, in essence is in a position to impose them without consumer backlash. Others such as Republic Bank charge similar rates of interest. They constitute a powerful propertied class.

The effects of this dynamic on property values are wide-ranging (Obeng-Odoom 2011a, 2013; Arku et al. 2012; Akaabre et al. 2018; Ehwi et al. 2019). To obtain such private bank loans, potential credit-seekers – whether they are aspirant investors, homeowners or property developers – tend to talk up their property values. Professional valuers are caught in-between the banks (which seek to give out more credit for higher rates of interests) and potential debtors (who try to access such loans). The valuers grapple with the additional conflict of interest dilemma which arises because their professional fee is charged as a percentage of property value. The higher the property value, the more they earn. In practice (Owusu-Ansah et al. 2018), the resulting vibrant property market is characterised by cumulatively higher land values.

These resulting increases create the impression that property values increase ad infinitum. Media representations embellish this imagery. It encourages the process of speculation, too. As demonstrated by Hyman Minsky (1992), more banks are built when opportunities for private money creation and enrichment abound (see also Bezemer and Hudson 2016: 27–32). So, banks transform from simply extending hedge financial credit to giving out speculative credit. In a race to the bottom, this financialisation turns into a grand Ponzi Scheme. Some of these 'absentee owners' (Veblen 2009 [1923]), are shareholders of transnational property development companies. Others are part-owners of the banks in Accra, most of which are foreign-owned (Sulemana et al. 2018).

One effect is colonial uneven urban development. Another is an increase in household debt. Often neglected in urban research in Ghana, indebtedness is a major feature of urban households in Accra. Successive surveys show that between 2006 and 2013, the share of indebted households in Accra increased from 14 per cent to 41 per cent. Crucially, most people in 2013 were taking loans for land acquisition and housing, not business (cf. Ghana Statistical Service 2013: Round 6, p. 165 and Ghana Statistical Service 2008: Round 5, p. 113).

Increasing household debt has several implications (for a detailed analysis, see Montgomerie 2019). The direct cost of the debt in the form of compound interest is often the focus of discussion for mainstream. The sterile discussion about what is and what is not a good debt among mainstream accountants illustrates the point. Anxiety and uncertainty are additional outcomes. Of far more importance for Georgist political economists, however, is the *opportunity cost* of servicing a growing household debt. Such costs relate to health, education and other family expenditures that have to be neglected in order to amortise escalating loans. Servicing such debts, therefore, prevents the economic ripple effects often called 'the Keynesian multiplier'. Clearly, the money which could have been injected into the economy to trigger *additional multiplier effects* and investment into capital goods such as factories is (mis)directed to the payment of speculative ventures including speculative land adventures (Gaffney 2015). Over the long haul, therefore, land-based debt, fuelled by speculation, can throw the entire economy into crises.

At the individual level, the effect is most felt by the defaulting mortgagee. Often, this spectre of default is increased because of the largely inflated nature of the property prices. For that reason too, the high-risk interest that attaches to the loans must be further discussed. The banks do not have the security or certainty to be able to recoup their investment through foreclosure, however. That is not just because Ghanaian laws make foreclosures difficult; rather, it is mostly because such properties, with inflated prices, stand little chance of being sold in the open market even when advertised at the reserve price. Consequently, not only the households, but also the banks in Accra, have become risky ventures. They could undermine themselves, throwing households into multiple crises, including saddling them with debts which become albatrosses around their necks even in their old age. The entire Ghanaian economy risks falling into depression, too.

Sensing these risks, the Ghanaian state has taken so-called remedial steps. Not only has the Bank of Ghana revoked the licences of banks, but it has also amalgamated several others into one grand bank overseen by the state. Subsequently, the Bank of Ghana has increased the minimum payment required to start and maintain banks (Addison 2018). The Bank of Ghana is also promising to be more stringent in its supervisory activities to detect risky behaviour.

The Ministry of Finance, on its part, has pledged to co-operate with the Central Bank, while the Government of Ghana has sought to absorb the debt of the private banks by paying off debtors (Ministry of Finance 2018). The state has justified socialising private bank problems on the grounds of restoring confidence in the market, trying to prevent joblessness, maintaining economic growth, and avoiding economic crises. Nevertheless, this bailout package is problematic. The direct cost is often easiest to pinpoint in the form of money lost to the state. These state resources are themselves generated from debt contracted from overseas sources which impose harsh terms and increasing indirect taxation. Unlike direct taxation, which the majority of people in the urban informal economy can escape (Obeng-Odoom 2011c), indirect taxation is paid by both formal and informal workers, rich and poor, and wealth-poor labourers, workers and other residents. Indirect taxation on essential goods and services penalises the poor. They pay disproportionately more of their income as tax, which falls more heavily on them. Direct taxes penalise workers for doing productive work, while neglecting unearned rents. In turn, such taxes encourage speculative behaviour (George 2006 [1935]: 226–235). The state itself acknowledges that it could have used the resources invested in the bailout for social services such as health and education, but it neglects the double effects on public debt. Servicing the growing public debt, itself securitised by landed resources such as oil, is diverting resources from strategic urban and national investments.

Clearly, increasing the current public debt by bailing out private banks cannot be a sustainable strategy. At a deeper level, the misdiagnosis of these social problems is worrying. Identified as a 'banking crises', the attempts to address them have centred almost exclusively on the banking sector to the neglect of the root cause: the commodification of land and the private appropriation of socially-created land rent.

I have illustrated this process with the experience of Accra, Ghana, but it is common more generally, especially in South Africa and Uganda as I have shown elsewhere (Obeng-Odoom 2013: 175–198). The details differ, of course. South Africa, with a housing loan penetration rate of 5.4 and a much more advanced banking system, would align more closely with Ghana, whose housing loan penetration rate is 2.8. On the other hand, Kampala in Uganda, with a less advanced mortgage system and a housing loan penetration rate of 1.2, differs in its experiences of indebtedness (Badev et al. 2014: 45–46). With a total population of 40 million and a mortgage market of only 5,000 mortgages, in Uganda it is mainly microcredit institutions that securitise land (*Economist* 2019: 58–59). They may not insist on formal land titles, but land is still the required collateral security.

The repayment period of one to three years is much shorter in Kampala than in Accra's financialised mortgage market, but the microcredit institutions would foreclose mortgages that are not amortised anyway. In this environment, stress levels are particularly high, as entire families work under harsh conditions to repay their loans. Recent surveys in East Africa show that, although taking such microcredit loans helps in improving the quality of housing, stress levels of the mortgagees have remained unchanged even for those with a decent home (*Economist* 2019: 58–59). If anything, the rise of microfinance institutions, engaged in fraudulent lending practices, has heightened uncertainty and anxiety (Wiegratz 2016: 278–279).

The wider political-economic ramifications of transferring money from real work to pay absentee owners create fundamental problems. Henry George himself considered the issues (George 1966 [1883]: 161–170). Public debt, often contracted under usurious terms, he argued, could be put to public improvement purposes, but it could also be put to war-making, extravagant spending and tyrannous purposes. Even public uses of debt tend to be characterised by inefficiencies and corrupt tendencies given the loose accountabilities between the public and the debt-contracting state. 'Public debt', therefore, is particularly problematic because it tends to be put to private purposes, while still being securitised by land, which is common property.

Public debt also binds future generations to paying for the wastefulness of the present population. 'It is not', George wrote, 'the case of asking a man to pay a debt contracted by his great-grandfather; it is asking him to pay for the rope with which his great-grandfather was hanged, or the fagots with which he was burned' (George 1966 [1883]: 165). Not only does it advantage the present over the future, but debt also makes the wealthy wealthier, as they are able to privately appropriate debt for their own uses, while socialising its re-payment.

Not only does this process entail creating cumulatively escalating debt-driven inter-group inequality between Africa and the rest of the world, but it also transfers socially-created rents into the hands of absentee private landlords. The rules of debt creation are written, re-written, and abused by rich countries. Powerful private and landed interests are co-authors. They say one thing for themselves and another for others. 'Ken Ofori-Atta, Ghana's finance minister, pointed out in a webinar hosted by Harvard University that rich countries were taking extraordinary measures to protect their economies, while telling Africans to stick to the rules. "You really feel like shouting: I can't breathe", he said.' (*Economist* 2020, p. 28).

If land commodification advocated by mainstream economists as a panacea is malign, not benign as claimed, is rent control the answer? Popular across the world, this alternative is often hurriedly imposed to defuse potential uprisings resulting from worsening social problems. That was evidently the case when, on 18 June 2019, legislators in Berlin voted to impose a freeze on rents for five years after residents of Karl-Marx-Allee demanded liberation from their urban economic crisis, central to which was the housing problem. Rent controls are in force in Spain, Barcelona and Amsterdam (*Economist* 2019: 21–22), as they are in Accra, where, in addition, there is even a Rent Control Department. However, as the evidence considered in this chapter suggests, rent control is no panacea. This attempt at re-regulation can simply be ignored by a powerful landlord class, as it was recently in San Francisco (*Economist* 2019: 22), where citywide rents rose by 5 per cent. Georgists (George 2006 [1935], 1966 [1883]; Stilwell and Jordan 2004; Gaffney 2015) propose to address social problems by institutionalising the right to land.

The right to land

This right is much deeper than the legal pursuit of the 'right to housing'. The right to land comes in three forms: the right to the fruits of one's labour; the common rights to socially created rents, which, in Georgist political economy, can only be put to public and common uses; and, most fundamental of all, the common rights to land.

To guarantee the right to land, George taught that public debt, obtained under usurious and careless conditions offered by the lenders and securitised by land, should be repudiated. Thus, he provided early insights into the contemporary debates about odious debt (Ndikumana and Boyce 2011). Taking inspiration from Thomas Jefferson, George noted that 'one generation should not hold itself bound by the laws or the debts of its predecessors ... measures which would give practical effect to this principle will appear the more salutary the more they are considered' (George 1966 [1883]: 167). Clearly, controlling the value of land makes the wages of the labourer hostage to the wishes of landlords because land rent reduces the size of wages. Incentives for hard work can be killed in this process, too. War, hunger, disease, crime and grime stem from the drive to control land. Finally, the power of rent, or of landlords to extract rent, makes landlords masters over the poor, indeed over all.

By guaranteeing that the fruits of labour are not taxed nor taken away by capitalists, and by taxing land rents or land value, the situation can be addressed. Analytically, the land question can be answered by Georgist political economy. It is an approach that can also contribute to resolving the policy question. Returning to the public what is socially created is one way. Committing net revenues from land to public purposes is another. Placing a tax on inherited land is a third. In these ways, the privatisation of currently common land such that the problem that breeds further inequality is confronted, both existing and intergenerational poverty, inequality and uncertainty can be addressed. Beyond offering analysis and policy solutions for present problems, the application of principles from Georgist political economy, as one approach to urban political economy, could make the urban economy more inclusive, more prosperous, and more sustainable. Through the provision of incentives for self-employment, quality wage employment, and comprehensive social protection programmes in which urban housing is framed as a merit good, Georgist political economy provides avenues for a new research agenda.

Note

1. I gratefully acknowledge excellent and very helpful feedback from Bill Dunn whose invitation to contribute to the book is also warmly appreciated.

References

Aalbers, M.B. (2020) Financial geography III: the financialization of the city, *Progress in Human Geography*, 44(3): 595–607.
Abusah, S. (2004) Access to land for housing development: a review of land title registration in Accra, Ghana, MSc thesis submitted to the Department of Infrastructure, KTH Royal Institute of Technology.

Addison, E. (2018) Address by the Governor of the Bank of Ghana, given at the Annual Dinner of the Chartered Institute of Bankers, Accra Marriot Hotel, 1 December.

Akaabre, P.B., Poku-Boansi, M. and Adarkwa, K.K. (2018) The growing activities of informal rental agents in the urban housing market of Kumasi, Ghana, *Cities*, 83: 34–43.

Arku, G., Luginaah, I. and Mkandawire, P. (2012) 'You either pay more advance rent or you move out': landlords'/ladies' and tenants' dilemmas in the low-income housing market in Accra, Ghana, *Urban Studies*, 49(14): 3177–3193.

Badev, A., Beck, T., Vado, L. and Walley, S. (2014) *Housing Finance across Countries: New Data and Analysis*, World Bank Policy Research Working Paper 6756.

Bezemer, D. and Hudson, M. (2016) Finance is not the economy, *Progress*, Winter: 5–10, 27–32.

Bonizzi, B. (2013) Financialization in developing and emerging countries: a survey, *International Journal of Political Economy*, 42(4): 83–107.

Bourdieu, P. (2005) *The Social Structures of the Economy*, London: Polity Press.

de Soto, H. (2000) *The Mystery of Capital: Why Capitalism Triumphs in the West and Fails Everywhere Else*, New York: Bantam Press.

Dunn, B. (2009) *Global Political Economy: A Marxist Critique*, London: Pluto Press.

Dunn, B. (2014) *The Political Economy of Global Capitalism and Crisis*, London: Routledge.

Economist (2019) Microfinance: one brick at a time, 20 July.

Economist (2020), The fire this time: police violence, race and protest in America, 6-12 June: 28.

Ehwi, R.J. and Asante, L.A. (2016) Ex-post analysis of land title registration in Ghana since 2008 merger: Accra Lands Commission in perspective, *Sage Open*, 6(2): 1–17.

Ehwi, R.J., Morrison, N. and Tyler, P. (2019) Gated communities and land administration challenges in Ghana: reappraising the reasons why people move into gated communities, *Housing Studies*, DOI: 10.1080/02673037.2019.1702927.

Gaffney, M. (2015) A real-assets model of economic crises: will China crash in 2015?, *American Journal of Economics and Sociology*, 74(2): 325–360.

George, H. (1966 [1883]) *Social Problems*, New York: Robert Schalkenbach Foundation.

George, H. (2006 [1935]) *Progress and Poverty*, The Fiftieth Anniversary edition, New York: Robert Schalkenbach Foundation.

Ghana Home Loans PLC (2015) *Ghana Home Loans PLC – Programme Memorandum*, Accra: Ghana Home Loans PLC.

Ghana Statistical Service (GSS) (2008) *Ghana Living Standards Survey: Report of the Fifth Round*, Accra: GSS.

Ghana Statistical Service (GSS) (2013) *Ghana Living Standards Survey: Report of the Sixth Round*, Accra: GSS.

Grant, R. (2009) *Globalizing City: The Urban and Economic Transformation of Accra*, Syracuse, NY: Syracuse University Press.

Haila, A. (1988) Land as a financial asset: the theory of urban rent as a mirror of economic transformation, *Antipode*, 20(2): 79–101.

Haila, A. (2016) *Urban Land Rent: Singapore as a Property State*, Chichester: Wiley-Blackwell.

Leon, J.K. (2015) The role of global cities in land grabs, *Third World Quarterly*, 36(2): 257–273.

Liberti, S. (2013) *Land Grabbing: Journeys in the New Colonialism*, London and New York: Verso.

Lutter, M. (2018) Rendeavour: an interview with Preston Mendenhall, the Head of Corporate Affairs for Rendeavour, available at https://www.chartercitiesinstitute .ort/post/rendeavour, accessed 5 January 2020.

Ministry of Finance (2018) *2019 Financial Year Presented to Parliament on Thursday, 15th November 2018*, Ministry of Finance, Accra.

Minsky, H.P. (1992) *The Financial Instability Hypothesis*, Levy Economics Institute of Bard College Working Paper No. 74.

Montgomerie, J. (2019) *Should We Abolish Household Debts?*, Cambridge: Polity Press.

Ndikumana, L. and Boyce, J.K. (2011) *Africa's Odious Debts: How Foreign Loans and Capital Flight Bled the Continent*, London and New York: Zed Books.

Obeng-Odoom, F. (2011a) Private rental housing in Ghana: reform or renounce?, *Journal of International Real Estate and Construction Studies*, 1(1): 71–90.

Obeng-Odoom, F. (2011b) Real estate agents in Ghana: a suitable case for regulation?, *Regional Studies*, 45(3): 403–416.

Obeng-Odoom, F. (2011c) The informal sector in Ghana under siege, *Journal of Developing Societies*, 27(3 & 4): 355–392.

Obeng-Odoom, F. (2013) *Governance for Pro-Poor Urban Development: Lessons from Ghana*, London: Routledge.

Obeng-Odoom, F. (2014) Urban land policies in Ghana: a case of the emperor's new clothes?, *Review of Black Political Economy*, 41(2): 119–143.

Obeng-Odoom, F. (2016a) *Reconstructing Urban Economics: Towards a Political Economy of the Built Environment*, London: Zed Books.

Obeng-Odoom, F. (2016b) Understanding land reform in Ghana: a critical postcolonial institutional approach, *Review of Radical Political Economics*, 48(4): 661–680.

Obeng-Odoom, F. (2016c) Informal real estate brokerage as a socially embedded market for economic development in Africa, in Abdulai, R.T., Obeng-Odoom, F., Ochieng, E. and Maliene, V. (eds) *Real Estate, Construction and Economic Development in Emerging Market Economies*, London: Routledge, pp. 224–238.

Obeng-Odoom, F. (2018a) The gated housing hierarchy, in Fredriksson, M. and Arvanitakis, J. (eds) *Property, Place, and Piracy*, London: Routledge, pp. 187–201.

Obeng-Odoom, F. (2018b) Transnational corporations and urban development, *American Journal of Economics and Sociology*, 77(2): 447–510.

Obeng-Odoom, F., Elhadary, Y.A. and Jang, H.S. (2014) Living behind the wall and socio-economic implications for those outside the wall: gated communities in Malaysia and Ghana, *Journal of Asian and African Studies*, 49(5): 544–558.

Obeng-Odoom, F. and McDermott, M. (2018) *Valuing Unregistered Land*, London: RICS.

Obeng-Odoom, F. and Stilwell, F. (2013) Security of tenure in international development discourse, *International Development Planning Review*, 35(4): 315–333.

Ouma, S. (2020) *Farming as Financial Asset*, Newcastle upon Tyne: Agenda Publishing.

Owusu-Ansah, A., Ohemeng-Mensah, D., Talinbe, R. and Obeng-Odoom, F. (2018) Public choice theory and rental housing: an examination of rental housing contracts in Ghana, *Housing Studies*, 33(6): 938–959.

Ryan-Collins, J., Lloyd, T. and MacFarlane, L. (2017) *Rethinking the Economics of Land and Housing*, London: Zed Books.

Stilwell, F. (1995) *Understanding Cities and Regions*, Sydney: Pluto.

Stilwell, F. and Jordan, K. (2004) The political economy of land: putting Henry George in his place, *Journal of Australian Political Economy*, 54: 119–134.

Sulemana, M., Dramani, J.B. and Oteng-Abayie, E.F. (2018) Foreign bank inflows: implications for bank stability in sub-Saharan Africa, *African Review of Economics and Finance*, 10(1): 54–81.

Turner, J.F.C. (1977) *Housing by People: Towards Autonomy in Building Environments*, New York: Pantheon Books.

Veblen, T. (2009 [1923]) *Absentee Ownership: Business Enterprise in Recent Times: The Case of America*, New Brunswick and London: Transactions Publishers.

Watson, V. (2014) African urban fantasies: dreams or nightmares?, *Environment and Urbanization*, 26(1): 1–17.

Wiegratz, J. (2016) *Neoliberal Moral Economy: Capitalism, Socio-Cultural Change and Fraud in Uganda*, London and New York: Rowman & Littlefield International.

World Bank (2003) *Land Policies for Growth and Poverty Reduction*, Washington, DC: World Bank.

14 The political economy of displacement governance: the case of refugees in the European Union

Ali Bhagat and Susanne Soederberg

The period 2015–16 saw more than 2.5 million asylum claims lodged in the European Union (EU) signalling the so-called European refugee or migrant crisis. The alarmist crisis terminology – used by media, policymakers and government officials – often imparts blame. Refugees are accused of clogging welfare systems and displacing the homeless while media portrayals of refugees have referred to them as a 'flood', 'swarm', 'flock' and as 'marauders', likening these migrants to animals, barbarians and natural disasters (Shariatmadari 2015). Employing a critical political economy (CPE) lens, the main objective of this chapter is to interrupt the refugee crisis by identifying and explaining some core silences around EU migrant governance. To this end, we focus on the role of space, scale, race and class in shaping the survival of refugees by which we mean their struggle to access basic material needs on a day-to-day basis, particularly low-income housing.

To decentre the refugee crisis, we highlight racial and class characteristics of refugees in their host cities (Rajaram 2018). By race and class, we follow Rajaram in our assertion that refugees are embedded within extant racial and class-based hierarchies that place refugees among the most marginalized people in their societies of relocation. As Robinson (1983) and others suggest, capitalism has always been racial and refugee governance in the EU further emphasizes the inseparable violence of race and class.

Second, we apply this understanding of refugees to the power and politics involved in the multi-scalar governance of survival in two major urban centres in the EU: Berlin and Paris. In using a multi-scalar perspective, we are able to emphasize the continually overlapping scales of governance as refugees navigate from country of origin to detention centre to other forms of cyclical displacement in their attempts to settle in major urban centres in the EU. In effect, we assert that urban scales of survival surrounding housing – a key site of struggle as it pertains to refugee survival – are inseparable from national and global tensions of xenophobia and austerity. In this second feature of our analysis, we focus on housing in capitalist political economy in Berlin and Paris.

Pulling the two analytical prongs together in a CPE framework, we argue that the governance of refugees in the EU has been shaped historically by multi-scalar modes of racialized and class powers. Multi-scalarity has converged most evidently on the urban scale (Darling 2016), where housing presents a visible battleground for survival within the context of the latest rounds of austerity. The latter describes a set of political-economic policies aimed at reducing government deficits through cuts in welfare spending and bolstering the private sector – a definitive feature of neoliberalization (Peck and Tickell 2002). The EU Commission, for example, declared that after nine years of budgetary constraint, France has finally cut its public deficit to an acceptable level[1] but must apply 'continuing rigour' (rFI 2018) to further reduce this debt (European Commission 2019) – reiterating that the onslaught on public expenditure in the aftermath of the 2009 Eurozone crisis is continuing to this day. The EU's push for austerity has urban ramifications too. For example, and as we will detail further below, the Berlin Senate engaged in ongoing privatization of public utilities through the slashing of public budgets and services (Davies and Blanco 2017: 1518; cf. Peck 2012). In short, it is impossible to divorce the difficulties of refugee survival and governance from the context of urban neoliberalization.

Refugee survival in this current moment of global displacement returns us to the core questions in CPE: 'who benefits and why?' and 'what are the nature and sources of power?'. In attempting to address these central concerns in political economy, we confront one methodological issue and two related theoretical premises in the context of the EU. We organize our chapter in the following way: first, in terms of methodology, we are concerned with how scalar analysis can be brought to CPE. To address this, we emphasize scales of racial governance in global capitalism where the urban is linked to national and regional forms of racial exclusion. Second, we highlight spaces of racial governance in global capitalism in our framing of shelter as survival governance. Third, we apply our theoretical premises to two major urban centres in the EU, where Berlin and Paris show inherent contradictions between racial governance in the context of urban austerity. We conclude by reiterating our core argument that refugee survival is underpinned by multi-scalar racial exclusion and CPE must thus pay more attention to the combined pressures of race and class that are most evident in cities of relocation.

Raced spaces in global displacement governance

We launch our conception of scale following Brenner et al., who note that 'neoliberalism is now deployed as a basis for analysing, or at least characterising, a bewildering array of forms and pathways of market-led regulatory restructuring across places, territories, and scales' (2010: 183). Indeed, neoliberalization is understood as uneven, polymorphic and multi-scalar. As process, neoliberalization is simultaneously transnational, national and urban. Rather than viewing neoliberalism as a meta-theory, it is important to consider it as successive waves of regulatory experimentation that are both contextually specific and consolidated through disruptions and conflict (Brenner et al. 2010: 198). The refugee crisis trope is placed within this context of multi-scalar neoliberalization creating a multiform response from the EU, national-level states and municipal governments. Instead of addressing material issues of survival, regulations surrounding refugee management focus on detention, deportation and border security. Neoliberalized refugee governance should be seen as a façade that provides very little in terms of welfare support for migrants and instead relies on racialized tropes to smooth over the tensions in capitalist political economy. These racial tropes have emerged in the face of the Eurozone crisis and resultant austerity, where jingoism has replaced progressive politics which could potentially address issues of urban poverty, particularly surrounding housing.

Thus, a multi-scalar conception of neoliberalization needs to be placed in conversation with emerging theories of race and International Political Economy (IPE). We echo Robinson's (1983) assertion that the reality of the capitalist system and any resultant resistance must pay closer attention to the complexities of race. As such, scales of neoliberalization cannot be separated from racialized governance. By drawing attention to raced scales, we are able to shed critical light on the ways in which displacement governance is an embodied set of regulatory functions motivated by strong borders and anti-migrant sentiment. In doing this we show how capitalism and racism buttress one another. Racism is the vehicle through which violence is justified; it also serves to mask the tensions in capitalist political economy. Shilliam's (2018) book, *Race and the Undeserving Poor*, shows the long history of so-called deserving and, often racialized, undeserving poor in the context of the UK from abolition to Brexit. Shilliam rightfully points out that 'class has returned to the diet of parliamentary and public discourse as a constitutively racialized phenomenon' (2018: 4). The demarcations between deserving and undeserving poor – while shifting through time and geographic context – are driven by elite actors, who strategically incorporate various working classes, nationalities and colonial histories to consolidate power and cut across popular discourses of the political right and left. As it pertains to migrants, we will show how their racialization places them among the most marginalized in society. Migrants themselves are not a homogenous category: many groups are ascribed racialized character-istics, which in turn impact their material access to survival in their cities of relocation, notably housing.

To explore housing as an integral feature of raced spaces, we heed Tilley and Shilliam's (2018) contention that race is structural and agential in reproducing social conditions and markets, by which we mean that displacement govern-ance operates in a racialized market from detention to ongoing relocation. In particular, we see the governance of displacement as a mode of 'classifying, ordering, creating and destroying' (2018: 537) spaces of survival for refugees. As Bhattacharyya (2018) reminds us, migration governance does not solely exist at checkpoints in the global North, but these confrontations occur at the site of departure and within state and non-state institutions as well. Indeed, economic exploitations and racist othering reinforce and amplify one another (2018: 102; cf. Melamed 2011; Bhambra and Holmwood 2018). We expand upon these considerations by making two related interventions: first, we look at the urban scale of analysis as a way of encapsulating the tensions of national and global displacement governance (Danewid 2020). And second, we show the 'actually existing' features of racial neoliberalization (Bhagat 2019) with regard to housing in our empirical cases in Berlin and Paris.

In naming housing as a raced space, we highlight the multi-scalar dimensions of refugee survival at the urban battleground. EU policies remain mostly silent on shelter upon migrant relocation and thus delegate it to national-level states, which in turn place the responsibility of housing on the urban scale of governance. Despite this, housing is a central feature of political economy and of refugee survival (Aalbers and Christophers 2014; Soederberg 2019). In highlighting the racialized dimensions of housing access, we see the lack of coherent policy at the EU scale and the ineffective deployment of short-, medium- and long-term shelter strategies at the national and urban scales as a purposeful erasure that reifies logics of cyclical displacement (Soederberg 2018). The erasure of adequate housing not only points to unaddressed ine-qualities in urban capitalism, but also reiterates that refugees are unwanted and must fend for themselves in their new cities.

We twin shelter survival in racial neoliberalism with other relevant issues of survival such as work. As Rajaram (2018) points out, refugees struggle to valorize their body power in capitalist modes of production: 'these are groups who lack the skills or cultural nous to be incorporated into the front stage operations of capitalism' (2018: 628). Importantly, while EU policies and mainstream news outlets frame refugees as useful labour, the tensions surrounding race and the framing of migrants in general as 'job-stealing others' prevents a coherent multi-scalar response for meaningful employment. The discursive construction of the 'refugee other' renders them simultaneously 'job-stealing' and a drain on the welfare system – they are 'undeserving' of access to basic survival support. While accessing the job market is hindered by language and other cultural barriers, refugees must quickly transform themselves into productive members of society either through work or entrepreneurship (Bhagat 2020). Understanding housing as a raced space in displacement governance hinges on other important vectors of survival such as labour. However, and in following the work of Aalbers and Christophers (2014) on centring housing in political economy, we assert that housing is a central feature of the urban battleground of refugee survival. Without basic shelter, refugees struggle to find meaningful employment.

Applying raced spaces to CPE

Germany and France are two of the most powerful actors in the Eurozone and their capital cities, where rental housing is the dominant tenure, have experienced neoliberal-led austerity even prior to the 2008 crisis. Berlin and Paris are also the top destinations for urban refugees in the EU, as we have explored elsewhere (Bhagat and Soederberg 2019). In Germany, 860,000 people are homeless and in France 140,000 people live on the streets and an additional 3.5 million live under precarious housing conditions. These cities have adopted variegated strategies of refugee management. Austerity, which has been present in Berlin since the early 2000s, has led to market-led solutions as the Berlin Senate had no choice but to turn to the global consulting firm McKinsey & Company to troubleshoot their shelter strategy. In Paris, refugees are expelled from the city's core on an ongoing basis due to a similar shortage in social housing, emergency housing and beds. Indeed, displacement does not have an endpoint – it is an ongoing cycle from country of origin, to refugee camp, to major city, and potential deportation. In the following two empirical snapshots we examine raced spaces on the urban scale. The cases illustrate the combined pressures of race and class, where housing is seen as the key site of struggle as a raced space in urban capitalism.

Snapshot 1: raced spaces in Berlin

Berlin has absorbed the highest number of forcibly displaced war refugees in comparison to any other city in Western Europe (Eurocities 2016). As is the case with other cities in the EU, securing affordable housing in Germany's capital had become challenging for many low-income households even prior to the influx of migrants in 2015 (Holm 2016). Newly arrived refugees must thus traverse raced spaces marked by growing levels of extant displacement in terms of evictions and rising homelessness (Housing Europe 2017; Soederberg 2018). The Berlin case illustrates the racialized and classed nature of refugee governance, where refugees are placed in precarious housing situations that mask pre-existing systemic inequalities in the German capital city.

While the German federal government determines where refugees are to be distributed and which refugees are permitted to remain in the country, how refugees are to be housed falls under the purview of each Land. In the case of Berlin, the Berlin Senate and its 12 district governments are responsible for providing refugee shelter (Foroutan et al. 2017). There are three main types of refugee accommodation made available by the Berlin Senate: (1) mass dwellings in the form of emergency shelters, (2) communal dwellings, and (3) rental housing. Due to existing racial exclusions and neoliberal restructurings, many refugees have been excluded from the more secure form of rental dwellings, and thus predominantly reside in emergency shelters and communal housing years after arriving in Berlin.

Emergency shelters are temporary mass dwellings that are intended to prevent homelessness and to ensure that German authorities are aware of the whereabouts of refugees during their application process. According to German asylum law, refugees are required to remain in the emergency shelters (*Notunterkünfte*) for at least six weeks and a maximum period of six months (Wendel 2014). Once refugees have fulfilled their required time in the emergency shelters and are approved for temporary residence by the German state (the Federal Office for Migration and Refugees, also known as BAMF), they are required – at least in theory – to move into either communal shelters or rental housing. The latter represents the tenure in which 85 per cent of Berlin's residents live (Holm 2013).

BAMF's approval for temporary residence permits means that refugees are granted the same status as Germans with regard to the social insurance system, including monthly housing assistance from the Federal Employment Agency (*Bundesagentur für Arbeit*), which has branches (*Jobcentres*) throughout Berlin's 12 districts. Yet, even armed with these welfare benefits, refugees find it difficult to secure affordable rental housing in Berlin. Instead, refugees continue to use their allocated rental housing allowance to pay their lodging in communal shelters. In many cases, primarily due to the lack of sufficient communal dwellings, refugees have been using these state benefits to pay for rent in emergency shelters (Refugees Welcome 2017).

The majority of refugees reside in communal shelters. In contrast to emergency shelters, communal dwellings offer less overcrowding, more privacy and provide more independence (curfews, designated mealtimes, security checks and so forth) than emergency shelters. Nonetheless, due to spatial and privacy limits, these shared dwellings are not suitable for long-term occupation, especially for families. The Berlin Senate has sought to deal with the housing crisis by providing various types of assistance based on marketized approaches (read: not building and managing social housing units). One solution, for example, involves a rental subsidy to incentivize the housing market to rent to refugees. In this programme, federal Jobcentres provide a 20 per cent top-up in rental support for refugees who are successfully approved by BAMF.

Two immediate problems emerged from this subsidy, both of which reflected the racialized spaces of neoliberal governance in Berlin. First, the state rental support for refugees was met by growing resentment among non-refugees, who were in hot pursuit of affordable housing. The media, for instance, argued that with this subsidy, the state was giving preference to refugees over other groups (primarily native Germans), who were also disadvantaged in the housing market, namely students and the homeless.

Second, in addition to the high rental rates and the need to compete with around 50,000 Berlin residents, including native Germans, who are also vying for an affordably priced flat, refugees had to contend with discrimination by landlords, language barriers, lack of knowledge of the legal working of the Berlin rental system, long lag times between finding a suitable flat and obtaining approval from the State Office for Health and Social Affairs (Landesamt für Gesundheit und Soziales – LaGeSo) to overtake the rental payments, and so forth (Flüchtlingsrat Berlin 2016). The combination of these structural barriers to accessing permanent housing and understaffed government agencies has resulted in longer waits for refugees residing in emergency and communal shelters – two types of shelter where, as noted above, 28,000 of the registered 80,000 refugees in Berlin continue to reside (Foroutan et al. 2017).

Both problems need to be contextualized within the wider neoliberal restructurings in Berlin, especially with regard to its social housing. Although Berlin – like other German cities – was subject to a fresh round of austerity measures with the advent of the 2008 financial crisis, Holm (2013) points out that the capital's experience with austerity dates back to 2001 when the BGB, Berlin's largest banking house at the time, was bailed out by Berlin's Senate after incurring high losses due to risky real estate deals in which public finances were used in speculative activities. The Berlin Senate's unilateral – and hence undemocratic – decision to socialize private banking debt transformed the banking crisis into a wider fiscal crisis. Neoliberal rollbacks were quickly scripted as the only viable response to the fiscal crisis, due to market pressures by creditors, investors and rating agencies (Peck 2012).

To meet its goal of balanced budgets, the Berlin Senate engaged in the ongoing privatization of public utilities and housing as fiscal necessities, including low-income housing provision (Aalbers 2016). Under the neoliberal rubric of market fundamentalism, the Berlin Senate incrementally retrenched its commitment to social housing by selling off many of its municipal housing companies to the private sector. By 2008, the Berlin Senate owned only six municipal housing companies or 15.8 per cent of housing stock (Fields and Uffer 2016). The result was that the price of rental units owned by municipal housing companies not only increased rapidly but also reached higher levels than private housing companies (Aalbers and Holm 2008). This trend inevitably culminated in increased housing insecurity for many Berliners, as manifested in a growing number of evictions and a rise in homelessness, which now include refugees (Berner et al. 2015; Soederberg 2018). Berlin also has the dubious reputation of being the homeless capital of Germany. It is in this context, forged by past rounds of neoliberalism, that refugees are compelled to seek places of survival within the structural violence of racialized and material spaces of exclusion.

Snapshot 2: raced spaces in Paris

The Paris case contrasts that of Berlin as migration governance in France emphasizes displacement away from the City of Paris to rural areas of the country or back to the port of entry through the use of the Dublin III Regulation – a EU-wide policy used to determine refugee hosting responsibility per the refugee's initial country of entry (EU Migration and Home Affairs 2016). The usage of the Dublin regulation shows how racial exclusion underpins the migration governance regime on the regional and international scale. Indeed, Dublin buttresses aforementioned policies that keep refugees in detention centres in Libya where the EU is funding states in the Middle East and Africa to prevent migrants from entering its borders (Council of the European Union 2019).

When refugees do manage to make it to urban centres like Paris, they face further relocation and adversity in terms of accessing housing and finding fulfilling employment. Indeed, unlike Berlin, where there were clear administrative channels of control (Berlin Senate), the national-level state, as opposed to the city and individual civil society organizations, use piecemeal strategies in the face of housing shortage and unprecedented homelessness (Abbe Pierre Foundation 2018). Refugee status is continually denied: only 13,020 refugees received status out of 100,412 applications in 2017, where black African refugees received higher rates of rejection than their counterparts from the Middle East (INSEE 2017). This is clear evidence of racial indexing, where black bodies are more likely considered inauthentic or irregular migrants. Paris has a long history of displacing its poor, and the creation of the banlieue racialized suburbs is a stark example of displacement as a long-standing feature of capital accumulation in the city as discussed by Harvey and other urban geographers (Harvey 2003; Smith 2008 [1984]). The so-called urban refugee crisis in Paris, due in part to the constant closure of shanty towns and informal shelters in Calais, overlaps with France's unprecedented crisis of housing insecurity and homelessness. Thus, the City of Paris has enacted disjointed strategies of racialized refugee management.

At the onset of increased migration in 2015, the city provided refugees with tents, blankets, basic supplies and even wi-fi under the metro stations Stalingrad and Juarez. As this was less than ideal as a location, these makeshift camps were shut down by national-level police and the City of Paris opened the 'Bubble' refugee processing centre. This marked a shift in refugee policy: if refugees wanted a more permanent home, they would either have to accept relocation by bus to rural areas of France as processed by the Bubble or have to await a decision on social housing in the extremely backlogged waiting list in Paris. Since Paris is an economic hub where refugees can also maintain kinship ties, many refugees choose to stay on the streets of Paris or find overcrowded homes where they are exploited in terms of rent by landlords. Other refugees must compete for resources with the homeless in emergency shelters (Bhagat 2019). The refugee crisis trope masks the realities of urban precarity in Paris and instead blames refugees for housing backlog, sexual violence and slum housing on the streets of the city (Dikeç and Swyngedouw 2017). Paris's expulsion of refugees is not a sharp departure from the city's history of displacing working class and racialized people from the city's core.

In conjunction with the EU's push to turn refugees into valuable labourers – a desire that is yet to be backed up by solid policy-based strategies on the regional scale – many Community Service Organizations (CSOs) in Paris focus on integrating refugees through the provision of language training and employment skills. As it stands, only 34 per cent of refugees are employed in France and, of these, only 17 per cent of females entering France for the purposes of family reunification have found employment (Bèque 2012). Indeed, only a third of refugees entering France have advanced knowledge of French – an important factor indicating poor employment prospects as knowledge of the host country's language upon relocation is a key factor for integration (Social Europa 2016). Statistics on refugee employment are difficult to find as many of these people find informal work. For example, fieldwork conducted in France in 2017 with a Women's and LGBT organization observed many refugee clients engaging in sex work in order to sustain themselves or even find shelter for a night (interview with Homelessness NGO in Paris, 8 June 2017 – A. Bhagat interviewer). Naming labour as a raced space – a space that is in fact linked to housing access – necessitates qualitative research at the level of the local scale. Since there is no coherent strategy for integrating refugee labour in Paris, the experiences of migrant survival are variegated. Undoubtedly, access to labour occurs on racial lines, where refugees are the most precarious populations seeking employment due to their lack of language skills.

As our argument set out, housing is the key indicator of survival in capitalist political economy, and other indicators, such as work or access to healthcare and education, are hinged on refugees attempting to get themselves off the streets of Paris. Since refugee housing (along with social housing in general) is facing a severe backlog in the city, the national-level state has created the Asylum Seeker's Allowance that amounts to around seven euros per day and an additional four euros if the state has not provided the person with accommodation. However, average rent in Paris exceeds 1,000 euros a month for a studio apartment (Errard 2019), making it very difficult for refugees to find a place in the city. The combined pressures of unfettered neoliberalization along with urban austerity in Paris have resulted in a raced market of housing that displaces the racialized poor from the city's core. For many refugees, the racialized dimensions of asylum management at both national and urban scales also prevent them from securing formal employment. This in turn makes it nearly impossible for migrants to afford Paris, as they receive very little welfare support in terms of housing. The focus on job training and language skills by many CSOs acts only as a piecemeal Band-Aid solution as the realities of survival in urban capitalism within extant crises of homelessness are too difficult to tackle without a co-ordinated national and regional strategy. Instead, refugees continue to be targets of police violence, detention and deportation on the streets of Paris (Schaeffer 2018).

Conclusion: multi-scalar governance and everyday life

This chapter has shown the relevance and potential future avenues for research in CPE that takes seriously the dimensions of scale and space. As we have argued, international and national dimensions of global displacement converge on the urban scale, where the raced spaces of housing and labour are rendered most visible. Our theoretical focus on raced spaces responds to cutting-edge research agendas in CPE, which call for the combined analysis of race and class. In so doing, we have attempted to provide an overview of 'actually existing' raced spaces in our two city studies of Paris and Berlin. We emphasized the overlapping yet differentiated effects of raced spaces within the context of urban austerity in two major host cities. This allowed us to show how the refugee crisis trope is managed and reproduced as cities, national-level states and the EU is incapable of tackling key issues of urban capitalism that predate the influx of migrants. While the crisis trope imparts blame and denotes fear, it also points to key EU strategies of border security in favour of refugee support and welfare.

As such, the Berlin case shows the constraints impeding refugees from access-ing affordable and adequate shelter within the context of marketized social housing and austerity budgeting where the severely underfunded municipal agencies have been unable to process and provide adequate shelter to the forcibly displaced. In Paris, refugees face constant policing and ongoing dis-placement, when they are either forcibly moved from the city through state-led violence or systemically displaced from the city due to high rents and poor job prospects. Emergency and short-term housing solutions are all at capacity, causing refugees to cycle in and out of homelessness on the streets of Paris. In order to survive, refugees are pushed into precarious forms of employment, thus illustrating that housing and employment access are intertwined. Both the Berlin and Paris cases show us the importance of the urban scale in CPE. In both cases, refugees face racism and violence, indicating that the refugee crisis is reproduced through ongoing neoliberalization in the city. The racialized logics of refugee governance mean migrants are cast outside the purview of state and city-level welfare responsibilities, especially in light of rising poverty, evictions and homelessness in the EU.

Note

1. Below the EU's limit of 3 per cent of a nation's GDP.

References

Aalbers, M. and Christophers, B. (2014) Centering housing in political economy, *Housing, Theory and Society*, 31(4): 373–394.

Aalbers, M.B. (2016) *The Financialization of Housing: A Political Economy Approach*, London: Routledge.

Aalbers, M.B. and Holm, A. (2008) Privatising social housing in Europe: the cases of Amsterdam and Berlin, *Rooiijn*, 110(41): 58–65.

Abbe Pierre Foundation (2018) *Report on the State of Inadequate Housing in France*, Paris: Abbe Pierre Foundation.

Bèque, M. (2012) L'enquête Parcours et Profils des migrants: Une approche statistque orginale, *Reveue européenne des migrations internationals*, 25(1): 215–234.

Berner, L., Holm, A. and Jensen, I. (2015) *Zwangsräumungen und die Krise des Hilfesystems: Eine Fallstudie in Berlin*, Berlin: Humboldt-Universität zu Berlin.

Bhagat, A. (2019) Displacement in 'actually existing' racial neoliberalism: refugee governance in Paris, *Urban Geography*, https://doi.org/10.1080/02723638.2019.1659689.

Bhagat, A. (2020) Governing refugee disposability: neoliberalism and survival in Nairobi, *New Political Economy*, 25(3): 439–452.

Bhagat, A. and Soederberg, S. (2019) Placing refugees in authoritarian neoliberalism: reflections from Berlin and Paris, *South Atlantic Quarterly*, 118(2): 421–438.

Bhambra, G. and Holmwood, J. (2018) Colonialism, postcolonialism, and the liberal welfare state, *New Political Economy*, 23(5): 574–587.

Bhattacharyya, G. (2018) *Rethinking Racial Capitalism: Questions of Reproduction and Survival*, London: Rowman & Littlefield International.

Brenner, N., Peck, J. and Theodore, N. (2010) Variegated neoliberalization: geographies, modalities, pathways, *Global Networks*, 10(2): 182–222.

Council of the European Union (2019) Libya and the surrounding area: current situation and need for immediate action, available at https://data.consilium.europa.eu/doc/document/ST-11538-2019-INIT/en/pdf, accessed 9 June 2020.

Danewid, I. (2020) The fire this time: Grenfell, racial capitalism and the urbanisation of empire, *European Journal of International Relations*, 26(1): 289–313.

Darling, J. (2016) Forced migration and the city: irregularity, informality, and the politics of presence, *Progress in Human Geography*, 41(2): 178–198.

Davies, J. and Blanco, I. (2017) Austerity urbanism: patterns of neoliberalization and resistance in six cities of Spain and the UK, *Environment and Planning A*, 49(7): 1517–1536.

Dikeç, M. and Swyngedouw, E. (2017) Theorizing the politicizing city, *International Journal of Urban and Regional Research*, 41(1): 1–17.

Errard, G. (2019) The average Parisian rent reached 1079 euros for only 31 m², *Le Figaro Immobilier*, 2 April.

EU Migration and Home Affairs (2016) *Country Responsible for Asylum Application*, Brussels: Europa.

Eurocities (2016) *Refugee Reception and Integration in Cities*, Brussels: Europa.

European Commission (2019) *Country Report France 2019 – In-Depth Review on the Prevention and Correction of Macroeconomic Imbalances*, Brussels: European Commission.

Fields, D. and Uffer, S. (2016) The financialization of rental housing: a comparative analysis of New York City and Berlin, *Urban Studies*, 53(7): 1486–1502.

Flüchtlingsrat Berlin (2016) *Wohnungen für Flüchtlinge statt Massenlagern und Notunterkünften*, Berlin: Flüchtlingsrat Berlin e.V.

Foroutan, N., Hamann, U., El-Kayed, N. and Jorek, S. (2017) *Zwischen Lager und Mietvertrag: Wohnunterbringung von geflüchteten Frauen in Berlin und Dresden*, Berlin: BIM, Humboldt-Universität zu Berlin.

Harvey, D. (2003) *Paris: Capital of Modernity*, Paris: Psychology Press.

Holm, A. (2013) Berlin's gentrification mainstream, in Bernt, M., Grell, B. and Holm, A. (eds) *The Berlin Reader: A Compendium on Urban Change and Activism*, Bielefeld: Transcript Verlag, pp. 171–188.

Holm, A. (2016) *Social Housing Need in Berlin*, Studie im Auftrag.

Housing Europe (2017) *The State of Housing in the EU 2017*, Brussels: Housing Europe.

INSEE (2017) Migrations residentielles: 60% des arrivals dans la metropoles du Grand Paris ont entre 15–29 ans, Paris: INSEE: Analysis.

Melamed, J. (2011) *Represent and Destroy: Rationalizing Violence in the New Racial Capitalism*, Minneapolis, MN: University of Minnesota Press.

Peck, J. (2012) Austerity urbanism: American cities under extreme economy, *City*, 16(6): 626–655.

Peck, J. and Tickell, A. (2002) Neoliberalizing space, *Antipode*, 34(3): 380–404.

Rajaram, P.K. (2018) Refugees as surplus population: race, migration, and capitalist value regimes, *New Political Economy*, 23(5): 627–639.

Refugees Welcome (2017) Offener Brief der flüchtlingspolitischen Initiativen an den neuen Berliner Senat, Berlin: Refugees Welcome, available at http://willkommen -in-wilmersdorf.de/index.php/2017/05/07/offener-brief-der-fluechtlingspolitischen -initiativen-an-den-neuen-berliner-senat/, accessed 24 May 2020.

rFI (2018) EU gives France deficit all-clear but wants more austerity, *rFI*, 23 May.

Robinson, C. (1983) *Black Marxism: The Making of the Black Radical Tradition*, London: Zed Books.

Schaeffer, J. (2018) Paris police clear out migrant camp at centre of debate, *National Post*, 30 May.

Shariatmadari, D. (2015) Swarms, floods and marauders: the toxic metaphors of the migration debate, *The Guardian*, available at https://www.theguardian.com/ commentisfree/2015/aug/10/migration-debate-metaphors-swarms-floods -marauders-migrants, accessed 9 June 2020.

Shilliam, R. (2018) *Race and the Undeserving Poor*, Newcastle upon Tyne: Agenda Publishing.

Smith, N. (2008 [1984]) *Uneven Development: Nature, Capital, and the Production of Space*, Atlanta, GA: University of Georgia Press.

Social Europa (2016) *How Are Refugees Faring on the Labour Market in Europe?*, Brussels: European Council.

Soederberg, S. (2018) The rental housing question: exploitation, eviction, and erasures, *Geoforum*, 89, Spring: 114–123.

Soederberg, S. (2019) Governing global displacement in austerity urbanism: the case of Berlin's refugee housing crisis, *Development and Change*, 50(4): 923–947.

Tilley, L. and Shilliam, R. (2018) Raced markets: an introduction, *New Political Economy*, 23(5): 534–543.

Wendel, K. (2014) *Unterbringung von Flüchtlingen in Deutschland: Regelungen und Praxis der Bundesänder im Vergleich*, Frankfurt am Main: Förderverein PRO ASYL.

15 Thinking beyond capitalism: social movements, r/evolution, and the solidarity economy

Julie Matthaei

Introduction

"It was the best of times, it was the worst of times; it was the age of foolishness; it was the age of wisdom": Dickens's famous opening sentence for *The Tale of Two Cities* well describes the present historical conjuncture. We live in a time of epic crises. Climate change and a high risk of nuclear war together threaten the very future of human life on earth, while rising inequality and corruption, and the concomitant rise of fascist regimes, are sabotaging humanity's efforts to solve them, and perpetuating injustice and poverty in the midst of plenty. At the same time, the present is, as well, a time of widespread (if partial and mostly invisible) economic and social transformation towards a more peaceful, sustainable, egalitarian, and democratic post-capitalist economic system, a shift which represents an epoch paradigm shift from millennia of inequality-based societies towards a new, solidarity-based paradigm of social life. Foolishness is pervasive among mainstream economists, especially neoliberal ones, as they maintain that there is no possibility of a better economic system than capitalism – and even claim that regulations of the "free market" are unnecessary and problematic – while social movements and their academic counterparts are busy deconstructing inequality in all of its dimensions, and investigating egalitarian, cooperative, sustainable alternatives.

In this chapter, I want to encourage radical/critical political economists who are not already so engaged to become active participants in this revolutionary shift through their research and teaching. First, I will discuss some of the basic ways that radical/critical political economists need to be more radical, in terms of centering an analysis of revolutionary economic transformation or system change. Then I will introduce the solidarity economy framework, which economists and social scientists around the world are using to visibilize, analyze, and propagate post-capitalist economic practices and institutions, while comparing it to the Marxist model of revolution, and outline aspects of a solidarity economy research program.

My analysis derives from my experience as a radical political economist in the US. While it speaks especially to radical/critical political economists who are working in capitalist countries, where economics is dominated by neoclassical economics, I hope it will be useful to my radical economist colleagues across the planet, including in the global South.

Be a *radical* radical political economist[1]

In my home country, the US, radical political economics was born out of the progressive social movements of the 1960s, especially the anti-war and civil rights/anti-racist movements. It has continued to develop with the evolution of these movements, and the emergence of others, such as the feminist and ecology movements, as have similar strains of critical political economy around the world. In my view, it is key for radical political economists to continue to see themselves as active participants in one or more of the progressive social movements of their time. That is what radical political economics is for! Movements for economic and social transformation need to define, understand, and document the inequalities and injustices they are confronting and trying to redress. They also need critiques of mainstream, neoclassical economics, and its claims that capitalist economies are essentially just and democratic, the best possible solution to the economic problem of naturally selfish, competitive, and infinitely needy humans confronting scarce resources. Finally, they need a vision of the economic future they should advocate and fight for. In their research, writing, and teaching, radical political economists can fulfill one or more of these roles, helping movements expose, document, and analyze the problems with capitalist economies which are ignored or rationalized by mainstream discourse, and supporting the necessary visioning of an economic path forward.

All over the world, mainstream economists claim that they are "objective," and disparage radical economists for their overtly critical view of capitalism, and feminist, anti-racist, pro-worker, and/or ecological stances. While it is crucial for radical political economists to use the highest standards of scholarship (and note that we are judged far more harshly than our neoclassical colleagues), it is important that we not feel pressured to give up or hide our association with social movements. Rather, radical political economists need to proudly affirm that we are striving to understand our economy from the standpoint of the oppressed, and to create liberatory knowledge. The philosophy of science has long since proved that objectivity does not exist – all research is biased due to the lens it applies, including what it looks at, and how it conceptualizes what it sees (Harding 1995). We need to be on the side of – and part of – liberatory movements, and proud of it.

This said, I am aware that in many countries, mine included, there is tremendous discrimination against non-neoclassical economists, especially radical ones. It requires courage and commitment to speak truth to power in a world where economics continues to be dominated by apologists for capitalism. Many radical economists may feel the need to downplay or even avoid the radical, systemic-change-encouraging aspects of their research, at least until they receive tenure. One left-feminist-anti-racist colleague of mine shifted her research to quantitative analyses of gender and race discrimination in order to successfully avoid anti-leftist bias among journal referees. And both Stephen Marglin of Harvard and Jack Gurley at Stanford came out as radicals after receiving tenure – not a bad strategy, given the enormous power differential between tenured and untenured faculty. In the mid-1970s, my fellow graduate students at Yale warned me not to study Marxist economics with the one untenured Marxist there, David Levine – but I did, and ended up being hired for a position teaching radical economics at Wellesley College which the students had demanded be created, and eventually tenured. (It also helped that, as a left feminist, I wrote my dissertation and first book on women in US economic history and ended up helping to create the field of women's studies!) The fact that so many continue to do radical/critical political economy in the face of blatant discrimination by the profession, especially in Western countries, is a testament to the strength of progressive social movements.

Indeed, one of our important roles as radical political economists in assisting systematic economic transformation is to expose the ways in which mainstream economics is biased in favor of the current economic system. For example, its core theory of income distribution, marginal productivity theory, assumes the absence of discrimination, and ignores the hugely unequal distribution of "factors," in particular of wealth, and the historical processes of colonization and slavery which created it. It ignores the qualitative difference between working and owning (especially when one's wealth is inherited, without effort), and neglects to mention the ways in which the concentration of wealth in the hands of a few, the natural tendency of capitalist economies left on their own, corrupts the democratic process. Its analysis entirely disregards the fact that capitalist firms, where most people spend most of their lives, are structured not as democracies, but rather as dictatorships, in which workers are obliged to obey their bosses.

A final, enormous bias of mainstream economics is that it takes capitalism as a given in its analysis, in spite of its manifold failings, never considering the possibility that qualitative changes in economic agency, practices, or institutions could evolve and improve it. If pushed, mainstream economists will use the invisible hand metaphor, claiming (against the growing findings of behavioral and feminist economics) that people are narrowly self-interested and materialistic by nature, requiring markets and inequality and profits to motivate them to contribute to the whole. We only have to refer to our sister discipline, sociology, to point out how social institutions – including economic ones – construct us as human beings, creating possibilities for other forms of identity and agency to accompany more egalitarian and cooperative economic institutions. For example, cooperative behavior would be far more widespread if people were not always presented with zero-sum economic situations. And people would not be as focused on consumerism, and "infinitely needy" as mainstream economists assume, were they not bombarded since childhood by marketing and advertising. Pointing these biases out through our research and teaching helps open minds to both the necessity and the possibility of systemic change, helping them "think beyond capitalism."

This leads me to another way in which radical political economists need to strive to be radical: by continually striving to be aware of, and counteract, our biases. Radical/critical political economics is still dominated by white, heterosexual, class-privileged men, as least in the North and West, and this positionality introduces bias into our research. Those who benefit from systems of privilege – be they gender, race, class, or nationality – tend to ignore or underplay these systems. Awareness of such biases, and the commitment to work to overcome them, is crucial if radical political economics is to continue to play a politically progressive role, and keep pace with the evolution of social movements. At the same time, it is crucial for radical political economists to be open to, familiar with, and indeed supportive of criticism of their research from those outside mainstream radical/critical political economics, particularly of research by members of subordinated groups. This holds also for researchers who are members of one subordinated group – such as white Western women who are feminist economists – who need to be aware of their racist and classist biases. This awareness of standpoint bias – or the contributions of research undertaken from the "standpoint of the oppressed," as Sandra Harding (1995) termed it – requires that radical political economy, to be truly radical, actively encourages research by members of oppressed groups, on the subject of inequality as well as other topics. While membership in an oppressed group does not, of course, necessarily bring with it a liberatory stance (all economists of color are not anti-racist, nor are all women economists feminist), we can expect that special insights which help radical political economics be more radical and transformative will come from economists who are members of a subordinated group or groups. At the same time, economists from privileged groups can do liberatory research if they are explicit about taking a multi-dimensional, anti-oppression stance. For example, to make my perspective clear, while I call myself a radical political economist, I also define myself as a Marxist–feminist–anti-racist–ecological economist, because none of these stances can be assumed within radical political economy (Matthaei 1996). Actualizing such a liberatory stance is not simple – even oppressed people internalize oppressive worldviews – but expressing the intention to pursue liberatory knowledge in all its dimensions is a first step, without which radical/critical political economists will tend to reproduce inequalities because the dominant economic discourse reflects and reproduces a white/male/class privileged point of view.

A final way I want to encourage radical/critical political economists to be more radical – and this is the central focus of the remainder of this chapter – is to move beyond critique of capitalist institutions to discuss better alternatives, and ways forward towards them. Mainstream economists, and conservatives and liberals in general, have countered radical critiques of capitalism with the assertion, made famous by Margaret Thatcher in the 1980s, that "There Is No Alternative." And indeed, until the 1990s, the anti-capitalist imagination was dominated by Soviet-style socialism, whose many economic achievements were seriously undermined by a lack of workplace or political democracy. The radical economists who criticized this model as "state capitalism" had little to propose as an alternative. While the dissolution of the Soviet Union in 1991 brought proclamations that capitalism had won – famously termed "The End of History" by Francis Fukuyama (1992) – it also coincided with the emergence of the solidarity economy framework for moving beyond capitalism, as we will see below. My main point here is that the radical research agenda must include a relentless search for alternative economic values, practices, institutions, and systems – throughout history, and around the globe – along with a vibrant discourse about yet-untried post-capitalist possibilities, to help bring social movements together around a shared vision of economic transformation.

Envisioning radical economic transformation: the solidarity economy framework

If, as I have argued, radical political economists need to focus more attention on system change beyond capitalism, what theoretical framework can they use? Radical analyses of system change have tended to be grounded in Marxist theory, in particular Marx's theory of historical materialism, which postulates a revolutionary shift from capitalism to socialism, motored by organizing by the working class. This framework has lost credibility for a number of reasons, including the conservative nature of the working class in many advanced capitalist countries, and the failings of the socialist countries which have been created, including the perpetuation of inequality and a lack of democracy. In the rest of this chapter, I will discuss a theory of economic and social transformation that builds on, but substantially transforms, the Marxist theory of revolution: the solidarity economy framework.

The solidarity economy framework, and the associated solidarity economy movement which advocates for the development of the solidarity economy, emerged in the 1990s, both in Europe and in Latin America, and spread globally through the World Social Forum movement (Allard et al. 2008; Kawano et al. 2010; Utting 2015). The concept of the solidarity economy, and these associated movements, overlaps with the New Economy movement, Sumak Kawsay/Buen Vivir (Hidalgo-Capitán and Cubillo-Guevara 2017), and the Community Economy movement (Gibson-Graham 2006), among others. The Intercontinental Network for the Promotion of the Social Solidarity Economy (www.RIPESS.org) connects, visibilizes, and promotes solidarity economy organizing on all continents.

The solidarity economy framework identifies liberatory economic practices and institutions already existing within capitalism-dominated market economies and treats them as parts of an emerging integrated "solidarity economy." Some of these institutions are recent creations, while others revive pre-capitalist, cooperative forms, often with indigenous roots. The basic criteria for inclusion in the solidarity economy is the values embodied by the economic practice or institution. The list of solidarity values includes cooperation, equity in all dimensions, participatory political and economic democracy, sustainability, and diversity/pluralism. The framework recognizes that any particular practice or institution will not be a perfect fit for all or even any particular value. Instead, each of these dimensions of the solidarity economy lies on a spectrum. The struggle for systemic transformation involves moving our economic practices and institutions along the spectrum, from inequality towards solidarity.

While cooperatives of all sorts – worker, consumer, and producer – comprise a key building block of the solidarity economy, so, too, do efforts to promote socially responsible consumption patterns, shift investment towards social and environmental goals, and redesign enterprise for community benefit. Many of the practices showcased, from community gardens, to the takeover of abandoned factories or lands, to the creation of community currencies, arise as people come together in response to the failure of capitalist economic institutions.

The solidarity economy framework retains many key aspects of the Marxist view of revolution. First, in contrast to neoclassical economics, it views people as socially constructed and hence able to become less materialistic and competitive, and more cooperative, as they create social practices and institutions which encourage this type of behavior. Thus, a more egalitarian and cooperative economy is possible. Second, it focuses on the inequality, domination, and exploitation that are at the core of capitalism, and views organizing against them as the major motor for economic transformation. And third, related to the other two, it believes that a superior, more evolved form of economics can and will evolve out of the contradictions of capitalism, based on this organizing.

At the same time, the solidarity economy framework suggests some essential revisions in the Marxist theory revolutionary change which I want to point out and encourage radical political economists to incorporate into their analyses of system change.

1.   From class to gender/race/class

A key difference between classical Marxist views of revolution and the solidarity economy framework is the expansion of the categories of oppression. Marxist analysis centers on class as the key type of oppression in capitalism, and on class struggle – workers' struggle against their capitalist oppressors – as the motor for revolutionary transformation. The solidarity economy framework postulates a similar understanding of revolution being motored by an oppressed group's struggles for liberation, but adds gender, race, and other forms of oppression to the analysis, seeing them also as playing key roles in moving beyond capitalism to a solidarity economy. Thus feminist, anti-racist, ecology, LGBTQ, and other forms of social movement against oppression are all motors in transforming economies from capitalism to solidarity economy. And each – as a movement combatting and transforming a particular inequality upon which capitalism is based – is necessary to capitalism's full transformation. Radical political economists are part of these transformative movements and, as I argued earlier, must strive to take into account and critique all forms of inequality in their research, as well as to be vigilant about eliminating bias in their research.

2.   From identity politics to solidarity politics ...

Marxist theory of worker-led revolution is based on "identity politics" – that is, it claims that a person's economic or social identity, as a worker or capitalist, determines their political position and activism. Workers struggle against capitalists and for revolution; capitalists struggle to dominate and exploit workers, and to maintain capitalist institutions. Anti-racist and feminist movements largely adopted this same, identity-politics view of transformation, positing feminism as a struggle of women against men and patriarchy, and anti-racism as a struggle of peoples of color against whites, white supremacy, and neocolonialism.

At the same time, however, as these movements – and worker movements – matured, they began to experience internal divisions and fragmentation because of inequalities among their members. For example, because women are made unequal by class, race, sexuality, and other inequalities, these inequalities were reproduced within feminist organizing, as well as differentiating the ways in which women experience womanhood and discrimination. This not only recreated inequality and oppression based on class, racial-ethnicity, and sexuality within feminist organizing, but it also differentiated the ways in which women experienced discrimination, and hence their ways of constructing feminist politics. The same differentiation and inequality have occurred within worker and anti-racist movements. In the US, feminist women of color took the lead in confronting white feminists on the anti-racism, homophobia, and classism within their writing and organizing (hooks 1981; Moraga and Anzaldua 1981). African American feminist legal scholar Kimberlee Crenshaw (1989) coined the term "intersectionality," now widely used in women's studies, to describe the differentiation of womanhood by these other forms of oppression, and the need for feminists to take it into account, rather than assume a sameness among women. Since white middle-class feminist women, who dominated the feminist movement, were committed to liberating women via their identity politics, they were forced to recognize that women in their movement were also oppressed by race, class, and heterosexism, and to extend their feminist values to include anti-racism, anti-classism, and pro-LGBTQ. Similar changes have been occurring in worker and anti-racist movements.

In this way, the practice of Marx's identity politics, when it was extended across the different, intersecting inequalities that characterize capitalism, began to transcend itself. White feminist women, for example, took on the challenge of striving to become anti-racist when their sisters of color confronted them on their racism. Unions began to strive actively against the racism and sexism which their members experienced both on the job and in union organizations. Anti-racist organizations are experiencing similar transformation. Social movements have begun to practice what I have termed "solidarity politics" – standing against all forms of oppression, even those which they are not directly experiencing, in solidarity with others who are. Two recent examples of solidarity politics in the US are the Women's March, which is explicitly opposed to all major forms of oppression of women, and Black Lives Matter, which affirms feminism and LGBTQ rights in its core values.

Another root of solidarity politics has been the practice of solidarity between movements when they act in coalition to address a shared problem, including but not limited to the multi-dimensional and interconnected inequalities created by late 20th-century globalization. In the US, solidarity politics burst onto the scene in 1999 with the famous "Battle of Seattle," which brought union workers and environmentalists together against the World Trade Organization (WTO). It was codified in the principles of the associated World Social Forum movement in 2001 (México Foro Social Mundial de las Migraciones 2018), which oppose all forms of oppression, bringing into being the exciting emergence of what has been called a "movement of movements," a coming together of social movements in opposition to all forms of oppression.

Solidarity politics is of central importance to radical political economists as we visibilize and analyze progressive movements for radical transformation. Marxist identity politics reproduces race, class, and gender divisions as it strives to end inequality and oppression. It divides the working class into opposing races and genders; women into opposing races and classes; and people of color into opposing classes and genders. While identity politics represents a required stage in the movement against inequality and for solidarity, only solidarity politics can bring people together across the differences and inequalities that racist patriarchal capitalism produces, so that we can achieve the mass base necessary to bring about, democratically, systemic economic and political change. Solidarity is rightly at the core of the term "solidarity economy," expressed in its value of equity in all dimensions, that is as opposition to all forms of inequality. Only solidarity politics can provide the multi-faceted critiques of our economic practices and institutions that will lead to a fully realized solidarity economics, a new economics based on a striving to reverse all forms of inequality, and the search for economic solutions that work for all.

It is important to underscore the fact that solidarity economics does, like Marxism, represent a rejection of capitalism. Feminist and anti-racist movements have tended to get co-opted by an equal opportunity view of liberation, which takes capitalist class hierarchies as given, and seeks movement up them by women and people of color, respectively, who were historically segregated into the lowest paid, lowest status, positions. The election of Barack Obama in 2008, and the almost election of Hillary Clinton in 2016, represented, for this equal opportunity form of organizing, the ultimate success: access of members of previously subordinated groups to the pinnacles of power. However, the limitations of this equal opportunity strategy for the liberation of all women, or all people of color, were made patently clear in this process, as gender and racial inequality in incomes and poverty rates have persisted, and racial wealth inequality has increased dramatically (Asante-Muhammad et al. 2017: 5). Solidarity politics – particularly politics in solidarity with class-oppressed women and people of color – has been leading US social movements to question the desirability of capitalism's view of equality – equal opportunity – and to begin to search for, create, and participate in emergent solidarity economy practices and institutions. A similar transformation has been happening in the ecology movement, as it realizes that the organization of production around the profit motive and consumerism is a major source of ecological destruction, necessitating new, post-capitalist economics.

3.   From revolution to r/evolution, within market economies

The Marxist view of systematic economic transformation beyond capitalism envisions a revolutionary change of systems – including the elimination of classes, the ending of private property in the means of production, and the elimination of markets – which happens rapidly, when workers take over the state. In contrast, the solidarity economy framework envisions a gradual process of deep, qualitative transformation, a process which I describe as r/evolution, using a term popularized by the James and Grace Lee Boggs Center, based on their 1974 book, *Revolution and Evolution in the Twentieth Century* (Boggs and Boggs 1974). Economic practices and institutions which embody solidarity economy values – such as worker-owned cooperatives, community currencies, socially responsible consumption – are already emerging within market economies, alongside and even within capitalist institutions. They are being fed by social movements, especially those practicing solidarity politics, and they reconstruct the social relations of production, to use a traditional Marxist term. Political changes to a pro-solidarity-economy political regime, such as Chávez's Venezuela, can bring a leap forward, but in all cases, it takes years, if not decades, to transform people, economic practices, and economic institutions. One major lesson of the feminist and anti-racist movements is that unlearning sexist and racist programming – "consciousness-raising" – is key to progressive transformation, and this takes time. So does the process of learning to cooperate with others and develop mutually beneficial solutions. Without the development of an engaged and united population, practiced in participatory democracy, cooperation, and solidarity economic practices and institutions, a political regime change towards solidarity and socialism is vulnerable to being hijacked by a small minority, who can reimpose capitalist institutions.

What history has been showing us is that neoclassical economists are clearly wrong in assuming that only narrowly self-interested materialistic individualism exists in market economies. Different kinds of agency can exist within markets, and to different degrees. Socially responsible firms and cooperatives can coexist with capitalist ones, especially if favored by public policy. More and more, people are learning how to bring their concern for the well-being of others and of the planet into their economic decisions, as consumers, workers, producers, and investors, "internalizing externalities."

4.   Beyond historical materialism

A central aspect of Marx's theory of revolution was the primacy of the "material" sphere of the economy. The mode of production determined the other spheres – for example, the family and the state – which were deemed "superstructural." Struggles for change, Marxists argued, should focus on changing the forces and relations of production. In contrast, the solidarity economy framework views r/evolution as, at its base, a transformation of values, brought on by progressive social movements. The family, the educational system, and the media also play central roles in programming us into a way of thinking that reproduces the capitalist system – or in teaching us how to think for ourselves, and critically, and how to practice mutuality, cooperation, and solidarity economy agency. Thus, the transformation of these spheres is as indispensable to r/evolution as is transformation of economic practices and institutions. Similarly, state policies can support the emergence of solidarity economy values, practices, and institutions in a plethora of ways, including changing or abolishing corporate charters, and the establishment of economic human rights.

5.   Beyond reform versus revolution

A key distinction established by the Marxist theory of revolution was that of reform versus revolution. Changes which did not fundamentally alter the structure of capitalism – anything less than a full revolution or organizing workers in support of such – were dismissed as reforms. Because reforms offer piecemeal improvements in workers' conditions, Marxists argued, they can end up disadvantaging workers in the end by dampening their revolutionary fervor. In contrast, the solidarity economy's r/evolutionary framework leads it to advocate for partial changes or reforms, especially when they embody solidarity economy values, and are put forward as part of a larger, integrated program of systemic change.

Towards a solidarity economy research agenda

As I argued at the beginning of this chapter, visibilizing superior alternatives to capitalism and a way to get there is, I believe, one of the most important tasks that radical political economists can undertake. We are at a time in history where capitalism is beset by severe crises, and the ruling class is cultivating racial-ethnic and other divisions so as to divide and conquer the 99 percent. The solidarity economy framework brings into awareness the possibility of a movement forward, towards equality and solidarity. I will end here with a list of various areas needing research.

1. MAPPING. A basic aspect of solidarity economy research is mapping: identifying different types of solidarity economy practices and institutions; noting their location and number; quantifying their impact on people and the economy (Borowiak et al. 2018; Pavloskaya 2018; Safri 2015; https:// solidarityeconomy.us).
2. BEST PRACTICES. As solidarity economy practices and institutions emerge and grow around the world, it is helpful to identify common problems, and best practices, that is, to create blueprints and manuals, as it were, for those involved in their construction. One important area of study is

solidarity economy forms of firms, including socially responsible management and businesses (Scharmer 2007; Waddock 2008), social enterprises (Bornstein 2007), and worker-owned cooperatives (Pencavel 2013).

3. GROWING THE SOLIDARITY ECONOMY. Another important question to explore is what conditions and forces lead to the growth of various solidarity economy practices and institutions? How have social movements been involved? How can the transformation of parenting, education, and the media help? When and how have economic crises contributed to the growth of the solidarity economy? What type of policies have been implemented, and what were their strengths and weaknesses (Utting 2017)?

4. COMPARATIVE SYSTEMS 2.0. During the Cold War, the field of comparative systems compared capitalism's successes to the failings of the Soviet and Chinese "command economies." Comparative systems 2.0 compares and contrasts capitalist and solidarity economy values, practices, and institutions, showing that capitalism is not, indeed, the last and best economic system (see, for example, Magne 2017; Navarra 2016).

5. BEHAVIORAL SOLIDARITY ECONOMICS. Much of behavioral economics has focused on types of behavior other than the narrow materialistic self-interest assumed by mainstream economics. When undertaken within the solidarity economy framework, the study of cooperative, altruistic, socially responsible behavior is indeed the study of the emergence of solidarity economy agency. And when undertaken with the Marxist/sociological understanding of the economic and social construction of individuality, behavioral economics can become radical political economics, arguing that a shift to a more egalitarian and cooperative economics is possible, and is happening! Emily Kawano (2018) has coined the term "homo solidaricus," which she contrasts to the "homo economicus" assumed by mainstream economists.

Conclusion

We radical political economists find ourselves in a challenging historical conjuncture – challenging not only because of the crises our economic system is creating, but also because we are challenged with the opportunity to make a real contribution to the forward movement of economics on the planet.

In most countries on the planet, it is not easy to be a radical political economist. Neoclassical economics predominates, an economics which is entirely lacking in the ability to think beyond capitalism, even in the midst of its manifest failings. The solidarity economy framework provides radical political economists with a way to visibilize and help grow emergent post-capitalist economic values, practices, and institutions. While this framework shares a good deal with the Marxist theoretical framework, making it subject to being dismissed out of hand in many countries, it has moved beyond Marxism in a number of important ways, which make it more appealing to mainstream economists, social scientists, and people in general, even in conservative countries like the US. The values at its core – especially equity, democracy, and sustainability – are values which capitalism itself has generated yet been unable to realize. The vision it presents is not utopian "pie in the sky," but rather a concrete, practical road forward that is already in the process of being built, a process of practical radicalism. It can be studied using the same quantitative tools as mainstream economics, including behavioral economics (as well as other, qualitative methods). Finally, its mode of transformation is not a violent revolutionary overthrow of capitalism, but rather a nonviolent, democratic process of displacing and transforming it. With the solidarity economy framework, the mechanisms for creating change and the values they embody are entirely consistent with the end goal of a cooperative, equitable, sustainable economy and society.

Note

1.   I am referring here both to radical political economics and to critical political economy, as well as to other forms of leftist, Marxist or neo-Marxist economics.

References

Allard, J., Davidson, C. and Matthaei, J. (eds) (2008) *Solidarity Economy: Building Alternatives for People and Planet*, Chicago: Changemaker.

Asante-Muhammad, D., Collins, C., Hoxie, J. and Nieves, E. (2017) *The Road to Zero Wealth: How the Racial Wealth Divide Is Hollowing Out America's Middle Class*, Washington, DC: Institute for Policy Studies.

Boggs, G.L. and Boggs, J. (1974) *Revolution and Evolution in the Twentieth Century*, New York: Monthly Review Press.

Bornstein, D. (2007) *How to Change the World*, Oxford: Oxford University Press.

Borowiak, C., Safri, M., Healy, S. and Pavlovskaya, M. (2018) Navigating the fault lines: race and class in Philadelphia's solidarity economy, *Antipode*, 50(3): 577–603.

Crenshaw, K. (1989) Demarginalizing the intersection of race and sex: a black feminist critique of antidiscrimination doctrine, feminist theory and antiracist politics, *University of Chicago Legal Forum*, 1989(1): Article 8.

Fukuyama, F. (1992) *The End of History and the Last Man*, New York: Free Press.

Gibson-Graham, J.K. (2006) *A Postcapitalist Politics*, Minneapolis, MN: University of Minnesota Press.

Harding, S. (1995) Can feminist thought make economics more objective?, *Feminist Economics,* 1(1): 7–32.

Hidalgo-Capitán, A.L. and Cubillo-Guevara, A.P. (2017) Deconstruction and genealogy of Latin American good living (*buen vivir*). The (triune) good living and its diverse intellectual wellsprings, in *Alternative Pathways to Sustainable Development: Lessons from Latin America*, International Development Policy series No.9, Geneva and Boston, MA: Graduate Institute Publications and Brill-Nijhoff, pp. 23–50.

hooks, b. (1981) *Ain't I A Woman: Black Women and Feminism*, Boston, MA: South End Press.

Kawano, E. (2018) Solidarity economy: building an economy for people and planet, The Next System Project, The Democracy Collaborative, available at https://thenextsystem.org/learn/stories/solidarity-economy-building-economy-people-planet, accessed 17 February 2020.

Kawano, E., Masterson, T. and Teller-Elsberg, J. (eds) (2010) *Solidarity Economy I: Building Alternatives for People and Planet*, Amherst, MA: Center for Popular Economics.

Magne, N. (2017) Wage inequality in workers' cooperatives and conventional firms, *European Journal of Comparative Economics*, 14(2): 303–329.

Matthaei, J. (1996) Why feminist, Marxist, and anti-racist economists should be feminist–Marxist–anti-racist economists, *Feminist Economics*, 2(1): 22–42.

México Foro Social Mundial de las Migraciones (2018) *Principles of the World Social Forum*.

Moraga, C. and Anzaldua, G. (eds) (1981) *This Bridge Called My Back: Writings by Radical Women of Color*, New York: Persephone Press.

Navarra, C. (2016) Employment stabilization inside firms: an empirical investigation of worker cooperatives, *Annals of Public and Cooperative Economics*, 87(4): 563–585.

Pavlovskaya, M. (2018) Critical GIS as a tool for social transformation, *The Canadian Geographer*, 62(1): 40–54.

Pencavel, J.H. (2013) *The Economics of Worker Cooperatives*, Cheltenham, UK and Northampton, MA, USA: Edward Elgar Publishing.

Safri, M. (2015) The politics of mapping solidarity economies and diverse economies in Brazil and the Northeastern United States, in Roelvink, G., St. Martin, K. and Gibson-Graham, J.K. (eds) *Making Other Worlds Possible: Performing Diverse Economies*, Minneapolis, MN: University of Minnesota Press, pp. 296–321.

Scharmer, C.O. (2007) *Theory U: Leading from the Future as It Emerges*, Cambridge, MA: Society for Organizational Learning.

Utting, P. (ed.) (2015) *Social and Solidarity Economy: Beyond the Fringe*, London: Zed Books/UNRISD.

Utting, P. (2017) *Public Policies for Social and Solidarity Economy: Assessing Progress in Seven Countries*, Geneva: International Labor Organization.

Waddock, S. (2008) *The Difference Makers: How Social and Institutional Entrepreneurs Created the Corporate Responsibility Movement*, Sheffield: Greenleaf Publishing.

Index

absentee owners 186, 188
accessibility
    price of 153
    value of 153
accumulation
    capital 36, 38, 43–4, 66–7, 72, 156,
        203
    competitive 38
    by dispossession 66, 72, 158
    Harvey's notion of 158
    objectives of 37
    of wealth 26, 35–6, 136, 138
affordable housing 168, 200–201
African neo-colonialism 66
agents' asset portfolio composition 136
Alff, Kirsten 67
Allende, Salvador 41
Amazon 167, 169
ambiguity, notion of 138
Amin, Samir 66–7, 70
Amsden, Alice 42
analytical nihilism 9
anti-capitalist politics 72
anti-discrimination laws 22
anti-racist movements 210, 216–19
asset choice, theory of 142
asylum management 204
Asylum Seeker's Allowance 204
austerity 44, 196–7, 199, 201–2, 204–5

Baker, Daniel 173
ballot-box democracy 114
Bandung Conference (1955), Indonesia
    69
Banerjee, Abhijit 92
bank deposits 48, 51, 53
banking crises 187

bank loans 142, 185
    Ghana Home Loans (GHL) 185
Bank of Ghana 187
banks' risk assessments 146
Battle of Seattle (1999) 217
behavioral solidarity economics 221
Belt and Road Initiative (China) 159
best practices, in solidarity economy
    220–21
between-group interactions, incidence
    of 108
bike-sharing services 174
biopolitics 159
Bitcoin 50
Black Lives Matter movement 217
blockchain technology 50
booms and busts cycle 146
borrowing and lending, system of 144–5
Breman, Jan 96
Bretton Woods institutions 155, 157
BREXIT referendum 109
business start-ups 172

capital accumulation 36, 38, 43–4, 66–7,
    72, 156, 203
capital-intensive production 98
capitalism
    constitutive of 158
    emergence of 68
    in Europe 66–7
    existential crisis for 159
    globalized 153
    human social relations under 37
    imperialism and the history of 67–9
    and labour exploitation 43
    Marxism concept of 43, 158
    proponents of 36